From Chauffeur
to
Brigadier

Brigadier-General C. D. Baker-Carr, C.M.G., D.S.O.

From Chauffeur
to
Brigadier
Founder of the Machine Gun Corps &
Pioneer of the Development of the Tank

C. D. Baker-Carr

LEONAUR

From Chauffeur to Brigadier
Founder of the Machine Gun Corps & Pioneer of the Development of the Tank
by C. D. Baker-Carr

First published under the title
From Chauffeur to Brigadier

Leonaur is an imprint of Oakpast Ltd

Copyright in this form © 2014 Oakpast Ltd

ISBN: 978-1-78282-451-0 (hardcover)
ISBN: 978-1-78282-452-7 (softcover)

http://www.leonaur.com

Publisher's Notes

Contents

MARY RUNDELL, (NEE BAKER-CARR),
IN HER "ONESIE" TANK SUIT!

A Foreword on Behalf of the Author's Family

It gives me great pleasure to write this introduction to the republication of Great Uncle Christopher's book, *From Chauffeur to Brigadier*. It is exactly 100 years since Christopher came back from Canada to rejoin the army—the point at which his book begins.

It should be no surprise that Christopher Baker-Carr would become a soldier and one who would thrive in times of war. Among our family forebears was Major-General Sir George Teesdale of the 1st The King's Dragoon Guards who we believe assumed command of the cavalry of the Household Brigade during the final stages of the Waterloo Campaign in 1815. During the Crimean War, the 22 year old Lieutenant Christopher Teesdale (later to become Major-General Sir Christopher Teesdale—*aide de camp* to Queen Victoria and Extra Equerry for 30 years to The Prince of Wales) won the Victoria Cross for gallantry at the Battle of Kars and in so doing became the first South African born recipient of that honour.

You will see from the photographs in this book, the evolution of "his" tank, the Mk IV (see page 175 of book) and "ours", a 16th/5th The Queen's Royal Lancers, Chieftain in 1970. You will also see Uncle Christopher, looking very smart in his uniform and a successor, me, in my "onesie" tank suit! The next generation, our daughter, Sarah, aged 4 is being shown the workings of the tank.

In February 1917 Christopher was appointed as the first commander of the 1st Tank Brigade. The ensuing Battle of Cambrai became synonymous with the formation of the Tank Corps—later the Royal Tank Regiment. And it was Uncle Christopher who commanded it—a glorious episode in our family history. He joins our other ancestors, Teesdale of the K.D.G. at Waterloo and a later Teesdale

Sarah Being Shown the Workings of the Tank

V.C. at Kars in the pantheon of illustrious forebears.

It is therefore with great pride that I write this foreword. It was always thought in our family that Christopher did not receive the recognition he deserved during his lifetime—but his legacy—machine guns and tanks—speak eloquently for his influence on Great War strategy and subsequently on military thinking for generations to follow.

The republication of Christopher's book I am dedicating to our daughter, Sarah Louise McAlpine, and to our son, James David Teesdale Rundell. Both have been spared the horrors of war so vividly described in this book.

Mary Rundell (nee Baker-Carr)
November, 2014

An Introduction to the New Edition of 'Chauffeur to Brigadier'

by The Leonaur Editors

Some ten years ago, when we conceived the notion of Leonaur, we were motivated to attempt to rescue from almost certain oblivion some of the many fine books which had been long out of print on the subject of military history in all of its forms.

This particular editor had ever a fondness for the 'first-hand account' narrative—the voice from the past. That these voices would be personally silenced by inevitable mortality is beyond anyone's influence. However, we reasoned, the written words of the authors of these books could and should certainly be preserved for posterity.

All of these books have merit for there is something in every one of them that is unique. In each one a person has written of a particular time in history from the perspective of his own education, place in society, rank and about the people he knew, his own place on a campaign, on the battlefield, in the regiment, in the company or possibly in the platoon to which he specifically belonged.

So on one level there need be no more explanation or justification as to why Leonaur would republish Christopher Baker-Carr's book especially in the centenary year of the outbreak of the First World War. Apart from all other considerations, the subject matter of his book deals with the development of tanks in the Great War which we know to be of particular interest to modern readers.

Inevitably, there is more to the republishing of this book than those reasons. Leonaur has, thank goodness, its own small cadre of enthusiasts and supporters. The circumstances that connect us to the individual who brought this book to our attention are interesting but convoluted and a digression which would take too long in the telling here.

CHRISTOPHER, GEORGE AND HENRY BAKER-CARR

Truthfully, at the time he raised the subject we have never before heard the name, 'Christopher Baker-Carr' and so we were attracted initially to the book for several other reasons. They were firstly that it seemed incredible that anyone would rise in rank so quickly from a civilian driver to a Brigadier. This alone must mean the subject of the book would be an exceptional person. Secondly, this very consideration put us in mind of Robertson's excellent book, *From Private to Field-Marshal* which Leonaur publishes and which, coincidentally, was brought to our attention by the same person who now championed Baker-Carr's cause. Thirdly, we had recently published our own, *A Twilight of Centaurs*, by Frederic Coleman which is the first hand account of another civilian chauffeur (and one who it transpired was a colleague of Baker-Carr's) on the Western Front. Finally and simply it seemed no one else was currently publishing this book, our confederate thought it was a good idea and he had a close association with the descendants of the author who were also enthusiastic about its republication. This bears precisely on why—as explained at the outset of this introduction—we publish books.

It was suggested to us that the title of this book, *From Chauffeur to Brigadier* was a particularly evocative one. So it is, for it promises a personal Cinderella story which is perennially compelling—rags to riches as it were. What could be better?

The answer is that this book, the man who wrote it and the incredible accomplishments he achieved are far more important than a tale of meteoric personal success. Though the book's original title has been retained, having read it we rather regret the author's choice for it disguises (and frankly rather minimises) the reality of an incredible man and enormous events and issues he influenced. This is, in fine we discovered, not just a good book by all the criteria we apply to decide these matters, but actually a very important book and one that it was essential to be republished.

The author of this book, Christopher Baker-Carr was commissioned into the Rifle Brigade in 1898, becoming a Captain and seeing action in South Africa and at Omdurman until 1906, at which time he terminated his military career to take up farming, firstly in South Africa and subsequently in Canada. We do not know exactly why he left the army after such a comparatively short time, given he came from a family which had a long and esteemed military tradition, though future events provide valuable clues as to the personality of the man and why that might have made for an uncomfortable life for a junior

THE AUTHOR OF THIS BOOK,
CHRISTOPHER BAKER–CARR
IN HIS UNIFORM, 1906

officer. His book makes it plain that he found it difficult to respect or defer to anyone he felt did not merit either consideration by his own estimation of them regardless of rank.

The march towards a European war in the first years of the twentieth century was inexorable. Several informed military men knew it was coming, who would instigate it and some knew when that would happen and how and where that would occur. Regrettably, the chasm between the heralds and potential listeners of influence remained, as usual, wide enough for the message to remain if not unheard—then by all accounts disregarded.

It was clear to many military thinkers that a war with Germany— by this point a major European power—was coming because it was a late developer as a nation to the extent that it had 'missed the boat' of imperial expansion, colonisation and global influence in politics and trade. Simply, Germany needed to 'catch-up' and by this time there was no other way to achieve that objective other than by conquest. Former soldiers knew that this war—a modern war in every way—would bear no relationship to the mostly small wars of the Victorian age that had been fought by the British since Wellington had defeated Napoleon on the slopes of Waterloo a century before terminating the last 'great war' to be fought across the globe. They believed, justifiably, that every man with military experience would be needed in such a war.

Baker-Carr rushed to offer his own services to the cause in 1914, and, in common with many former officers at the time, was told there was no duty and no place for him.

At this point in Baker-Carr's account the reader will begin to glean the measure of the man behind the words, for he was possessed of an extraordinary determination that was not to be curtailed by mere rejection or obstacles. He resolved to become actively involved in the war and to achieve that objective he was prepared to do anything that would be of use to anyone. So he became a civilian volunteer driver with The Royal Automobile Club contingent the members of which, mostly driving their own cars, travelled to France to put themselves and their vehicles at the disposal of staff officers. This proved to be an interesting and perilous occupation particularly in the early stages of the conflict when there was an ever present danger of driving head-long into enemy positions or patrols. Nevertheless, his time as a 'chauffeur' gave Baker-Carr an *entrée* into military life once again and access to the connections he was seeking.

It would not be unfair to Christopher Baker-Carr to suggest that he was something of a maverick particularly in military circles. It is quite clear that he was a free-thinking man within a world that fostered traditional obedience and an adherence to endorsed practices as they applied to the field of battle. Baker-Carr was not a product of the Staff College of his day and he maintained (for what seemed to him very sound reasons which are hard to dispute by those of us with the benefit of hindsight) a perennially jaundiced view of those of his contemporaries who were. This most especially bore, from his perspective, on the ability of influential commanders to appreciate and react to the quickly evolving requirements of the battlefield in what he knew to be a great and pivotal conflict of the industrial age. His particular concern was that the enemy had clearly learned the lessons the British Army yet remained reluctant to acknowledge and that this might lead precipitously towards defeat.

At the outbreak of the war the German forces certainly possessed a massive superiority in aircraft, artillery pieces and automatic weapons compared to any army which opposed them.

This was a time when the machine gun, though no new phenomenon, was generally considered to be something of a nuisance by the British Army. Infantry battalions did not possess many of them, they were poorly regarded by senior commanders and the machine guns were regularly dispatched to the sidelines in pre-war exercises to where they could not interfere with the 'proper business' of military manoeuvres. How different the philosophy of the German Army was on the matter in 1914 the B.E.F quickly discovered to its cost.

It is perhaps time on this centenary anniversary of the First World War's opening shots to place Christopher Baker-Carr in his rightful position in the history of his nation, of the British Army and in the development of modern armament and warfare. There can be no doubt he was an under-rated officer and one who, after the end of the Great War, all but faded from military history. Indeed, it is certain that many contemporary readers have been drawn to his book by an interest in its subject matter rather than through any prior knowledge of the man whose wartime activities it so entertainingly describes. However, our view is that in military terms Christopher Baker-Carr was a great man and one who is owed a debt of gratitude by his country which has never possibly been fully acknowledged.

Baker-Carr knew beyond any doubt how vital the machine gun was to the dominance of the battlefield and how essential it was that the weapon was employed effectively in large numbers by skilled troops under independent and specialised command. This conviction led him on a campaign to bring about the creation, under his management, of the Machine Gun Training School which produced thousands of competent gunners where previously there had been virtually none and no immediate potential that there would be any more. He was, furthermore, instrumental in securing the extensive manufacture and widespread distribution of the machine gun in the British Army and, indeed, the creation of the Machine Gun Corps itself. Beyond doubt all of these initiatives came into being as a consequence of Christopher Baker-Carr's single-minded resolve.

This alone should have been enough for one man to achieve and for history to have indelibly marked him. It is surely astonishing that he is today largely forgotten when one considers the potential consequences for the Allied cause had not this one man come to his vital conclusion and fought a crusade to see his vision come to fruition.

If that was all there was to the story of Christopher Baker-Carr it would be been more than enough. It was not enough for Baker-Carr himself, however, because the principle that motivated him to champion the cause of the machine gun was not limited by the development of a single weapon, but by what it represented as an essential component which would potentially contribute to final victory.

Above all Baker-Carr understood with conviction that the stalemate of trench warfare was destined to persist and whilst the effective use of the machine gun would go some way to guarantee a *status quo* in such conditions, there never would be the opportunity to put the long wished for 'Gee in gap' for there was nothing in the prevailing arsenal or embodied in tactics that had the capacity to cross 'no-mans land' to breakthrough and so neutralise a long established strong defensive line.

Christopher Baker-Carr did not conceive the idea of the tank in the British Army, that honour goes to Swinton, but he instantly knew its potential. It was, in short—'the answer'—a turn-key solution that was entirely innovative which held the potential to end the deadlock of the war of trenches and the fruitless slaughter of the infantry attack as men were hurled against fixed positions.

He became the tank's champion and drove its cause forward resolutely. In the broadest sense almost everyone knows the outcome of Christopher Baker-Carr's efforts on automatic weapons combined with armour, and what effect they had on this and wars that followed. Certainly, Baker-Carr can justifiably be acclaimed as one of the founding influences of what became the Royal Armoured Corps and, given the position of the British Army as innovators in this field, of armoured mechanised warfare generally.

It has to be admitted that soldiers like Baker-Carr have never been especially popular in the British Army. It has ever been a conventional institution that does not encourage visionaries. The list of mouldbreakers is short (though too long to feature here) however, it is worth mentioning, given Baker-Carr's views, that one of them was John Le Marchant without whom there would have been no Military College at the time it was formed. That list contains other names which have become abidingly famous for these were exceptional people who really made a difference against the odds within a conservative system that demanded conformity as the prerequisite to all that made it function.

In the end, there is but one way to achieve the unpopular in the face of resistance which is to stretch ones boundaries to breaking point, interpret (or misinterpret) orders and permissions loosely and to take advantage of every opportunity however slight to achieve what you believe to be right. Those who did this were always men who took risks and walked a fine line between personal success and disaster.

Of course, the introduction of the tank did not win the Great War though Baker-Carr could only know that would be so after the event. Hostilities lasted just four years and within that time the tank was under constant development. The potential of the weapon was evident to those with a willingness to see it, but experimentation combined with battlefield application is never an ideal scenario. Consequently, the patchy, unreliable and indecisive performance of the tank in battle in 1916 was not seen by commanders to be the weapon upon which they might depend as an instrument of fundamental change in the attack. Byng's decision to employ tanks in large numbers at Cambrai in late 1917 provided something of a wake-up call. The machines themselves were still undependable but Napoleon's principle that, quantity has a quality all of its own, was well proven. Certainly the demoralising effect on the enemy in the face of an attack of massed tanks was plain to see and invaluable.

Ultimately the Great War was to be a war of attrition. Germany was literally worn down in every definition of the term. German commanders knew that once the United States of America had joined the fray with its vast resources of men, materiel and manufacturing the only way to slow down the inevitable outcome was to disrupt the logistical flow as it crossed the Atlantic Ocean. For once this mighty resource arrived in Europe it would not simply assist in fighting the war, but would supply the means to certainly win it. When the day of the U-Boat was ended by the proliferation of naval destroyers operating from either side of the Atlantic the imminent end was in sight. Germany attempted one terrifying last throw in the West to avert defeat, but it was not enough.

During the 'Hundred Days' offensive leading to the Armistice the tank came into its own. It was now 1918 and numbers of the latest and best tanks built were in commission and available to be employed on a battlefield which, once more, offered fluidity of movement. Now the tank was able to be used to its best effect thus far in the war that gave birth to it, but there had been too little time between the inception of the battle tank and the close of hostilities for it to be realised to its full potential. So those who were responsible for bringing the tank to the battlefield never saw the tanks achieve their full potential. Understandably, after four years of appalling loss of life no one was minded to mourn that particular shortcoming. That would come later.

Demonstrably, the introduction of the tank was a 'game-changer' on the battlefield for there has never been a war defined by mud, wire and the unchanging lines of trenches again. It is, perhaps, chilling to note, that the first time the world actually saw what tanks could really do they were deployed against the British Army among others in the hands of the very nation Baker-Carr and the other tank pioneers had worked so hard to defeat.

None of this was Christopher Baker-Carr's concern. All that can be expected of any soldier is that he serves his country and fights its enemies. So much is recognised by all military men as 'duty'.

Of course, some soldiers have always by ways and degrees 'gone above and beyond' duty and medals are struck and presented for it. We admire such people as is proper and perhaps, despite the apparently 'exceptional' character of their actions that is what everyone wants and expects, because we understand the kinds of deeds that define the term. Every so rarely a military man goes 'above and beyond' in the service of his country's cause because he knows what is needed to be done irrespective of whether anyone approves of it or him. In his time and place, thankfully, Christopher Baker-Carr was such a man. May we never cease to produce men and women like him.

Please enjoy his book. It will in all probability be a revelation.

The Leonaur Editors

This book is dedicated to
The Officers and Non-Commissioned Officers
Of the Staff of the Machine-Gun School
In France, 1914-1916
And to
The Staff of the First Brigade, Tank Corps
1917-1918
In Affectionate Gratitude for Their Constant
Support and Unfailing Loyalty, without
Which Nothing Could Have Been
Accomplished

Foreword

It was my unique privilege during the Great War to be closely associated with the development and organisation of the most important defensive weapon, the machine gun, and of the most important offensive weapon, the tank.

Today, perhaps, it will seem incredible that the High Command failed to appreciate the true value of the machine gun and the tank in the early stages of their development. It will seem even more incredible that, at a later period, it was necessary to scheme and struggle against official lukewarmness, at times almost indistinguishable from hostility, in order to secure the increase in the numbers of these arms, which, as was evident to everybody else, had proved themselves to be the greatest preservers of life yet discovered.

In the following pages I have endeavoured to set down an account of the difficulties encountered, of failures and successes, of high hopes brought to the ground by lack of faith and vision, of the ultimate recognition at long last, of the superiority of machinery and metal over beef and brawn.

Much of what I have written, especially in the earlier portions of the book, is, of necessity, a personal narrative, and I have described events and occurrences as I, myself, saw them.

The Great War is still a recent memory. It is not yet history. Many of the chief personages in that vast tragedy are living or have only recently passed away. Not yet has emerged the truth, the whole truth and nothing but the truth.

Vision is still blurred by proximity, but, as the years go by, that vision will become clearer and more sharply defined, until, at length, persons and events will stand forth in their true perspective.

None of those who took part in the war will live to read the impartial verdict of history. If this book succeeds, even in the most infinitesimal degree, in throwing some new light on certain aspects, its object will have been achieved.

C. B.-C.

September 1929.

CHAPTER 1

Departure for the Front

1

On the fifth of August 1914 England awoke to find herself at war. After days of agonising suspense and uncertainty regarding the attitude of the Cabinet, a united people breathed a deep sigh of relief when at last their path lay clear before them, all doubts and hesitations swept into oblivion by the violation of Belgian neutrality.

Thousands upon thousands of men, of every class, profession, and age, already thronged the recruiting offices. Tens upon tens of thousands of others were waiting only until such time as they could find out where to present themselves for enrolment.

When I arrived at the War Office that morning, I found it besieged by officers, active, retired, or on leave foreign service, begging and beseeching to be employed.

Having left the army some eight years previously and not belonging to the Reserve of Officers, I realised that there was little or no hope of my being able to rejoin my former regiment. My only real claim for immediate employment was that I had been on the Instructional Staff at the School of Musketry at Hythe, but I was aware that this qualification, if pressed, might tend rather towards a post at some training centre in England, a thing I was determined to avoid at all costs.

I knew that I should be met with the inevitable, stereotyped instruction to put my request in writing, but I also knew that, as a last resort, I could apply to Sir John Cowans, then Quartermaster-General, upon whom a brother Rifleman could always rely for help.

First of all, I paid calls on one or two other old brother officers on the War Office Staff, who, though exceedingly pleasant in spite of their overwhelming work, could only suggest that I should put in a written application for employment. (I might mention here that I did so and, three months later in France, received a reply that my application would receive due consideration.) It soon became evident that I must stake everything on my last hope. I therefore sent up my card to Cowans, asking if I could see him for a minute.

I waited in fear and trembling till, after a few minutes' absence, the messenger returned.

"Would you please step this way, sir?" he said. Eagerly I followed him upstairs to the O.M.G.'s department. After a moment's waiting, I was shown into his office.

"Sit down, Baker, and tell me what's your trouble," said Cowans, who, as was his custom, appeared to have unlimited time at his disposal and to be concerned only with the affairs of the person with whom he was talking.

I briefly explained my position.

"Have you put in your application?" he asked.

"You know what that means," I said. "I want to be in this show. I may be too late."

"You won't be too late, old boy," replied Cowans.

"There'll be lots of room for everybody." He thought for a moment. "Do you mind in what capacity you go if I can work it?"

"I don't care a bit, as long as I get out at once."

"I'll manage it somehow. Go to the R.A.C. and register your name as a driver. They've offered to send cars to France and I probably can use them. I'll let you know at the club later."

He waved his hand in a cheerful farewell and turned back to the enormous stack of files, documents, etc., which had been held up for my convenience.

I went straight to the R.A.C., where I had a talk with the official in charge of the registration of cars for war service, and was enrolled as a volunteer driver. I had no car at that time, but the official informed me that an elderly patriot had registered his car at the R.A.C. for service abroad, if a driver could be found for it. I proceeded immediately to the house of the owner, who gladly agreed for me to take his car, if the War Office decided to avail itself of the offer of the R.A.C.

I waited as patiently as I could for developments.

On the afternoon of the 16th August, I sat in the club and listened, for the hundredth time, to the various conjectures concerning the destination of the Expeditionary Force. Three years later, during the preparations for the Cambrai Tank Battle, it was to be brought home to me more fully that the Englishman is the only person in the world capable of keeping his mouth shut. Hundreds of people in authority and their subordinates had knowledge of the secret of the B.E.F., but I never met one single man in London at that time who even hinted that he was in possession of this information.

As I sat there listening, a waiter handed me a telegram. I opened it, hoping vaguely that it might contain some prospect of employment. It did; and more. It was an order to report the following day at Southampton with the car and proceed to France, where further orders would be received.

Full of excitement, I dashed off to Burberry's and bought a suit of khaki off the peg. The fit was moderate, but it was uniform. That was the one thing that mattered. I collected a few necessaries for myself and the car that night, including a new set of tyres, free of charge, from a German company that had been taken over by the British Government.

The next day I reported to the Embarkation Staff at Southampton, where I found a dozen other fortunate owner-drivers, who were also under orders for France. The cars were safely stowed away in the bowels of the ship and, after dark, we moved out silently and mysteriously into the Channel, in company with several other transports, under escort of destroyers. We carried no lights and even the striking of matches on the open deck was strictly prohibited.

In the smoking-room, where our little party had congregated, the wildest conjectures as to our future employment were being put forward. Some visualised themselves dashing wildly at eighty miles an hour through the German lines, the bearers of messages on which the fate of armies depended; others pessimistically were convinced that we should be employed as taxi-drivers on lines of communication.

It was a motley collection. It included several well-known racing drivers, Toby Rawlinson, brother of General Sir Henry (afterwards Lord) Rawlinson, Oscar Morrison, and Jimmy Radley. There was one, Coleman,[1] a full-blooded American, whom the Germans would have been fully entitled to shoot on sight. In his ill-fitting uniform he looked like a prosperous banker in unsuitable fancy-dress. There were, also, two or three retired officers who, like myself, had jumped at the

---

1. *A Twilight of Centaurs,* the opening campaigns of the First World War as witnessed by an American volunteer driver with British cavalry on the Western Front, by Frederic Coleman is also published by Leonaur.

first opportunity to rejoin.

Looking back after more than fourteen years on that little scene, I wonder if there entered into any of our minds the slightest conception of the strange adventures in which we were to take part. Soon the little band was to be dispersed forever on their different tasks. All of us, sooner or later, received commissions and took a more direct and personal part in the war; but those first experiences, in many cases wilder than our wildest dreams, will never be forgotten and will be treasured up as long as memory lasts.

2

At Havre next morning we disembarked our cars and were instructed to proceed to Amiens. All along the roads up from the coast we were received with loud cheers and acclamations in every village through which we passed. Flowers and fruit were hurled into our cars and at least one member of the party suffered from a black eye, caused by an apple thrown by a too-enthusiastic admirer to him while travelling at a speed of fifty miles an hour. At Neufchatel we stopped for an hour for lunch.

Up till then we had travelled as a convoy. The white dust, which lay inches deep on the road, had turned us all into the semblance of flour-millers. It was therefore agreed during lunch that, on the next stage to Amiens, where we were to receive further orders, we should travel independently and reassemble a few miles before reaching our destination.

There was a general scramble to get away first. The racing drivers, with their racing experience, were quickest off the mark. Their cars roared up the long hill in a cloud of white dust, the open exhausts chattering like machine guns.

Everybody went "all out." To this day I cannot conceive why there were not a dozen accidents. Not a breath of wind stirred on that blazing August afternoon and most of the time one was driving through a pall of dust, as thick as a London fog, thrown up by the preceding car. My personal recollection of that drive is that I started from Neufchatel ninth, arrived at the rendezvous fourth, and, to the best of my knowledge, I had passed only two cars belonging to our party on the way.

As soon as the reassembly was complete, we proceeded demurely, in convoy fashion once more, into Amiens, where we arrived at five o'clock in the afternoon. There six of us received instructions to push on at once to Le Cateau, where British G.H.Q. was established. After a short stop to fill up with oil and petrol, we took the road again and arrived late at night in the courtyard of the school at Le Cateau, which had been taken over by the General Staff as offices. Nobody seemed to know that we were coming, but we were welcomed with open arms as G.H.Q. was suffering from a serious dearth of cars. A number of W. & G. taxis had been brought over from London, but they had not been designed for the service demanded of them and, in a few days, they had met with an untimely but glorious end.

My first few days at Le Cateau remain in my mind as a confused blur of driving night and day, of short snatches of sleep, little time to wash or shave, and hurried meals in wayside *estaminets*. As soon as I had brought one passenger back to G.H.Q., I found another waiting impatiently for a car to proceed in haste on business, urgent and pressing. Several times, when returning from some mission empty, I was commandeered by an excited officer who had to get somewhere at once and possessed no means of locomotion. One morning I spent several hours searching for the lost Transport Column of the 19th Brigade, who had had no supplies or food for two days.

On another occasion, I was hailed by an excited general officer, who seized me and ordered me to drive him to G.H.Q. "as hard as God will let you." He got in beside me and I did my best to carry out his instructions. I did the five miles to Le Cateau in about six minutes and drove into the little town at fifty miles an hour. As we neared the bottom of the hill, a long line of horse-transport suddenly appeared from a side street, moving directly across our front. It was quite impossible to stop. I jammed on all my brakes and, twisting the steering wheel sharply to the left, skidded the car on to the pavement of the side street. I missed the nearest wagon by at least a foot, grazed a lamp-post, and finally emerged on to the roadway safe and sound, not a little pleased with (as I thought) rather a pretty piece of fancy driving.

"Stop," shouted my general. "Stop, blast you!"

I pulled up.

My general descended. He was trembling with rage and hatred.

"You —— —— ——," he said.

"I thought you were in a hurry, sir," I replied meekly.

He glared at me a moment.

"My God, my God!" was all he could ejaculate, as he gave me one parting look of loathing and walked away briskly in the direction of the General Staff Offices.

Thank heaven, the next time we met he failed to recognise in the *commandant* of the Machine Gun School the dirty, unshaven chauffeur who had driven him a year before. For my part, I preserved a discreet silence, thinking it wiser not to recall our little adventure to his recollection.

3

I kept no diary and events followed one another in, such quick succession that it is difficult to set down, with any accuracy, details of those first experiences. One or two minor incidents, however, stand out with startling clearness.

The first German prisoner. I was standing outside the General Staff Offices, waiting for a passenger, when I heard a murmur of angry voices, broken by an occasional scream of execration. Having nothing to do for the moment, I went outside the gates to see what was going forward.

Up the street marched a dozen British soldiers. In their midst walked a boy, bare-headed and dressed in the "field-grey" uniform, which we were to know so well later. The wretched lad, not more than nineteen or twenty years of age, looked pale and drawn, but was attempting bravely to conceal his terror of the angry mob of Frenchmen and women who hemmed in the escort on every side. Now and then a woman would make a dash for the little party and shriek threats and abuse at the unfortunate prisoner. One of the escort would gently, but firmly, push the infuriated woman away, adding a few words about "giving the pore fello a chanst." I'm sure the prisoner heaved a sigh of relief when he found himself locked up in a cell, safe from the angry mob which, but for the escort, would have undoubtedly torn him to pieces.

The first German aeroplane. Suddenly one morning an aeroplane was seen in the clear sunlight, flying over the little town of Le Cateau. In those days the Germans were easily distinguishable by their hawk-like bodies, even at a height of ten thousand feet. There was the wildest excitement and, with one accord, everybody who possessed a revolver or a rifle started loosing off madly. Till the machine was out of sight, *feu-de-joie* continued, the last few shots being fired at a range of about five miles.

It was at this time that the first aerial combat in history took place and it is curious now to reflect that, on both sides, it was fought with revolvers. The revolvers were soon superseded by carbines, but it was

28

not till sometime later that the Vickers or Lewis guns became the recognised armament of aeroplanes.

During this uncertain and disorganised period, I drove anybody and everybody, as directed by the officer of the General Staff from whom I received my orders.

Once or twice I had the pleasure of driving the then Chief of the General Staff of the B.E.F., Sir Archibald Murray. A man of great ability and personal charm, his somewhat delicate health broke down under the terrific strain of the opening phases of the war. A few days later at St. Quentin he worked in the General Staff Office till past midnight, poring over reports and maps. Some member of his staff asked him a question and, receiving no reply, walked over to his chief's desk. The C.G.S. was sitting in his chair, his head fallen forward on to the table, in a dead faint. Later on, Sir Archibald, when Deputy Chief of the Imperial General Staff at the War Office, gave me most valuable assistance at the time when I was struggling to persuade the High Command in France that the machine gun was quite a useful weapon.

Sometimes I was sent out to find some division whose whereabouts was uncertain. This was usually a thrilling job, as the only thing of which one could be quite certain was that the place where the division had last been heard of had since fallen into German hands. In addition, parties of *Uhlans* were constantly reported, though I think that most of these reports, like that of Mark Twain's death, were "much exaggerated."

Almost all the roads were under shell fire, and on several occasions, after being pinned down by heavy shelling for an hour or so, behind a bank or in a sunken road, I wondered if, after all, a nice, quiet job as Musketry Instructor in England would not have been preferable.

My final exit from Le Cateau was a somewhat precipitate one. I had been out all day on various jobs and returned there late at night to collect my kit. The Expeditionary Force was falling back. Already G.H.Q. had moved to St. Quentin and, in a few hours, we knew that Le Cateau would be in the hands of the Germans.

Up till now, the inhabitants of the little town had preserved an almost child-like faith in the invincibility of the British Army, and when the news leaked out that we were falling back, consternation reigned among the townspeople. A hundred times a day I was asked if it were true that the British were retreating. One had to say "Yes"; it was so painfully obvious. Trenches were being dug on the hill north of the town and all the civilians, men, women, and children, lent a hand. The phrase *"reculer pour mieux sauter,"* with which one tried to soften the blow, brought but little comfort to the poor people. One of the many pathetic sights was that of an elderly housewife, busily scouring and whitening her front doorstep, when I knew full well that within forty-eight hours the house in all probability would have ceased to exist.

Shells were falling plentifully in the town and already many of the houses were in flames. The exits to the south and west were blocked with the fleeing inhabitants, their belongings hastily thrown into every sort of vehicle from a farm-wagon to a Sunlight-soap box on bicycle wheels. It was curious to note the incongruous collection of articles snatched up at the moment of departure, ranging from kitchen utensils, feather-beds, and pieces of furniture to glass cases of wax flowers, stuffed birds, bunches of dyed pampas-grass, and imitation lace curtains.

It was raining hard and as black as ink. With difficulty I picked my way through the confusion, gathering eager passengers as I went. To this day I do not know how many people climbed on to the car that night, but I know that there were eleven women, besides several children, inside it.

It was terribly sad to see them. They were absolutely stunned. I have often wondered what was the fate of a poor old woman who was one of those seated in front beside me. She must have been at least seventy years old. She told me that she had managed to eke out a scanty livelihood in a tiny shop in a back street of Le Cateau. A shell had struck the house next door and set it on fire. Terrified, she wrapped a shawl about her head and walked out into the night. She had no relations or friends to whom she could look for aid; she had no money, everything in the world she possessed had been left behind in the little shop.

I set her down with the others at the *Mairie* in St Quentin, with a feeling of sorrow that I could do so little to help. The poor old woman wept silently as she tried to kiss my hand and, muttering a few broken words of thanks, turned away hopelessly into the darkness.

CHAPTER 2

With Sir John French

1

The retreat had begun in earnest.

Wherever I went, I met bodies of troops, ranging from organised units to little parties of ten or a dozen men. One of my multifarious jobs was to assist in directing these scattered parties to their brigades or divisions where they would find the remainder of the unit to which they belonged.

"Who are you?" I would call out, as a dozen tired and footsore men approached.

"We're the sole survivors of the Blankshire Regiment, sir," an old soldier would reply. "All the rest got done in yesterday. Not a soul except us is left alive."

"All right. Keep straight on for a couple of miles more and you will find three or four hundred other sole survivors of your regiment, bivouacking in a field."

This happened not once, but twenty times. On the first occasion or two, one was inclined to place some credence in the statement of the "sole survivors," but after a while one became so used to the description that it developed into a joke. It is, however, easy to understand how the expression was employed in the utmost of good faith. The fight was always a moving fight. Isolated parties of men often put up a desperate resistance, not knowing that their regiment had received orders to retire. They fought on and on till almost surrounded and forced to abandon the position which they held. Then, finding themselves alone, they drifted away along some road or track, in the firm belief that all save themselves had perished.

The spirit of the men was unconquerable. They plodded wearily along the roads, footsore, hungry and thirsty. Whenever I could, I used to carry food and drink in my car and many a time did I have a talk with half a dozen of them, as they stood around and munched the French bread and bully-beef I provided.

"When are we going to attack, sir?" was always the first question. "We gave them hell yesterday. Why don't they let us have a go at them?"

I would murmur something about strategical retirements, conforming to the French or our old friend *"reculer pour mieux sauter,"* in English this time. But that was no good to them and they would walk off, muttering to themselves something about being able" to take on a dozen lousy Germans."

One day I stood with Sir Horace Smith-Dorrien by the roadside, as the retreating columns trudged past. As each company drew near, the word was passed back that the corps commander was watching them. Caps were straightened, the poor tired feet made a brave effort to march in step, as each man turned his haggard, unshaven face towards the spot where Sir Horace stood gravely at the salute. The rain was pouring down in torrents, but he stood there till the last man had passed. Then he turned away in silence. At that moment I do not think he could have spoken.

Nobody in the fighting line appeared to realise how desperate was the situation. In a moving battle of such enormous extent the actual fighting man knew little or nothing of what was going on less than half a mile away. Even divisional commanders were not fully cognisant of the constantly changing situation, and it was only at G.H.Q. that one fully appreciated the significance of the remorseless retirement.

Some of the rapid and abrupt removals of G.H.Q. were not without their humorous side.

In St. Quentin, for instance, Sir Nevill Macready, the adjutant-general, sat in his extemporised office working far into the night. His faithful assistant worked beside him.

"There seems a lot of traffic in the streets tonight, Fido," said Sir Nevill. "Go and see what it is."

In a few minutes "Fido" returned with the news that G.H.Q. was on its way to Noyon and had forgotten to inform the adjutant-general!

Hastily every available vehicle was collected. Typewriters, files, and documents were hurled into them and the A.G.'s office started off in pursuit of its careless guardian angel.

For a few days I was taken from my other work to augment the number of cars for the personal use of Sir John French. His A.D.C.s, the late Lord Brooke (afterwards Earl of Warwick), Fitz Watt, and Freddie Guest, were all naturally very concerned about the safety of the C.-in-C., especially as Sir John thoroughly enjoyed going into the fighting area where he had no business to be. In addition, the position of our troops varied from hour to hour and at times there were huge gaps in our line through which a determined cavalry leader could have thrust large bodies of mounted troops. As it was, cavalry patrols often rode through these gaps, though their purpose was solely to gain information and not to fight.

Rumours of large bodies of *Uhlans* on the road between Noyon and Ham were particularly rife at the moment when G.H.Q. started to move from the former to the latter town. That day my car was being used by the C.-in-C.'s personal staff, and after lunch, I was taken aside by Brooke and told that we were going through to Ham. A lot of *Uhlans* had been reported on the road and we should have to keep a sharp look out.

Off we started, Freddie Guest with a couple of passengers in his car leading the way; Sir John in a covered Rolls next; then my car, with Brooke beside me. We proceeded along the road for a mile or two, filled with a tense feeling of excitement.

As we approached the spot where the body of *Uhlans* had been reported, we saw a car come tearing over the hill in a cloud of dust from the direction of Ham.

"Great Scott!" exclaimed Brooke. "Something's up. Back your car off the road."

I stopped the car and backed almost into the ditch.

"Let Sir John's car go by first and then we'll do a bolt back to Noyon," said Brooke, as the approaching car came nearer.

Guest stood in the middle of the road to stop it. It pulled up with a grinding of brakes.

"What's up?" asked Guest anxiously, as he recognised the Duke of Westminster's chauffeur, the sole occupant of the car.

We all listened breathlessly for the answer.

It came.

"His Grace left his cigar-case in his billet, sir. He sent me back to get it."

No other *Uhlan* passed that way!

3

I was still more or less attached to the C.-in-C.'s retinue when G.H.Q. was at Compiègne, though I was doing a lot of other driving as well. Things were very critical on that day, as Sir Douglas Haig's First Corps had been almost surrounded and annihilated in the Fôret de Mormal.

At eight a.m. I arrived in the C.-in-C.'s house, where I found the A.D.C.s in deep discussion as to how Sir John could be safely got away in the event of a *débacle*. Brooke told me to go upstairs and have a wash in his bedroom before breakfast. In the middle of my toilet, in walked Sir John, in a blue dressing-gown, whistling cheerfully. He asked me if I had everything I wanted, and wished to know where I had been and what I had seen. Then, remarking that it was time for him to dress, he walked off to his own room, whistling cheerfully once more.

Sir John French may not have been a great soldier in the modern sense of the word, but he was a great leader of men. His unfailing cheerfulness and courage at that time were of inestimable benefit in keeping up the morale of the soldiers, and if ever he realised the desperate plight of the army under his command, he never showed the slightest sign of it.

That night, on instructions from Brooke, I slept in my car outside the C.-in-C.'s house, a wise precaution in the not impossible event of a sudden cavalry raid.

It has often since then occurred to me how half a dozen fast and reliable tanks would have given an easy victory to the Germans in 1914. Once through our very sketchy lines, they could have destroyed railway bridges, telegraph communications, ammunition and supply dumps, and played general havoc with Army and Corps Headquarters. The morale effect would have been incalculable. Even a dozen armoured cars, such as then were actually in existence, handled by a resourceful an intrepid commander, could have accomplished almost the same result.

To those whose experience is confined to trench warfare this may seem to be an absurd statement; but on no less than five occasions of which I know, and probably on several others when I was ignorant of the fact, I passed outside the British lines and on only two of these occasions was I challenged on my return. There is not the least doubt that several times German cars, containing men disguised in British uniform, moved about freely behind our lines.

Although it is anticipating considerably, I should like to mention here as a confirmation of my statement that, during the final overthrow of the German Army in September 1918, some of the armoured cars of the Tank Corps penetrated so far behind the enemy line that they became entangled with the retiring German convoys. The cars took their places quietly in the line of traffic and religiously conformed to the orders of the German military policeman who controlled the stream of vehicles. It would have been useless to open fire, and the cars remained among the German traffic till they could extricate themselves on reaching a village, where they turned about and drove back to our lines in safety.

To Compiègne came "Papa Joffre," a grand, burly figure that inspired one with complete confidence, a curious type of commander-in-chief for an impetuous, nimble-minded race, for Joffre impressed by his calm stolidity. During all those days and weeks of agonising suspense, the French nation pinned its faith to "Papa Joffre." The French are somewhat apt to make a hero of a man and put him on a pedestal. Having put him there, they then proceed to hurl mud at him. Joffre so far has escaped the mud and his name will always be remembered with gratitude, not so much for his attainments as a soldier as for the spirit of calm, indomitable fortitude with which he inspired the French people at a crucial moment in its history.

4

For a few brief hours Dammartin was a stopping-place of G.H.Q. The less said about the departure from it the better.

I shall never forget the sight of Henry Wilson, Brigadier-General of the General Staff (afterwards Field-Marshal Sir Henry Wilson), clad in a dressing-gown, riding-breeches, and carpet slippers, standing on the steps of the *château* where General Staff was established, waiting for his car. As usual he was perfectly calm and collected, though many of the other members of the staff appeared somewhat "rattled." As, also, was his custom, he kept firing off sardonic little jests at all and sundry within earshot. Behind that heavily lined, kindly, humorous mask was hidden the keenest brain in the British Army. After many vicissitudes of fortune, he was destined, before the end of the war, to hold with conspicuous success the highest post in the British military world.

Nobody could fail to appreciate his remarkable abilities, but not a few mistrusted him, some because he was so brilliantly clever (for cleverness in the British Army is always regarded with suspicion), others because they considered that he was too great an admirer of the

Sir Henry Wilson

French. One thing, however, is quite certain: he was the only soldier capable of holding his own with the nimble minds of political opportunists with whom later he had to deal, when Chief of the Imperial General Staff.

The departure from Dammartin was a panic-stricken flight. Rumours of thousands of *Uhlans* in the woods nearby arrived every moment. Typewriters and office equipment were flung into the waiting lorries, which were drawn up in serried ranks in front of the *château*.

It was a pitch-black night, lit up by a hundred dazzling headlights. With much difficulty I collected my quota of passengers and got clear of the seething mass of vehicles. Having deposited my load at the next halting-place, I returned once more to Dammartin, where I had left some washing-which I could ill afford to lose. Everything in the little town seemed quiet and peaceful, so, seeking out my previous billet, I went to bed and enjoyed a good night's sleep.

5

During the retreat I had been called upon on one occasion to drive Major Shea (now General Sir James Shea, K.C.B., K.C.M.G., D.S.O.), who was acting as liaison officer between G.H.Q. and the Cavalry Division.

At this time I knew Shea only slightly, but the time was to come when later, as his permanent driver, I was to know him intimately and to conceive for him personally a great affection and the deepest admiration for his remarkable *sang-froid* and cheerfulness under the most disturbing conditions.

One night I was summoned to G.S. offices to drive him out to General Allenby's Headquarters. I waited outside the office till the door opened and Shea appeared.

"Where to?" I asked him, as he got into the car beside me.

"Cavalry Division," he replied. "I'm not sure where they are. All I know is that they were reported in such-and-such a village at four o'clock this afternoon. It's perfectly certain they're not there now. The Boches are probably there. We'd better go and find out."

I glanced at him sideways to see if he was joking. Not a bit of it. His eye-glass was firmly fixed in his eye and there wasn't the vestige of a smile on his face.

"This is a nice sort of bloke," I thought to myself, as I swung out on to the main road.

Mile after mile we drove, almost in silence, till the map told us that we were not far from the village in question. We had not met a living soul nor had we been challenged one single time.

"It's only half a mile on," said Shea, as we came to a cross-road. "Up here to the right."

"Don't you think it might be as well if we approached backwards?" I asked. "The Germans are put up a barricade in front of the village if they're there and the road is too narrow to turn in quickly."

"Good idea, old boy," replied Shea.

I reversed the car and we moved slowly up the road, both of us peering backwards into the darkness. We could see no lights and could hear no sound whatever. The place seemed absolutely deserted. I was about to make some remark when suddenly a burst of rifle fire broke out fifty or a hundred yards away. We could see the flashes of the rifles and hear the vicious crack of the bullets as they flew past.

"I think the Germans are here, old boy," said Shea calmly. "Perhaps we'd better clear out."

Already I had my forward gear in mesh and the car bounded forward, as if it had been pricked from behind with a sharp pin. Fortunately, I had extinguished my headlights when I had reversed the car and, although the bullets were too close to be pleasant, we managed to get away undamaged.

"Where to now?" I asked, as we arrived once more at the cross-roads.

"We'd better get back inside our own lines and see if we can get any information. Keep straight ahead."

I switched on my headlights again and drove cautiously down the road. I was considerably perturbed as to how we were to get back through our own lines without accident, as everybody's nerves were on the jump and all sorts of rumours of disguised German cars were rife.

After ten minutes' travelling we caught sight of two figures in khaki, standing on a little culvert fifty yards ahead. At the same moment a challenge rang out.

Automatically I pulled up with a jerk.

"It's all right, sentry," shouted Shea. "We're General Staff from G.H.Q."

"Drive up slowly," called back the sentry.

I let in my clutch and crawled up to the little bridge, leaning out with my pass held in my right hand. Shea leaned out of the other side, also displaying his pass. I stopped on reaching the sentries, who took our passes from us to examine them.

Without the slightest warning, an officer appeared in the glare of my headlights six feet in front of the radiator, pulled out his revolver and fired two shots at us point blank. The first shot went between Shea's head and mine; the second smashed one of my headlights.

I don't quite know what I said to that officer, but it was not half so efficacious as the quiet, blistering sarcasm with which Shea addressed him. By the time Shea's homily on the danger of firearms in the hands of inexperienced people and on the desirability of not losing one's head on active service was ended, I was terribly sorry for that young man.

"All right, old boy," said Shea, turning to me when he had finished. "We must get on."

I don't mind admitting that these two little incidents in the course of ten or fifteen minutes had shaken my nerve a bit and I drove along the road at about ten miles an hour, one foot resting lightly on the clutch pedal, the other ready at a moment's notice to jam down the brake.

"We've got to push on a bit faster, old boy," said Shea. "We shan't meet any more sentries now."

Hardly were the words out of his mouth than a man leapt from the ditch not thirty yards ahead and knelt in the road, his rifle at his shoulder. In the light of my remaining headlight, I could see his finger trembling on the trigger.

"Halt!" he shouted. "Don't you move or I shoot."

The car was at a standstill before he had uttered the first word. I sat motionless at the wheel, wondering where he would get me.

Out of the corner of my eye I could see another khaki-clad figure, creeping up the ditch by the roadside. As soon as he was level with us, he made a dash for my side of the car and rammed his bayonet up against my ribs.

"Oo are yer?" he demanded fiercely.

I explained to him that we were quite harmless individuals in search of the Cavalry Division. After examining our passes, he stood back and saluted.

"It's all right, Bill," he called to his comrade, who was still kneeling in the road, his rifle pointing somewhere about the pit of my stomach. He turned to me with an ingratiating grin. "I only did that to frighten sir!" he said.

"My friend," I replied, as I let in my clutch with a trembling foot, "you succeeded beyond your wildest expectations."

CHAPTER 3

The First Battle of Ypres Begins

1

When at last the retirement had reached its southernmost point and the German onslaught was spent, it seemed as though it must be months before the Expeditionary Force would again be in fighting trim. The casualties had been enormous and the survivors were worn out with fighting and marching. Boots, clothing, and equipment were in a terrible condition. Several times I heard it stated by senior officers that it would be at least six or eight weeks before the army would be fit to take the field. Actually it was less than ten days before it went into action once more and played an important part in the Battle of the Marne.

During the few days between the end of the retreat and the commencement of the Marne offensive, I was sent to Paris by Sir John French with dispatches for the British Ambassador. I had to remain there for two or three days for a reply and enjoyed to the utmost the luxury of baths, good food, and a comfortable bed.

It was on the day after my arrival that the French Government decided to leave Paris for Bordeaux. Consternation reigned in the city. Everybody was convinced that this precipitate departure meant that Paris was about to be besieged. Thousands upon thousands of people thronged the approaches to the Gare de Lyons; every vehicle, horse and motor, was at a premium and huge sums were offered for them by would-be refugees. Then, on the following day, came another bombshell in the shape of a government order that no one was to leave Paris without a special permit. This order, however, was cancelled within twenty-four hours and thousands of Parisians sought safety in flight.

For a day and a night I was the sole guest at the Ritz Hotel. As I ate a final lunch before leaving for the front, I was surrounded by the few officials and waiters who had not been called up. Time after time I was asked how soon I thought Paris would be shelled and whether the city would be captured.

Outside the fortifications frantic efforts were being made to put Paris in a state of defence. Barbed wire was being erected by the mile, trenches were being dug, buildings and trees were being razed to the ground where the field of fire was impeded. In view of what one knows now, one realises how fatuous were these preparations. If it had ever come to pass that Paris had been besieged, the Germans could have systematically blasted it to pieces from a range of ten miles or more and never risked the life of a single soldier in making an assault.

Paris was a city of the dead. There was not a single vehicle in the Champs Elysées between the Place de la Concorde and the Arc de Triomphe. Not a living soul was to be seen, except occasionally a woman or an old man who hastened along, looking neither to the right nor to the left. All the hotels and shops were closed and a deathly silence brooded.

Outside the Porte Maillot, however, there was feverish activity. The Bois de Boulogne was filled with thousand of sheep and cattle; tons upon tons of stores were being piled; mountains of hay and forage were stacked everywhere.

As I drove through the city on my way to the Porte St. Denis and passed by the Place Vendome I looked up at Napoleon's column and wondered whether for a third time it would be pulled down and, if so, whether it would ever rise again.

It is easy to be wise after the event, but it seems now almost incredible that the German High Command failed to appreciate the fact that the Channel ports at that time were theirs for the taking. Later on they expended tens upon tens of thousands of lives in their vain efforts to capture them. At the end of August 1914, patrols of *Uhlans* actually rode unmolested into the outskirts of Boulogne and departed.

The only explanation is that the German Government was so obsessed by the name of Paris, and was so confident that its capture would bring the war to a rapid and successful conclusion, that they were unable to realise how much the possession of the ports would mean.

On my return, I found G.H.Q. on the move again, this time forward to Coulommiers. The miracle had taken place, and the Germans had hurled away the first of the three certain chances of victory vouchsafed to them.

During my few days' absence, a remarkable change had taken place. The gloom and depression of the last three weeks had departed and an atmosphere of optimism reigned in its stead.

2

Much to my delight, I was now allotted permanently to Shea and for the next few weeks I spent my time in driving him between G.H.Q. and Allenby's Headquarters.

Almost my first job was to drive him from Coulommiers to Cavalry Corps Headquarters the night before the beginning of the Battle of the Marne.

We had been out all day and, after an early dinner, I had retired to bed in the billet which Shea and I shared. At eleven o'clock I was awakened by Shea's servant, Pitney, with the news that the car was wanted as soon as possible.

In a few minutes I was dressed and stood waiting outside the G.S. office.

"We've got to hurry up, old boy," said Shea, as he sat down beside me. "I want to get out as quickly I as I can."

It was a bright, clear night, warm and still. As I turned out of the square on to the main road, it was difficult to realise that there was a war going on. In those days of open warfare the night shelling was almost negligible and a deep peace seemed to reign everywhere, although within a few miles thousands of men were waiting to spring at one another's throats.

The road was lined, like most of the highways of France, with tall poplars, which cast deep shadows across the white, dusty surface. The rhythmic chatter of the exhaust was thrown back from the trees, and the flickering of the alternate light and shade exercised an almost hypnotic effect on the senses.

Already the faithful Pitney, who always accompanied us on our night trips after our previous experiences, had covered himself with his blanket and, rolled up on the floor in the back of the car, was snoring loudly. From time to time Shea made some remark, but he, too, was beginning to succumb to the influences of the night.

"You've got to put out your headlights now, old boy," was his last remark in a sleepy voice. "It's all right, though; you can see the road. Push along as fast as ever you can."

I switched off the lights and, although I could see fairly well, I had to concentrate my full attention in order to drive without mishap at fifty or sixty miles an hour.

Gradually I felt the weight of Shea's body pressing against my left side. I glanced at him and saw that his eyes were closed, his eye-glass firmly fixed in his left eye. Almost imperceptibly his head drooped towards me, and in a few minutes it was comfortably resting on my shoulder. He, too, began to snore softly.

There is nothing that accentuates a sense of loneliness more than to be the only wakeful person. I drove on, my eyes on the road, but my thoughts a thousand miles away. The low hum of the engine, the steady flickering of the shadows, the rush of the cool, fresh air on my face began to produce on me a somnolent effect. Once or twice I found myself nodding over the wheel and I had to concentrate all my will-power in order to keep awake.

Suddenly, without the slightest warning, a white cow stepped from behind a tree and walked straight into the middle of the road. It was impossible to pull up and, at the speed at which we were travelling, it would have been suicide to swerve. I kept straight ahead and struck the animal broadside on with my radiator and mudguard. It seemed to fly in the air, and there were four violent jolts as the wheels passed over its body.

"What was that, old boy?" asked Shea, waking suddenly and sitting up with a start.

"A cow."

"Did you kill it?"

"I think so."

"Well done, old boy!" said Shea, as his head slipped back on to my shoulder and the gentle snoring recommenced.

On I drove, chuckling to myself and wondering whether anything in the world could ever disturb his equanimity.

3

The next few days were days of hope and exultation. Nobody doubted but that the beginning of the end had come. The enemy had shot his bolt and we had him on the run. Even Henry Wilson, the ablest thinker in the British Army, was prophesying a German *débacle* and talking about chasing them to the Rhine. Little did we dream that we had before us more than four years of misery, mud, and slaughter.

The German Crown Prince on the eastern wing of the invaders found himself in serious difficulties and von Kluck's Army, we heard, had been hastily dispatched to his aid. This movement entailed a march, during which his flank was exposed to an attack.

Without a moment's hesitation the Paris Army of Defence was hurled into the battle. Speed was the essential factor and to this end every motor vehicle in Paris was pressed into service. Taxicabs, motor-buses, delivery-vans, and private cars, filled to overflowing with soldiers, were rushed to the rendezvous. Along the road for many months afterwards could be seen the remains of broken-down vehicles, some still bearing the signs of their previous owners, Galeries Lafayette, Printemps, Louvre, etc., etc.

An incident occurred at this time which surely must constitute the shortest campaign in history. An officer of an Irish regiment, who had been left behind in England at the beginning, was ordered to rejoin at once in order to take command in place of the C.O., who had been killed in action. Much elated, the officer arrived in Paris and, by offering a large reward, managed to hire a car to take him to the front. The chauffeur drove him to a point beyond which he dared not go. The officer got out and was in the act of counting out the promised fare, when a high explosive shell burst not far away, wounding him in the leg. Replacing his money in his pocket, with the help of the driver he climbed back into the car and returned to Paris. From Paris he was sent to London, where, after several months in hospital, he was discharged as unfit for service in the field.

Gradually resistance stiffened till our advance was brought to a complete standstill on the River Aisne. In spite of desperate efforts to progress, our way was barred. The deadlock that was to last for nearly four years had begun.

G.H.Q. was now at Fère-en-Tardenois, no great distance from the line. In consequence there was little for the liaison officers to do and I had a good deal of spare time on my hands. Rheims was only forty or fifty kilometres distant and many times did I pay a visit there, often taking with me officers of G.H.Q. on a "joy-ride."

In Rheims I made the acquaintance of the managing director of G. H. Mumm & Co. (a German firm), who was most generous with his excellent champagne, and many were the dozen of the *Cordon Rouge* in their neat wicker baskets that I distributed among the messes of my friends at G.H.Q. One case I left at Henry Wilson's mess, where by chance Joffre happened to be dining that night. The marshal inquired as to whence the excellent wine had come and, on being informed, said that he, too, would like a dozen. The following day Henry Wilson repeated this conversation to me and, very shortly, I was able to deliver a case, receiving in return a charming note from Joffre in acknowledgment.

4

Before the Battle of the Aisne was over, Shea was given a command in the field and, much to my regret, our association was at an end.

The race for the Channel Ports had begun. At last, but too late, the Germans had realised the incalculable value of the coast and were making frantic efforts to possess themselves of it. We, too, had awakened to the danger and were desperately endeavouring to avert this catastrophe.

The British Government was urging the French to allow our army to take up its position on the left of the Allied Forces, resting on the sea. Whether the French did not trust us even at that early date and still regarded us as *"perfide Albion"* has never been divulged, but, until the last day of the war, we were never allowed to occupy the position which every consideration, geographical and strategical, rendered logical. Was it, as the Germans never wearied of telling them, that they were afraid that, if once we took possession of the coast, we would never give it up? Possibly this may not have been the case, but a hundred times I was assured by the French peasants that England intended to hold on like grim death to all the land in France that she could seize.

I was now allotted as permanent driver to Major Price-Davies, V.C., D.S.O. of the 60th Rifles, whom I had known for many years. The principal duty assigned to him was to keep G.H.Q. in touch with Gough's Cavalry Division, as it hastened northwards to cover the Channel Ports. Daily our journey to Divisional H.Q. became longer and longer as the cavalry approached the Belgian frontier, till at length the patrols came in touch with the enemy in the vicinity of Hazebrouck and Poperinghe.

The situation at this time was one of great anxiety. There was nothing between the Germans and the sea except two or three thousand mounted men, until such time as our army on the Aisne could be relieved by the French and moved northwards, a manoeuvre that could not be completed for many days. Every morning Price-Davies and I left Fère-en-Tardenois in the early hours, drove to Ypres or wherever Gough happened to be and, after spending some hours with him, made our way homeward, having covered a distance of some two or three hundred miles.

The first of many exciting adventures, which I met with during

45

RUINS IN RHEIMS, SHOWING THE CATHEDRAL IN THE
BACKGROUND, AUGUST 1915

my association with Price-Davies, was not long in coming.

One Sunday, for some reason or another, after eating our lunch with Gough, we were suffered to take our departure early. I turned the bonnet of the car southwards and headed for Compiègne, where we stopped for half an hour and enjoyed a cup of tea.

"Which way shall we go back?" asked Price-Davies, looking at his map.

"Let's go back along the Compiègne-Soissons road," I replied. "It's a splendid road. I came along it several times during the retreat. I'd like to have a look at it again."

We left the town by the Soissons Gate, outside of which hundreds of the *burghers* of Compiègne with their families were strolling about and taking the air that beautiful Sunday afternoon.

We sped along the road, gradually leaving behind us the suburbs of the town. I opened up the car and soon we were reeling off a steady fifty miles per hour. After travelling some ten or twelve kilometres, we were surprised to see a line of French soldiers, lying on the right or southern side of the banked-up road.

"What are these blokes doing?" I asked.

"Some sort of training, I expect," replied Price-Davies.

On we went quite unconcerned, till suddenly a French soldier jumped from behind a tree and signalled us to stop.

"What's the matter?" I asked, as I displayed my special pass.

"You wait here till the officer comes," was the reply.

Very soon a French captain appeared who, after, putting his revolver to my head, demanded to know what we were doing.

"What's all the trouble?" I asked, when we had at last after some difficulty persuaded him that we were respectable persons.

"There is a Mercédès car out on the road this afternoon with two Germans in it disguised as British officers. We have orders to shoot on sight. You had better be careful."

"This is pleasant!" I thought to myself. "This car's a Mercédès and there are two British officers in it. We've got to go slow."

Off we started again, keeping to a modest speed and exchanging salutations with the soldiers, as they lay on the bank within a few feet of the roadway.

After travelling thus for a few kilometres, the line of troops suddenly bent back southwards from the road.

"That's better," said Price-Davies. "We can get along a bit faster now."

Soon we were bowling along again at a steady fifty. I was thinking to myself that we would soon be home at this rate, when I heard *crack—crack—crack,* coming from the right side of the road.

"Those damned Frogs are plugging at us," I remarked.

"I can't make out what on earth they are up to," replied Price-Davies.

Before the words were out of his mouth, we heard *crack—crack—crack,* this time from the *left* side of the road.

For a moment we were completely fogged. Then suddenly comprehension burst upon us. We were between the French and the German lines. The troops we had seen after leaving Compiègne were the French front line.

"If we stop now they're bound to get us," I said.

"Let's push on and hope for the best," replied Price-Davies.

I put my foot hard down on the accelerator and soon had the car doing well over seventy. It was all right for me; I had lots to do to keep the car on the road, but Price-Davies, on the German side of the car, had nothing to occupy his mind. He sat beside me, carefully scanning the ground for signs of German trenches, occasionally consulting his map, as calmly and as carefully as though he were in his office. His face was a little more set than usual and the line of his mouth a little more determined.

"If we get hit in the tyres or the petrol tank, pull up on the right side of the road and we'll get down the bank on the French side," he said at last. "There are two villages ahead. They may be held by the Boches or the French. We shall have to chance it."

This was a cheerful outlook. Whoever held them, it was certain that a barricade would have been erected at either end, manned by soldiers who would loose off at us without the slightest hesitation. Furthermore, there was a sharp S bend outside both villages which would preclude any chance of observation till we were right on top of them.

However, there was nothing for it but to carry on. I took a long breath as we swung round the bend and my heart leapt as I saw the village street before me unbarricaded. Once more I trod on the accelerator and we tore through that empty village like a hunted cat. Neither of us spoke, but we simultaneously turned to each other and grinned. The other village still lay ahead of us, but, having passed one successfully, we were more hopeful about the second. The five or six kilometres between the two villages we covered in three or four minutes and once again I held my breath as we swung round the last corner. Not a sign of a barricade or a soldier!

Both sides had been popping off at us all this time, but, the far greater danger of the villages being past, the musketry practice had lost much of its terrors. The Germans now opened on us with field guns for a change, but we could afford to laugh at the shells that kept bursting a hundred yards or more behind us. Soon the town of Soissons came into view and the firing from both sides died down and ceased.

I was congratulating myself on our troubles being safely over when, fifty yards ahead, I was horrified to see a huge chasm dug across the road, completely blocking further progress. On the left side of the road stood a long line of ruined houses, on the right a cemetery wall ten feet high. I pulled up and got out of the car to make an examination to see what could be done.

On the far side of the chasm stood a sentry, an elderly French Territorial, who evidently regarded me with considerable suspicion as I crawled round the excavations towards him. As I got near to him, my eye caught sight of the butt of my revolver in the side-pocket of my British warm, where, early in the proceedings, I had slipped it in case of need. Cautiously I slid my hand down to put it out of sight. The sentry misinterpreted the movement and, throwing his rifle to his shoulder, loosed off a shot that whizzed unpleasantly near my head. I threw up my hands and shouted at him. He reloaded, but eventually allowed me to approach, though he kept me covered all the time.

"I want to drive into the town," I explained, as soon as he was satisfied of my *bona fides.*

"Where do you come from?"

"Compiègne."

"Well, then," he replied, "you've got to go back there."

"That I will *not* do," I said quite firmly. "Where is your officer?"

"Inside the cemetery."

I walked to the nearest loop-hole in the cemetery wall, where, after a long and heated argument, I managed to persuade the officer in command to open the cemetery gates that, fortunately, lay on the Compiègne side of the chasm. Cautiously I drove the car through the gate and, after a somewhat tricky obstacle race over graves and round monuments, I arrived at the other gate inside the town of Soissons.

Without further adventure we arrived at Fère-en Tardenois, where Price-Davies disappeared into the General Staff Office to make his report. As I sat waiting in the car outside, I was accosted by Johnny

Baird (now Lord Stonehaven), who was at that time employed in the Intelligence Department.

"Had a good drive, Baker?" he asked.

"Yes," I replied. "The last bit of the road from Compiègne to Soissons was a bit too exciting, though."

"You didn't come on the Compiègne-Soissons road!"

"We did."

"But you couldn't. The German trenches are within a hundred yards of it."

"We did, just the same, though I don't think they are as near as that."

Still he refused to believe me, until it was corroborated by Price-Davies himself, who came out of the G.S. office. I am sure that the German trenches were at least two or three hundred yards distant, but I found on examining the car that there were the holes of several bullets through the body.

5

Daily we paid our visit to Gough while the distance of our drives shortened as G.H.Q. moved by stages to St. Omer, where it settled down, there to remain for eighteen months to the great profit of the inhabitants and the local farmers.

Already the battle, known later as the First Battle of Ypres, had begun. The Seventh Division, under General Capper, strung out along a front with hopelessly inadequate numbers, was putting up an heroic defence which will remain one of the finest pages in the annals of the British Army. Without supports or reserves, without barbed wire or proper trenches, supported by insufficient artillery, they hung on day after day, night after night, week after week, continually under shell and rifle fire.

Looking back on this period of the war, it seems incredible that the enemy could not break through. Time after time a hole was made in our line, but somehow it was closed again and the position restored. Numbers dwindled daily. Battalions were commanded by captains, then by subalterns. Companies were commanded by sergeants and corporals, on one occasion by a private soldier. But still they held on.

Each day that we spent at Divisional Headquarters, dangerously pushed forward, we heard of one more member of the Staff who had been killed or wounded. Capper himself seemed to bear a charmed life. Day after day he exposed himself in the most reckless fashion. He wasn't brave; he simply did not know what fear meant. His steely blue eyes, beneath a thick crop of dark, wiry hair, stared at one with the look of a religious fanatic. One day, when I had spoken of the risk he was running, he turned on me almost fiercely.

"I consider it to be the *duty* of an officer in this war to be killed," he said.

In spite of his utter disregard of danger, he survived until the ill-fated Battle of Loos eleven months later, when he was killed a day or two after being promoted to the command of an Army Corps in recognition of his splendid services.

Many have been the discussions as to what extent the higher commanders should expose themselves to danger. It must always remain an open question. At times it is folly. At other times it is not only right but absolutely essential that they should do so. During the retreat from Mons Sir John French put heart into the men by going into places where, strictly speaking, he had no right to go. Sir Douglas Haig, accompanied by Johnny Gough (his Brigadier-General, General Staff) during the later stages of the First Battle of Ypres, did much by his presence to steady the line and create a feeling of confidence. Capper, without doubt, by his absolute fearlessness helped to inspire the unspeakable courage displayed by the Seventh Division.

The first time that we drove through the city of Ypres not a single shell had fallen in it. The Cloth Hall and the cathedral in all their glory stood there intact, though the enemy lay but a few thousand yards distant. Business went on as usual, except that trade had never been so brisk. Long lines of troops, transport wagons and lorries streamed through the town unmolested. Save for the distant roar of the guns, Ypres might have been a hundred miles from the front.

The only explanation of this immunity is that the *kaiser* intended to proclaim the annexation of Belgium as soon as the last few acres of its soil were captured and that he had given explicit instructions to leave intact the city in which he would deliver his message to the world. Was the subsequent smashing of Ypres till it was naught but a smouldering mass of bricks and rubble a military operation or merely an example of the emperor's childish petulance at not being allowed to have his own way? Later, tens of thousands of shells were hurled into the stricken city, breaking the already broken, smashing the already smashed, merely to satisfy the vengeance of a frustrated lunatic.

One early morning Price-Davies and I drove into Ypres soon after the arrival of the first shell that was ever fired into it. We pulled up near the railway station and walked over to examine the house which had been struck. It was a portent, but, even then, no one had the least idea that this was but the forerunner of ten thousand others.

Gradually the bombardment increased in volume in proportion as the German assaults on our stiffening line were repulsed. The divisions from the south were coming fast and filling the gaps. Soon the Indian Corps would arrive and bring the help so sorely needed.

A huge convoy of transports, escorted by warships, already had passed safely through the Suez Canal and shortly would land the welcome reinforcements at Marseilles, where everything was being prepared in readiness for them.

A few days before their arrival a wireless message was dispatched from the supply officer of the corps, asking the Mayor of Marseilles to procure a thousand goats for the native troops.

In some way the message was mutilated in transmission and the *maire* received the following:

Please procure a thousand girls for troops.

The *maire* scratched his head, but, after all, he thought, war is war. We must do our best for the gallant Indian soldiers who are coming to our aid. He got busy. The next day he was able to reply:

Have procured three hundred girls. Hope to have balance ready before your arrival.

Hastily a message was dispatched in answer:

Reference my cable of the nth inst., for 'girls' read 'goats.'

"*Mon Dieu!*" exclaimed the *maire*. Much ink has been spilled concerning the wisdom of employing Indian troops in France. It is only too true that they were hopelessly unsuited to the type of warfare prevailing there and the terrible climatic conditions in which they found themselves in the trenches, at times with the most disastrous results. At that moment, however, the situation was so desperate that we would have welcomed with open arms anything that could stand up in a trench and convey to the enemy the impression that a soldier was occupying it.

6

The last week in October and the first week in November were one continuous nightmare. Day after day the Germans flung masses and masses of their best troops against our attenuated line. Day after day these assaults were repulsed with frightful slaughter, but ground was lost by us, and thousands of casualties, irreplaceable at the moment, were sustained. Time after time breaches in our line were filled only by dint of the utmost courage and at heavy loss.

The Germans were able to hurl thousands upon thousands of shells against our wearied troops, lying in their hastily improvised, shallow scratches in the ground that in those days answered to the name of trenches. The back areas for miles were searched by heavy guns and all main thoroughfares and road junctions were kept constantly under a withering fire.

CHAPTER 4

An Awkward Situation

1

Gradually Ypres was deserted. Soon it was a city of the dead. Nothing remained alive in it save a few starving cats that clung faithfully to their homes. An oppressive silence reigned as one drove through the square, accentuated by the ear-splitting burst of heavy shells.

The Cloth Hall and the cathedral, standing in the centre of the town where all the thoroughfares met, appeared to be the main objectives of the bombardment. Every time that we passed by them, sometimes as often as six times in one day, another tower, another column, another window had disappeared. Huge, gaping holes yawned in the roads, houses crumbled and collapsed, water and sewage mains were burst asunder.

Sometimes, by a strange freak, the whole front wall of a house had been torn away, leaving the interior intact. The furniture stood there just as it had been abandoned by its fleeing inhabitants, the bedclothes still lay where they had been thrown back, plates and cutlery were strewn on the dining-room table, cooking-pots rested on the kitchen stove, whose fires had long since been dead.

The silence of the town pressed down on one's soul like a heavy weight. One felt as though one must do something to break it, shout or even scream. Then, in the distance, would be heard a deep boom and the silence is torn by the wailing shriek of an approaching shell. Louder and louder it screams till at last with deafening roar it bursts, scattering stones and *débris* a hundred yards around. Then silence, deeper and more pregnant than before, falls once again, filling the spirit with a sense of loneliness and oppression, almost unbearable in its intensity.

Every morning and afternoon for many weeks Price-Davies and I made our way from St. Omer through Poperinghe, Vlamertinghe, and Ypres, along the Menin Road to Hooge Château or wherever Capper's headquarters were established. The run as far as Poperinghe was uneventful, save for the ordinary pitfalls of greasy *pavé* and traffic-encumbered roads. A few shells fell at intervals in Poperinghe, but so rarely that no one took much notice. Then out on to the road to Ypres, past Vlamertinghe, which had suffered and was still suffering from bombardment, out on to the last stretch before reaching the city of desolation.

In the distance one could see great clouds of black smoke from the huge howitzer shells suddenly spring up and hang like a pall over the destruction. One knew that almost every shell was directed on the centre of the town through which one was compelled to pass, much against one's inclination, slowly and cautiously in order to avoid fresh pitfalls and the *débris* of recent explosions. As we approached the asylum, which stood in ruins a few hundred yards on the western side of the town, I used to take a long breath, as a swimmer does before plunging into ice-cold water.

Down the street we drove, down past the railway station, a mass of broken brick-work, charred wood, and twisted rails; down the narrow street beyond, every house of which was smashed and gutted; round the corner to the right; past the doomed cathedral into the Square where stood the disintegrating mass of the Cloth Hall. As quickly as was possible I drove, keeping a sharp look out for recent shell holes; out through the Menin Gate on to the road to Hooge, which ran straight from the German lines, east and west, and which it was the sole task of some of the enemy guns to keep under a continuous rain of shells.

3

At the beginning of the battle we drove as far as Hooge Château, where Divisional Headquarters were installed. From there we made our way on foot towards the front line where the general was usually to be found. Dugouts were unknown in those days and any shallow depression in the ground was designated a trench.

On one urgent occasion, however, in order to save time we drove along a narrow farm track, which was not far behind the front line. The position of our troops varied almost from hour to hour, and today

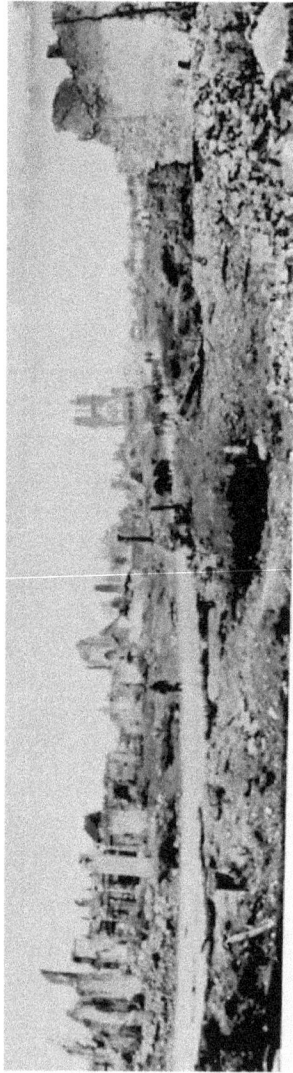

THE RUINS OF YPRES

it seems almost incredible that a car could move along a road, the ditch of which constituted our line. It lay just behind the crest-line in a thin belt of trees. At a spot more sheltered than elsewhere, Price-Davies got out of the car and, bidding me await him there, went off in search of Capper. In the ditch lay the remains of a company of the Scots Guards, weary, unshaven, unkempt, covered with mud, indomitable and undismayed.

I sat there in the car, wondering how much longer human endurance could last. It seemed as though the breaking-point must come soon. Would it come before reinforcements arrived and would all this gallant effort be in vain? When would the first——

"What the hell are you doing here?" an angry voice from the ditch broke in upon my meditations.

"Waiting for my passenger who's gone to see the general," I replied.

A wild-eyed, haggard officer crept from the ditch and walked to the car.

"Come out of there, you bloodstained fool," he shouted.

"I'm all right here."

"You sanguinary idiot! The Germans are only two or three hundred yards away, and here you are sitting in your blasted car as if you were in Piccadilly. Get out of it or I'll damn well pull you out."

Obediently I got from the car and lay down in the ditch beside him.

"Sorry I cursed you, old man," he said, as he accepted a cigarette from my case. "I'm just about all in. We've been in the front line for ten or twelve or fourteen days—I don't know how long it is. I'm the only officer alive in the company and I've only got about thirty men left out of two hundred. I haven't had a wink of sleep for over two days. Sometimes I think my brain's going."

We lay there for an hour talking, while I gave him all the encouraging news I could think of, till Price-Davies came back and I had to leave. The next day I heard that, within a couple of hours of our visit, a violent attack had been made on that part of the line. The attack was repulsed with heavy loss to the Germans, but my erstwhile friend and more than half his gallant band lay dead in the shallow ditch.

At last Capper was compelled to abandon Hooge Château. For many days his staff had been imploring him to go, but he had persistently refused until one day, while we were seated at lunch, a shell arrived and wrecked his bedroom overhead. Without asking his sanction, lorries were ordered and everything thrown hurriedly into them. We stood on the steps of the *château* watching the proceedings, when another shell arrived. A lorry was drawn up on the gravel drive four or five yards from the house. The shell passed through the cab of the lorry, sliced out the stomach of the driver and buried itself, without bursting, in the ground, within a few feet of the general and the rest of us, standing on the steps.

In those early days before a definite and continuous line was established, there was ample scope for spies. In Belgium especially the situation provided many opportunities to both sides for obtaining information. As the trench system was joined up and perfected, so it became increasingly difficult for spies to cross the line, and it was necessary to employ such devices as dropping agents, fitted out with parachutes, from aeroplanes some distance behind the trenches.

One day as Price-Davies and I were driving up the Menin Road, we were hailed by an excited private of the Royal Army Medical Corps who came running from a cottage. He babbled some incoherent story about a pigeon which it seemed advisable to investigate. Getting out of the car, we followed the man into the cottage.

On a chair sat a Belgian peasant, talking and gesticulating vehemently. Behind him stood another private of the R.A.M.C, holding a pigeon in his hand.

After much questioning, we elicited the fact that these two privates were billeted in the house and had their suspicions aroused by the behaviour of the owner. They had kept watch on him and at last had caught, him in the act of tying a piece of tissue paper to the pigeon's leg. The piece of paper was produced and on it we found was drawn a crude plan of some French batteries on the other side of the road.

As the batteries were not far distant, it seemed to be the best thing to hand over the peasant and his pigeon to the officer commanding for him to deal with. The matter touched them personally and we felt sure that they would deal more swiftly and effectively with the situation than the British.

In a few minutes the transfer was effected, much against the wishes of the prisoner, and Price-Davies and I proceeded on our way.

A day or two later we inquired what had transpired, but all we could discover was that the matter had been "disposed of satisfactorily."

There is no doubt but that, during the confusion of the advance to the Marne and the Aisne, many spies were left by the enemy on our side of the line, though in many cases the spies were not strictly speaking spies, in that they wore their uniform.

The spy who is solely actuated by patriotic motives, and not by the desire of money, is without doubt the bravest of the brave and worthy of admiration. Every man's hand is against him. One careless word, one thoughtless action, may be fatal. He never knows when he will feel a hand laid suddenly on his shoulder and he will be marched off and put up against a wall.

A curious incident occurred during the Battle of the Aisne.

The 9th Lancers were quartered in a farmhouse surrounded by several outbuildings. It was noticed that the enemy shelling in the neighbourhood seemed to be uncannily accurate and that a battery was no sooner shifted than its new position was immediately discovered.

One day, when some hay was being removed from a stack at the back of the farm, a telephone wire was discovered lying on the ground. An officer was called and the wire was followed up. It led the searchers into the centre of a rick where two German officers were found, ensconced in a small recess. A telephone instrument was also found, the wire of which ran through our trenches into the enemy lines. The Germans had lain inside the haystack for five days and five nights. Both were dressed in uniform, in consequence of which they could not be treated as spies, but merely as prisoners of war. I often wonder what would have happened if the position had been reversed and English officers had been captured by the enemy in a similar situation.

<h2 style="text-align:center">4</h2>

As our line gradually fell back, so did the high-water mark of my drives recede. Soon the village of Hooge was as far as it was possible to proceed and many nerve-racking hours did I spend there, while Price-Davies crawled and crept about in, or just behind the front line. He now refused to allow me to go with him, as he said it would do no good and was merely doubling the risk.

Often he was compelled to move over exposed ground within view of the enemy. It is a perfect mystery why he was not killed a dozen times a day. Often after waiting for him for two or three hours, I began to wonder whether I should ever see him again. Sometimes also when a shell arrived and half-filled my car with bricks and rubble, I wondered whether he would ever see *me* again.

On one of these days I sat in the car, trying my utmost to divert my attention from the shelling by the perusal of a copy of *The Times*.

A medical officer appeared from a fairly whole cottage, which served as a dressing-station, and invited me to come in and have a cup of tea. Gladly I accepted and followed him into the kitchen, where a kettle was boiling merrily on a little stove. Just as he was pouring the water into the teapot, there was a crash and a bang. The kitchen wall collapsed, upsetting the doctor and spilling our kettle of water.

"The fire's still going and the kettle isn't damaged," said the M.O. cheerfully, as he picked himself up. "I'll soon have another lot boiling."

Always, always there was a little stream of wounded men, trickling down the road. At times, when I knew that Price-Davies would not be back for an hour or more, I used to fill my car with wounded and carry them to the temporary hospital near the Menin Gate. The expressions of gratitude from the poor fellows were almost pitiful, considering how little one had done, and the stories they told filled one with a sense of pride that these men were one's fellow-countrymen.

The 3rd Cavalry Division, commanded by General Byng (afterwards Lord Byng of Vimy), were holding a portion of the line next to the 7th Division, and were now included in the domain of Price-Davies.

Byng's headquarters during the daytime appeared to be the deep ditch that runs on either side of the Menin Road. There he passed the day, always cheerful, never depressed in the slightest degree, however disconcerting was the news. On our way back from the 7th Division to St. Omer we were usually held up by him for a talk. I admit I used to dislike the time thus spent, as the hour of the evening hate was drawing near and the road was directly enfiladed. While Price-Davies and the divisional commander were exchanging views, some of the staff would gather round the car and tell me all the latest rumours.

At last the maps would be folded and put away; then, amid a chorus of goodnights, we would proceed on our way, through the City of Desolation, back to St. Omer and my comfortable billet, whence, after cleaning up, I repaired to the Hôtel de Commerce for dinner.

Every night there was a little party of five at our table, three permanent, the two others changing daily. Jack Seely (afterwards Major-General J. E. B. Seely, D.S.O.), Dalmeny (now Lord Rosebery), and myself were the permanents, the incoming and outgoing King's Messengers the temporaries. It was a cheerful party at all times with Dalmeny's forceful humour and Seely's more subtle wit and unruffled good-nature when his "leg was pulled." The King's Messengers, without exception, were welcome additions to our party and regaled us with all the latest news and scandals from London. Sometimes, too, we were enlivened by the presence of other distinguished visitors to G.H.Q. On one occasion a well-known Cabinet Minister, disguised as a staff officer, honoured us with his company and, after dining exceedingly well, insisted on displaying his vocal attainments and his abilities as a trick-cyclist on a machine stolen from the Signals Office. It was perhaps, fortunate for him that his hosts stood well with the Military Police, who, hearing the uproar, quickly appeared on the scene with the firm intention of taking official action.

5

My "chauffing" days were drawing to a close, but they were not to end without one last, hectic adventure.

The 3rd Cavalry Division was now holding the line near Klein Zillebeke and out we went to pay a call on Byng. We found him installed in a ramshackle, ruined cottage by the roadside. Quite a number of 5.9 howitzer shells were falling around, but, for the most part, in a field on the other side of the road where four or five peasant women were gathering beetroots, absolutely indifferent to the bursts about them.

On this day, of all days, my car had elected to give trouble. A tiny spring, which controlled the valve of the petrol pressure pump, had broken. As long as the engine was running the pressure kept up, but as soon as the engine stopped all the petrol ran back into the tank. The only real difficulty, however, was that two persons were necessary to start up the car, one to swing the starting handle while the other kept pumping up the pressure.

We spent an hour or two with Byng, at the end of which he departed, leaving us at the ruined cottage. It was now past one o'clock and time for our lunch. From the car I brought our hamper (one of Mumm's champagne baskets), in which we carried a tin of bully beef, fresh bread and butter, and some fruit; also a bottle of white wine and a thermos flask of coffee. Seating ourselves against the wall farthest from the enemy, we started our meal. We had not eaten a dozen mouthfuls before the shelling, which had been falling harmlessly in the soft fields a hundred yards away, was switched directly on to our shelter. We continued our lunch, hoping that the shelling would pass on; but not a bit of it; if anything, it got worse. Neither of us wanted to abandon our food, but, after one particularly well-directed shell had half-filled our hamper with bricks, we thought it time to move on. The car was somewhat difficult to start, but, after a little work, Price-Davies pumping the pressure, I swinging the handle, she started off and we proceeded on our way to Zonnebeke, where Price-Davies was to visit General Lord Cavan in a charming spot called "Cavan's Dug-out."

We drove down the narrow strip of greasy *pavé* that led into the village. It had always been an unhealthy spot, but on that afternoon it looked more than usually unpleasant. Not only were there large numbers of shells falling in the village itself, but there was a constant rattle of rifle and machine-gun fire.

"You'd better turn the car round and wait for me under cover here," said Price-Davies, as we reached the church in the centre of the village.

He got out and made his way in the direction of the front line, dangerously near which "Cavan's Dug-out" was situated.

This part of the line was a point of some danger, forming, as it did, the junction of the British and French Armies. The enemy, of course, was well aware of this fact and had chosen that particular afternoon to launch a heavy attack against it.

Within a few minutes of our entrance into the village, the assault began. Shells started to arrive in the most unpleasant numbers and the rattle of rifle fire increased ten-fold. Bullets were spattering against the walls of houses, and it did not require an expert ear to tell that they had been fired at no great range.

There is nothing more unpleasant than inactive waiting under such conditions. The minutes seem to prolong themselves into hours, and, in addition, I was anxious about starting up the car in the event of an emergency. I did not dare to take down the pressure pump and try to make any temporary repairs, fearing lest I might be called upon at any moment to make a hurried departure.

The village, when we had first entered it, had seemed absolutely deserted, but, after half an hour or so, I noticed several stragglers begin to drift down the street from the direction of the firing line, first one, then two or three at a time. They were French infantrymen, with here and there a *cuirassier*. I was wondering what this might portend when suddenly there dashed after them an infuriated French officer with sword drawn, who fell upon them, beating them with the flat of his weapon and shouting the most virulent abuse.

"This looks cheerful," I thought to myself. "The next thing will be a few Boches."

The officer returned towards the line, driving in front of him his little crowd of fugitives and telling them his candid opinion of their behaviour.

The next item was the arrival of a French artillery officer whose battery was concealed down a side street. He looked at me and at my car with evident disfavour.

"What are you doing here?" he demanded fiercely. "This isn't a proper place for a car."

"I was told to wait here," I replied.

"You get out at once. You are blocking the road with your cursed automobile. My battery must move and it cannot pass if you remain here."

There was no alternative but to shift, as the street in which my car was parked was only a few feet wide.

Most unwillingly I pumped up my pressure to its fullest extent and dashed in front to the starting handle. By the time I reached it, the pressure was gone. Feverishly I rushed backwards and forwards between the dashboard and the radiator, but not a kick could I get out of the engine. I was beginning to get anxious, as I could see the horses of the battery being led up to the guns to hitch in.

"Can I assist?" asked a French *poilu*, who had appeared on the scene from nowhere in particular. "I was a mechanic before the war."

"Yes, certainly. I will pump up the pressure while you turn the starting handle."

I pumped furiously till the pressure was full.

"Now!" I shouted.

The soldier caught hold of the handle. Before he could give one turn, he disappeared from view.

"What's up?" I called out.

There was no reply. I jumped from the car and ran to the front. My would-be helper was lying in the road, crumpled up, with a bullet through his forehead.

Hastily I dragged the body to one side. Already the horses of the battery were hitched in. In a moment the guns would be on the move.

Catching sight of another *poilu*, who seemed to have nothing to do, I called to him to come and help. He, too, seemed used to cars and, with his aid, at last I got the engine going.

Not a minute too soon. There was a yell behind me and a clatter of hoofs on the uneven *pavé*.

"En avant, sacré cochon!"

I glanced over my shoulder. There was the gunner officer, riding ahead of his battery and waving his drawn sword at me.

"They'll be on the top of me in a moment," I thought to myself. "They seem to be in a hurry."

Quickly I let in my clutch and started up the lane. As soon, as the battery turned into the main street, it broke into a gallop and I had to accelerate to keep ahead of it. There was not a chance to pull to one side to let it pass. The *pavé* was only a few feet wide and on either side was a quagmire of yellow mud without bottom.

On I drove, pursued by the guns, while all the time the commander howled imprecations at me. Not till we had covered nearly two miles was I able to pull aside and let the battery go past.

I was so relieved at getting clear of it at last that I entirely forgot about my pressure. Before I knew what was happening, my engine had stopped.

Cursing myself heartily for my carelessness, I started once more on the almost hopeless task of starting it up by myself. For half an hour I toiled, by the end of which time I had exhausted myself and my entire stock of expletives. It was the first time that I had ever failed Price-Davies and I should never forgive myself if I could not get back before he needed me.

Nobody passed up or down the road. It seemed as though I was stranded there forever. At last, however, to my joy I saw a car approaching, driven by an officer who, by a stroke of good fortune, was an experienced motor engineer. Quickly I explained my trouble to him. Out of his pocket he produced an ordinary rubber band, which he fastened to the valve of the pressure pump.

"There you are," he said.

I pumped up the pressure and eagerly watched the gauge. Not a sign of a leak. All was well.

Thankfully I started up the engine and was in the act of turning round to go back when I heard Price-Davies' voice behind me.

Briefly I explained what had happened, but, although he at once agreed that I had had no alternative, I have always been haunted by the feeling that in some way I had failed him.

6

The very last job on which I was employed was to drive Price-Davies out to select points of vantage from which Lord Roberts could view the battlefield.

It was not easy to find look-out posts from which a general view of the long-drawn-out line could be obtained, especially in the vicinity of Ypres, and it was only after much travelling that we found what we sought.

On the Hill of Kemmel, which lies not far behind the Salient, stood a half-ruined tower from which a vast panorama was visible.

Away to the north stretched mile upon mile of monotonous flat swamps as far as the eye could see. At times on a clear day the inundations, where the dykes had been opened in order to impede the enemy advance, could be made out; but mostly a thin, white mist lay like a cotton shroud over the landscape. To the east, the ground rose almost imperceptibly, till it reached the low line of hills above West Roosebeke and the Paschendaele Ridge from which the Germans looked down into our lines.

The whole world had the appearance of being forsaken and deserted by man. Not a single soul could be seen and it was difficult to believe that, within a radius of a few miles, tens of thousands of human beings toiled and fought, lived and died.

Along the forlorn, disused highways and canals, leafless and moribund trees, splintered and riven, seemed to keep watch as ghostly sentinels; where prosperous villages had stood, the roofless houses, smashed and shattered, showed up like hollow, rotting teeth; the once rich meadows, shell-pitted as though by smallpox, threw up a rank crop of reedy grasses; from the broken drainage ditches, so meticulously tended in times of peace, a noisome stream of yellow slime oozed slowly over the face of the land, till the whole countryside was transformed into one vast and bottomless quagmire of liquid mud.

Truly an abomination of desolation.

The coming of the great little field-marshal had, created considerable stir in St. Omer, not only amongst the British soldiers, but, also, amongst the French civilians. The short, slight figure, erect in spite of his; eighty-odd years, was eagerly watched for in the streets. Hats were reverently doffed as he passed, an unusual tribute to one of an alien race.

Within a few days the field-marshal was dead, dying as he himself would have wished to die, within sound of the guns and among the soldiers whom he had loved so well.

7

A few days later I was invited by General Capper, whose division had at last been withdrawn from the line, to attend a parade of one of his brigades and, afterwards, to lunch with him at his headquarters at Bailleul.

The parade took place in a field. It was a very small field, for little space was needed to hold the remnants of those four splendid regiments. One battalion consisted of one officer and fifty men, while the total strength of the brigade was some six or seven officers and less than three hundred men, all that was left of a hundred officers and four thousand rank and file.

It was a tragic and pathetic picture and brought home to one more than anything else could have done the magnificent and indomitable heroism of the 7th Division.

After the parade was over, I returned with General Capper to his house. During lunch the conversation chiefly turned to the reconstitution of the division and its training.

"You were Instructor at Hythe, Baker-Carr?" asked the general. "Why don't you come and do a real job of work? You've had a wonderful time driving your car, but I consider that you ought to do something more than that."

For some time past the same idea had been uneasily present in the back of my mind.

At the very beginning, nobody realised the gigantic proportions which the British Army would attain and few had any conception of the probable duration of the war. In consequence, in their enthusiasm to get into it somehow, many retired officers had undertaken jobs far below their capabilities. It was now becoming apparent that everyone with any special knowledge would be sorely needed for the training of men who were joining the colours by the tens of thousands.

"Yes, sir," I replied. "I've been thinking the same thing myself. I don't want to leave France and take a training job in England. Have you anything to suggest yourself, sir?"

"Come to my division and train some machine gunners for me. There isn't a single one left."

"I should be delighted, sir; if you can get permission from G.H.Q. I should like nothing better."

"All right," replied the general. "I'll telephone Billy Lambton, Sir John's Military Secretary, and arrange it with him."

I returned to St. Omer with a nebulous idea forming in my brain.

For the rest of that day and most of the night I turned it over in my mind. Before Lambton rang me up in the morning and asked me to come and see him, the idea had taken definite shape.

CHAPTER 5

The Genesis of the Machine Gun School

1

Until the beginning of the Great War, the subject of machine guns, for some reason, had never been taken seriously in the British Army, in spite of the lessons which might have been learnt from the Russo-Japanese War. It is safe to say that the German Army, alone of continental armies, was the one in which the possibilities of the weapon were fully appreciated.

Musketry in the British Regular and Volunteer Forces, on the other hand, had been brought to a pitch of excellence never before achieved; but the developments of fire-power by the use of machinery had been completely ignored. The reason for this phenomenon is somewhat obscure, but may be largely traced to the average Englishman's deep-rooted dislike and mistrust of machinery in general.

Although England has always been in the forefront of mechanical discovery, the actual use of the machinery, thus created, has often, in this country, lagged far behind invention. For instance, the replacement of the hand-loom by the power-loom was only brought about after violent opposition and considerable rioting; the evolution of the motorcar in this country was delayed for several years by childish legislation which made compulsory the carrying of a red flag by a man on foot in front of the vehicle; today, we are far behind every other civilised nation in the employment of electricity. This feeling of antipathy towards mechanical methods, as opposed to hand skill, may possibly go far to account for the widespread resistance which I encountered when striving to secure the recognition of the machine gun as one of the most important weapons of the foot-soldier. Later on, the same antipathy was to be displayed against the tanks, to be overcome, at long last, in face of the maddening want of vision on the part of those with whom decisions rested.

2

"General Capper has asked for you to be attached to the 7th Division Headquarters for the purpose of training machine gunners," said Colonel Lambton, when I entered his office the following day. "Would you like to go?"

"Well, sir," I replied, "I've been thinking it over and this is how it strikes me. The 7th Division has lost more heavily than any other, but I expect all of them are short of machine gunners. How would it be if, instead of training men for the 7th Division only, I trained them for all divisions?"

"That seems sensible," said Lambton. "I'll ring up the other divisions and ask. Come and see me again tomorrow."

For the next twenty-four hours I considered the problem from every angle. My ideas were still somewhat nebulous and I had not the slightest conception what far-reaching results would accrue from my little scheme; but I could see that at least I should be doing useful work, for which I possessed special qualification. For the moment I was fully satisfied.

The next day Lambton informed me that the divisions, without exception, had strongly advocated the idea. There appeared to be a complete dearth of machine gunners in the B.E.F.

"What shall I do to get started?" I asked.

"Go and see 'Uncle Harper,'" replied Lambton. "Fix it up with him."

"Uncle" Harper was, at that time, Colonel on the General Staff. Many times subsequently I was to come into the closest personal touch with him when he commanded the 51st Highland Territorial Division (whose divisional sign, "H.D.," stood for "Highland Division" or, more familiarly, "Harper's Duds," one of the finest divisions in the army) and, later, the 4th Corps.

Everybody loved "Uncle," who, with his black moustache and luxuriant crop of snow-white hair, was a well-known and striking figure at G.H.Q. Beneath a somewhat irritable and impatient exterior he was, in reality, one of the kindest-hearted of men. In later days, when I commanded the 1st Brigade of the Tank Corps, I was constantly

Major-General Sir G. M. Harper

engaged with him in wordy warfare at Army and Corps Conferences; but he never resented a frank and outspoken statement of opinion and usually ended up by allowing me an entirely free hand. Not long ago, (as at 1929), he met with a tragic death, being killed in a motor accident near Aldershot.

I walked into "Uncle's" office and touched my cap.

"Colonel Lambton told me to see you about training some machine gunners for the divisions, sir," I began.

"Yes," said "Uncle," "he telephoned to me about it. Why don't you get on with it?"

"I want some sort of authority before I can start, sir."

"All right," replied "Uncle," "you've got it. Now get on with it."

"But—" I began again.

"Look here, Baker," said "Uncle." "Are you running this show or am I? Go away and do what you like, but don't bother me. I'm busy."

This interview constituted the Charter of the Machine Gun School, which trained tens upon tens of thousands of machine gunners and provided the starting-point from which later sprang an entirely new unit in the British Army, the Machine Gun Corps.

I went back to my billet and did some serious thinking.

Some sort of organisation had to be got together and it was obvious that I could not look for much active assistance from G.H.Q. Not only had I to collect an instructional staff, but, in all probability, I should have to manufacture them myself. Guns for training purposes did not exist and I realised that it would be useless to endeavour to obtain them from England in the circumstances.

I cast my thoughts about in search of the most likely source from which to collect the raw material for the making of sergeant instructors. At once the Artists' Rifles (then at St. Omer, acting as G.H.Q. troops) came to my mind. I knew the commanding officer slightly and he had the reputation of always being ready to assist in any way possible.

No sooner had I come to this conclusion than I started off to the Infantry Barracks, in which the Artists were quartered.

The colonel was more than ready to help and at once offered me his entire Machine Gun Detachment.

"It's very good of you, sir," I replied. "But, to be quite frank, I'd much sooner have a dozen intelligent privates who know nothing whatever of machine guns and, therefore, have nothing to unlearn."

"Just as you like," said the colonel. "I'll order twelve first-class men to report to you tomorrow."

The next problem was the housing problem. When the first class assembled, I should have to be prepared for at least a hundred of all ranks, including twenty or thirty officers. The officers presented no great difficulty; I could find billets for them and they could get their meals at the various restaurants in the town; but the N.C.O.s and men were a far more difficult question. Not only must they be housed, but they must be fed. That meant barrack-rooms, cooking-pots, and a cook.

The Artillery Barracks in St. Omer were occupied at that time by odds and ends of the British Army, details of the Royal Engineers, Army Service Corps, etc., and I hoped that it might be possible there to find rooms into which I could squeeze my sergeant instructors and the students, when they arrived.

On reconnoitring the barracks, I found several rooms unoccupied. They had been left by the departing artillery in a filthy condition, but a little hard work would soon put that right. There was, also, a cook-house of sorts in which the R.E. cook, who appeared to be its presiding genius, graciously gave me permission to do my cooking.

So far, so good. But what about guns?

This problem exercised my mind for quite a long time, until I suddenly remembered that the remnants of an Irish regiment were also stationed at St. Omer. It was possible that they still might be in possession of their guns.

Hastily I went in search of the commanding officer and learnt from him that both their machine guns had been saved, though they had no machine gunners left.

Interpreting "Uncle" Harper's instructions very liberally, I told the officer that I had authority from General Staff to "borrow" the guns from him for a few months. He not only agreed to hand over the guns without demur, but he even promised to deliver them wherever I required.

Things were looking up. The only remaining difficulty was that of obtaining an up-to-date instructor to train my embryo instructors. It was possible that I might have managed to do it myself, although it was more than eight years since I had been called upon personally to instruct, but I knew how much other work there would be for me to do and probably my methods would be very antiquated. There was only one place from which I could obtain competent sergeant instructors, and that was the School of Musketry at Hythe. I must take a chance there and use my persuasive efforts to procure them without a direct order, which I knew was never likely to be given.

Obtaining three days' leave, I dashed over to England and proceeded to Hythe, where I found Colonel McMahon, *commandant* of the school. Without a moment's hesitation he agreed to let me have not one, but two sergeant instructors, both of whom I had known well during my appointment at the school. I came away almost bewildered by this piece of unexpected good fortune.

The next day I returned to St. Omer, where I found that my embryo instructors had swept and garnished the two barrack rooms which I had selected, and had also taken possession of another for themselves which they had cleaned and improved out of all recognition. In their spare time they had been learning what they could by the aid of a pamphlet on machine guns and the two borrowed guns, which had been duly delivered.

The embryos were still being fed by their unit, but I was determined that this was going to be a self-contained concern. We must draw our own rations and do our own cooking.

I didn't dare to ask "Uncle" for such trifles as cooks, etc. He would in all probability tell me to go to blazes and might even regret having ordered me to "get on with it." It was far safer to keep out of his sight and arrange matters myself.

The senior of the embryos, Bax, who later became Sergeant-Major Instructor and at all times lent the most valuable assistance, suggested that the Artists would also supply a cook; in fact, he knew of one of the candidates who had volunteered to come as an instructor and had been crowded out. With the sanction of the commanding officer, the "cook" arrived next day. He admitted frankly that he didn't know the first thing about cooking, but was quite ready to try. As I did not propose to eat his food and his fellow Artists would be the sole victims for the next few weeks, I had no objection to his trying his hand.

Early next morning, "Slushy" (as he was christened by his comrades) and I drove up in state in my car to the ration stand, much to the amusement of the other ration parties. We drew the meat, bread, groceries, etc., for the instructional staff and, having stacked them in the car, drove back to the barracks. I had already "borrowed" a few cooking utensils from my Universal Providers, the Artists' Rifles, and I told "Slushy" to get busy.

I cannot imagine anything more unappetising than the meals set before the embryos for the next few days, until "Slushy" became a little more familiar with the culinary art. I subsequently discovered that he was a scholar of Magdalen, Oxford, but, at the end of a week's cooking, I doubt if his own mother would have been able to recognise him during working hours. His face was smeared with coal-dust and perspiration, his clothes presented the appearance of having absorbed more than the major portion of the fatty contents of the day's ration. But "Slushy" stuck to his job like a man and eventually developed into a really first-class cook.

In a few days' time my two new assistants, Ward and Blomfield, arrived from Hythe and started work. No hours seemed too long for either them or their pupils, who must have dreamt of fusee-springs and feed-blocks. For ten days they worked without cessation, and so rapid was the progress made that I was able to give the General Staff a date on which the first class could be assembled.

In the meantime I had been unexpectedly reinforced by the arrival of Captain the Hon. H. R. Atkinson, lately an instructor at Sandhurst. I don't know to this day how he came or who sent him, but, whoever was responsible, I am eternally grateful, as his help and counsel, especially in the early "buccaneering" days, when the Machine Gun School was nobody's child and was regarded as a purely temporary expedient, were invaluable.

3

At last the great day arrived. Bus loads of officers, N.C.O.s, and men drew up outside the barracks. The twenty officers were directed to the billets already allotted, while the eighty N.C.O.s and men were shown to their barrack-rooms with most unsoldierlike politeness by their future instructors, now disguised as sergeants, temporary, acting, honorary, without pay, allowances or anything else. So far the school had no "establishment," that magic word, almost "Mesopotamian" in its blessedness, without which, in the military world, nothing can be obtained.

Officially, for several months to come, the Machine Gun School did not exist. The sergeant instructors were still carried as private soldiers on the strength of their unit, while the officers, Atkinson, Ward, Blomfield (for both of the latter I managed to get commissions very shortly after their arrival) and myself, were merely "temporarily employed on special duty."

It is more than likely that this lack of "establishment" was of the greatest value to me. If, in the early days, I had tried to put the school on an official footing, it would have been on a ridiculously small basis and every increase in staff, etc., would have been strenuously opposed; it is even possible that it might have been entirely suppressed. As it was, by hook or by crook, I gathered, without sanction from anybody, fatigue-men, assistants for "Slushy" in the cook-house, additional instructors from the Artists, and a large amount of equipment.

The instruction that I had decided to give was confined to the mechanism of the gun and a little shooting; the length of the course was fixed at fourteen days. No attempt was made to give any instruction in the tactical handling of the weapon, about which little or nothing was laid down officially. At that time, the sole mention of machine guns was confined to a dozen lines in the *Infantry Training Manual*. Nobody in authority concerned himself with this weapon of enormous potential importance and battalion commanders, before the war, frankly and cordially disliked it.

"What shall I do with the machine guns today, sir?" would be a question frequently asked by the officer in charge, on a field-day.

"Take the damned things to a flank and hide 'em!" was the usual reply.

At the end of the fourteen days, the first class returned to their units in the line, apparently fully satisfied with the instruction given and grateful for the comparative comfort in which they had lived. There was not even one complaint about the *chef.*

Naturally we, the officer instructors, had constantly supervised the squads at their work, but the sergeant instructors, all men of brains and education, had picked up the art of training with the most astonishing rapidity. Unconsciously they were using the very jargon and the little jests that Ward and Blomfield had employed in giving them their own instruction, and, after a few courses, it would have been difficult to distinguish them from old hands at Hythe. The only real difference was their superlative politeness and the consideration they displayed for the feelings of the denser of their pupils. There was an entire absence of impatience with stupidity, and often did I come across one of the sergeant instructors giving additional tuition out of hours to the more backward members of the squad.

A happy show is a good show, and it was on this principle that the Machine Gun School was conducted. In the early days, when it was a small concern, it was not difficult for me to keep in close touch with the entire personnel of the staff, and never was there a more enthusiastic or contented collection of men. Later, when the school developed into huge proportions and close personal contact became impossible, the spirit in which it had been inaugurated still persisted, and if, at times, some of the stricter canons of military procedure were disregarded, the results at any rate were eminently satisfactory.

I had been warned by Colonel Harper that the continuance of the school would be largely dependent on reports received from the divisions at the conclusion of the first course. Another class assembled within three or four days of the departure of the first and we all anxiously awaited the verdict on our efforts.

At last, about halfway through the second course, I was summoned to the General Staff Office.

"The divisions say that they are very satisfied with the instruction given, but all of them have made the same two complaints."

I waited nervously to hear wherein we had failed. Then I saw the little twinkle come into "Uncle's" eye and my anxiety disappeared.

"In the first place, they want to double the numbers. Secondly, they want you to give some tactical instruction."

"Very good, sir," I replied, knowing how inadvisable it would be to put forward my difficulties and ask for assistance. "I'll arrange to double the class the next course but one and we'll give some tactical instruction."

I touched my cap and walked out, much pleased with the result of my interview, but wondering how on earth I was going to carry out my promises.

Another dozen Artists were commandeered and given by Ward and Blomfield the same intensive training that the first batch had received. The extraordinary keenness and ability displayed by the original embryos had dispelled all my fears on the score of raw material, and I was assured, thanks to the wonderful enthusiasm of the commanding officer of the Artists, of an inexhaustible fund. The supply of guns, however, was a more difficult problem, but even the General Staff could be made to understand that it was impossible to give instruction in a weapon unless the weapon itself were available. Evidently I could rely on considerable support from the trenches, and that, at all times, was an extremely valuable stick with which to coerce G.H.Q. The guns would doubtless be forthcoming when required.

The question of tactical instruction was an entirely different affair.

Apart from the dozen lines with which the handling of machine guns in the field was dismissed in the *Infantry Training Manual*, there was absolutely nothing to guide one. Even at Hythe the subject had been treated somewhat sketchily, and the conditions under which machine guns would be used in France were utterly different from any previously contemplated. None of my officer assistants had had any experience whatever of fighting in the present war, and my own, up to the moment, had been confined to the role of interested spectator. It had, however, been very forcibly borne in on me what terrific power these weapons possessed in defence, if properly sited and handled.

Atkinson was as much an enthusiast as myself, and, with the help of Ward and Blomfield, we evolved a lecture on the Tactical Handling of Machine Guns, to be delivered in the Riding School of the barracks by the *commandant* on the last day of the class.

In due course the lecture was given, occupying some thirty minutes in delivery. It seemed to go down all right, if the rapt attention of the audience could be regarded as any criterion, but, looking back now, it seems hopelessly inadequate. The bases on which the lecture was founded were sound and, later, we found no cause to make any radical alterations, but many important points, not then appreciated, were dismissed in a few words and others left entirely untouched. Gradually, after the school became recognised as the source of all information on automatic weapons of every kind, a full and complete series of lectures was evolved, dealing with the Vickers and Lewis guns from every aspect. The exact number of these lectures has escaped my memory, but it certainly was not less than seven or eight.

4

The second class departed in its turn, and was replaced by a third. Still there was a cry from the divisions for more vacancies at the school. Again my staff of sergeant instructors was doubled, with the co-operation of the Artists. The administration of the establishment was becoming a serious question and the clerical work, nominal rolls, returns of all sorts, etc., was beginning to interfere to the detriment of the instruction. Not only were we responsible for the intensive training of officers and men from the trenches, while training at the same time thirty or forty fresh instructors, but we were trying to administer a constantly changing unit of three or four hundred, without any facilities whatever.

With considerable hesitation I approached "Uncle," but my very mild and tentative suggestions called forth such a torrent of half-jesting vituperation that I vanished from his presence with the utmost rapidity. The time was not yet come when I could speak openly with the enemy in the gate, and I must still rely on the gentle art of "wangling."

Yet again the Artists were summoned to my aid and a skilled shorthand-writer and typist appeared at the school, with typewriting machine complete. I often wonder whether the regiment would have been able to supply a deep-sea diver or a Hoogly pilot. In their ranks were to be found lawyers, musicians, opera-singers, painters, architects, music-hall artists, doctors, stockbrokers, clergymen (one of these was a sergeant instructor later, and held regular services on Sunday morning in the prescribed costume), engineers, chemists, etc., etc.

The Machine Gun School would have come into being even though the Artists' Rifles had never existed, but it is not too much to say that the success which the school achieved was largely due, in the first instance, to the loyalty and enthusiasm shown by the sergeant instructors who, for the first eighteen months, were drawn entirely from the regiment.

Christmas came and went. The number of students increased by leaps and bounds. Gradually I was able to add to my exiguous staff a few necessary oddments: an armourer sergeant, half a dozen permanent fatigue-men, an elderly sergeant (an ex-Regular serving in a territorial battalion) as sergeant-major. The school was forcing its way to recognition by G.H.Q., though, even now, official sanction for it had not been given. Between the courses Atkinson and I used to make tours of Corps and Divisional Headquarters, like a couple of commercial travellers pushing their goods. The fighting line, at any rate, had awakened to the realisation of the automatic weapon and many commanders were showing themselves eager to learn anything they could, which would help to strengthen their front without increasing the number of men.

Already I was urging the advisability of doubling the number of machine guns per battalion, *i.e.* raising it from two to four. I had put forward the suggestion very tentatively to G.H.Q. and had been promptly told to mind my own business. The commanders of larger units, such as armies and army corps, did not at that time appreciate the vast saving of man-power that could be effected by the substitution of machinery for brawn, and it was only when we got within the danger zone that the proposals drew forth a cordial response. "Propaganda" was an almost unknown word in those days, but the thing itself was exploited to the utmost by Atkinson and myself on all and every occasion.

Soon I was again reinforced and strengthened by the unlooked-for and welcome arrival of Major George Lindsay (now Brigadier G. M. Lindsay, C.M.G., D.S.O., lately Inspector-General of the Tank Corps) and Captain (now Lieutenant-Colonel) McGillycuddy. I had never applied for them and they themselves knew nothing beyond the fact that they had been ordered to report to me. Lindsay came from the School of Musketry at Hythe, McGillycuddy from the front line, a happy combination of theory and practice.

To all the staff, officers and N.C.O.s alike, I can never be sufficiently grateful. Nobody was ever better served, but it is to George Lindsay, more than to any other person, that my thanks are chiefly due. With a farsightedness, possessed by no one else at that time, he visualised developments in the use of the machine gun that, when first put forward, were regarded by the General Staff as the ravings of a lunatic. As *commandant* of the school, I was the official mouthpiece, and it was my duty to put forward our considered views on the subject. Enthusiastic though I was, it was essential that I should not run the risk of being written down as a machine-gun "crank," or what little influence I then possessed would be discounted. On the one hand, I was being constantly urged by Lindsay and the others to keep hammering away at the General Staff; on the other hand, I was being equally constantly urged by G.H.Q. to mind my own business. I knew full well that Lindsay was fundamentally right, but I also knew that one injudicious step on my part would result in the complete destruction of all our hopes and plans.

"One step at a time," I thought to myself, when far-reaching proposals were suggested. "This machine-gun business is a new problem. The military mind dislikes being made to think. I've got to proceed cautiously."

The first step on which I concentrated was to obtain sanction for the increase from two to four machine guns per battalion. Already I had broached the subject in all quarters. In the front line my suggestion was received with enthusiastic acclamation, but, as I progressed in a westerly direction towards St. Omer, the enthusiasm gradually wilted until, at last, at G.H.Q., it expired completely and was replaced by a cold hostility.

Thanks to the universal support from the firing line, the school was now becoming an accepted fact. Furthermore, queries on the subject of machine guns in general were frequently received by the

General Staff, who, unable to provide answers themselves, sent them on to the Commandant, Machine School, "for your views, please." One or two useful inventions, also, had emanated from the school and these had aided materially in bringing our activities into the public eye. Recently "Uncle" Harper had been given a command in the field and his place on the General Staff had been taken by General Percival, late of the R.A., who was more patient and readier to listen to reason than his predecessor.

After much striving and after enduring many snubs, I was at last instructed to put down on paper the reasons for my proposed increase in the number of machine guns. For weeks past Lindsay and I had been preparing a memorandum and, after allowing a decent interval to elapse, I forwarded it to G.H.Q. At last things seemed to be moving.

Week after week went by and nothing happened. We were beginning to feel almost desperate when at length the file, containing my proposals, was returned with the comments of army and corps commanders. Eagerly we opened it and scanned the views expressed.

When we read them, we nearly wept.

Not a single individual had had the courage openly to support our suggestion, not even those who had privately given it their cordial approbation; many had "hedged" badly; others were frankly hostile. One army commander gave his opinion that "the machine gun was a much over-rated weapon and two per battalion were more than sufficient." Another half-heartedly approved of the idea, but doubted if it could be carried out. A staff officer at G.H.Q., who has since achieved considerable fame as a fearless and outspoken military writer, was favourable to the increase in numbers, but definitely rejected the proposal on the grounds that it would be impossible to train the personnel in wartime!

For the moment we were defeated, though it seemed incredible to us that anyone could be so blind as to fail to realise the vast saving of men that could be effected by the use of machine guns. It seemed as though the High Command did not *want* to see, in spite of the fact that they were shrieking for reinforcements. Vainly I pointed out that one machine gun with a crew of six men represented the fire-power of forty or fifty rifles at the very lowest computation. It was no good.

Even today, (1929), the average Military Mind still "shies" at the substitution of men by machinery. More and more the army becomes mechanised, in spite of opposition in high places. Nothing stands still in this world except the Military Mind, which steadfastly refuses to look ahead, until it suddenly finds itself involved in a new conflict, having learned nothing, having forgotten nothing. In 1914, it still was thinking in terms of the Boer War; at the beginning of the Boer War, it thought in terms of the Crimea; at the beginning of the Crimea, it thought in terms of Waterloo.

As a matter of fact, to say that the Military Mind *thinks* is a misleading statement. It does not think in the true sense of the word; all it does is to react along certain well-defined, stereotyped lines. This is not the fault of the individual; it is the fault of the whole system. Nothing is more discouraged in the army than a departure from the well-worn path of tradition. The "good soldier" is one who does what he is told without thinking. I remember getting into terrible trouble during the South African War for deviating from this golden rule. I was instructed to erect a line of barbed-wire entanglements, presumably with the intention of keeping out the Boers.

Whilst doing it, it struck me how much more difficult it would be to climb over or through barbed wire which was irregularly spaced and loosely stretched. Without realising the enormity of my offence, I carried out the work on those lines. I was delighted with the result, until my superior officer came to inspect. Then I was sorry, not only for myself but also for my men, as, after being told a few home truths, I was instructed to undo the work and re-erect it strictly according to sealed pattern, dressing the uprights neatly by the left.

The chief trouble at G.H.Q. was that there was no one there who had time to listen to any new idea. Everybody was so busy writing "Passed to you," "Noted and returned," or "For your information," etc., etc., on piles and piles of "jackets," that no one had a moment to consider any proposal for altering the existing condition of affairs. If, what Ian Hay calls, "the Round Game Department" must exist, let it do so; but, for heaven's sake, let us have some branch whose chief duty it is to *think*.

There must have been many excellent ideas that never fructified through lack of encouragement. Speaking for myself, at times I became so despondent about getting anything done that I nearly gave up. If it had not been for the constant support of Lindsay and the others, it is possible that I might have succumbed altogether to despair and "thrown in my hand."

CHAPTER 6

Domestic Difficulties

1

In March 1915 the size of the classes at the school had increased to such an extent that the Artillery Barracks were no longer large enough to accommodate us.

Furthermore, there was no ground available in the vicinity for outdoor work and tactical exercises, and much valuable time was lost in marching to and from our miniature range, a mile or more from St. Omer. I therefore started to look about for a new home.

The first inquiry that I made led me to the convent near the village of Wisques, a couple of miles from St. Omer. The building was a huge pile of grey sandstone, standing in a commanding position on the top of a hill. All around lay rough, broken ground, covered with short turf, interspersed with gorse and heather. Beyond were woods and fields and prosperous farms.

The building was deserted and had remained unoccupied since the expulsion of the Religious Orders from France, some fifteen or twenty years previously.

I walked through the endless passages, visualising classrooms, messes, and offices. In the huge basement were several well-lit, well-ventilated rooms, suitable for an armoury and more classrooms. On the first floor were dozens of medium and small rooms, which would serve admirably for officers' bedrooms, while, above them again, extended vast attics where the N.C.O.s and men, attending the classes, could be accommodated in comfort. To crown everything, there was a large chapel attached, in which I estimated nearly a thousand people could be seated. What a magnificent lecture hall, I thought to myself! Could I possibly obtain possession of this gem of a place?

In the village I found out that the convent was the property of the local *seigneur* to whose *château* I was directed. I found him at home and laid before him my proposal to rent the building. I was terrified that he might ask such a price as would deter G.H.Q. from taking it.

"I shall be delighted to let you have it, *Monsieur le Commandant*," he said at once.

"But at what price?" I asked anxiously.

"*Mais pour rien!*" he exclaimed, almost indignantly. "You require it for your soldiers. It is yours. I am not one to make money from this war."

Alter shaking this unusual Frenchman warmly by the hand, and thanking him very heartily, I returned to St. Omer and reported my wonderful find at the Q.M.G.'s office.

Firstly, I was told it could not be done; secondly, that it was not my business to look for accommodation; thirdly, that these things must be done through the recognised channels.

All these contentions were perfectly correct, but, if I had always waited for things to be done for me instead of going out and doing them myself, the Machine Gun School would probably have never come into existence at all or, if it had, it would have remained for ever in the two dingy rooms at the Artillery Barracks, which, also, I had taken possession of without authority. Besides, "Uncle" Harper's original *dictum* "get on with it" appeared to me capable of the most liberal interpretation.

At last, however, by the good offices of the General Staff, it was agreed that the school might be moved to Wisques, provided always that the rent of the convent was not excessive! Eventually, after long and tedious negotiations between the Q.M.G.'s Department and the French Mission, charged with such matters, the building was taken over and an enormous monthly rent was thrust upon the owner, against his wishes and in face of his earnest expostulations.

Our whole attitude towards the French throughout the war reveals a curious state of affairs. Anyone would have thought, from our behaviour, that the French were conferring a great favour on us by allowing us to come and fight in their country. Not only did we pay the highest market-price for everything, but, not satisfied with that, we usually insisted on paying more. Every time a regiment was moved by rail to another part of the line, the British Government paid heavily for the train; every time an officer or man went on leave, the fact was duly noted and the fare paid; when, later, on their urgent representations, we took over more of the front line, we paid them for the wood in the dugouts and the barbed-wire entanglements, which, in all probability, did not exist.

In addition to the huge official payments made by the government, millions of *francs* were expended daily by officers and men. The shopkeepers in the towns had never known such prosperity. For example, the owner of a sporting-goods establishment in St. Omer told me that he had made more money in the eighteen months during which G.H.Q. was there, than he had made in the previous twenty-five years he had been in business.

Although G.H.Q. constantly reminded me that, in fact, the Machine Gun School was an institution of no real importance, they indignantly refused to allow me to close down for more than a week, in order to move into our new home and settle down.

Much had to be done to render the huge building habitable. On this occasion the housing of the rank and file was simple and "Slushy" and his minions could be relied upon to feed them properly. It was the question of boarding and lodging the officers which worried me, for, by this time, the classes numbered four or five hundred strong, including a hundred or more officers. There certainly were plenty of empty rooms in the building, but I was anxious to make the school not only a place of instruction but, also, if possible, a pleasant respite from the hellish nightmare of the trenches. The officers would need to be fed and I did not altogether approve of G.H.Q.'s suggestion that each of them draw his own rations and cook them in his mess-tin! Having been delivered of this brilliant suggestion, the General Staff returned with zest to the daily paper-chase.

Then I bethought myself of the local branch of Felix Potin, the great French provision merchants, managed most efficiently by two extremely capable women. After several days of almost delirious bargaining, I fixed up a contract with them, whereby they undertook to provide the officers with three meals a day at a total cost of five *francs* per head. They were to draw the officers' rations and supply linen, glass, cutlery, service, cooking pots and pans, etc., etc., while I, in return, granted them the sole right to sell wines and spirits to the messes and, in addition, I was to place at their disposal a large room in the convent for the purpose of selling groceries, wines, etc.

I do not suppose for one moment that this arrangement could be regarded as "based on sound Military Practice," but it worked, and worked most admirably, for the twelve months at Wisques and later when the school moved to other quarters. I never received a single complaint regarding the quality or quantity of the food, and on the many occasions when I paid surprise visits to the mess, I always found the fare excellent. On the other hand, I have no doubt that the contractors made a handsome profit, to which they were fully entitled.

Still I was not entirely satisfied, as there was no furniture whatever for the officers' sleeping-quarters. It is all very well to say that we were on active service, etc., but it has been found, time and time again, that comfortable conditions are essential, if the fullest value is to be obtained from instruction.

I took a car, therefore, for Boulogne, accompanied by my recently appointed interpreter (heaven only knows why I was provided with this appendage; I had never asked for him nor was there anything for him to do), who spoke most excellent French and about half a dozen words of bad English. I was really sorry for him. The poor fellow was so keen to help and had nothing to occupy his time, except to learn English.

Arrived in Boulogne, we visited all the furniture shops in turn, where I bought up every stick of bedroom furniture on terms that would have turned Mr. Drage green with envy. It is true that the goods were not "To be delivered in our own vans without our name on them," but the transport I should have no difficulty in procuring for myself.

My interpreter felt that at last his hour had come. First of all I explained to him my requirements in English. This was absolutely useless. Then I explained them all over again in French with the desired result, but, unfortunately, the *patron* of the shop also understood and the interpreter was reduced to playing the role of a Mrs. Plornish. However, he had had a good day out and had also improved considerably his knowledge of the English language.

On the appointed day, bus after bus drew up at the front gates and disgorged its cargo. Party after party was taken over, allotted quarters and told off into training squads. Detachments from distant portions of the line, or delayed by a breakdown, kept coming in till after dark, but at midnight all had safely arrived.

As we walked down to our house, having seen everybody comfortably settled in, we agreed that whatever might happen, the convent at Wisques would always provide ample accommodation for the classes. Little did we dream that, within less than twelve months, it would filled to overflowing and that, once again, we should be compelled to look for larger quarters.

2

At this point it is necessary to digress somewhat in order to appreciate more fully the strength and the weakness of the machine-gun situation at that time in France.

In the first place the Machine Gun School owed its genesis to a casual conversation between General Capper and myself. There had been no definite plan whatever when it had been started and it was regarded by everybody as merely a temporary expedient. Nobody at G.H.Q. had ever said, "Let there be a Machine Gun School"; in fact, few people there even noticed that there was any necessity for such an establishment.

If some of my readers who were at G.H.Q. at that time should say, "But of course we gave Baker-Carr every help and encouragement," my reply to that is that not one single member of the staff of G.H.Q. ever took the trouble to pay a visit to the school during the six months that it was quartered in the Artillery Barracks, a quarter of a mile distant from the General Staff Office. It was only after the school had been moved to Wisques that, at last, Major Hutchison (now Major-General Sir R. Hutchison, K.C.B., D.S.O.) paid us the honour of a visit and spent with us a brief half-hour. Every little improvement in the status of the Instructional Staff had to be fought for vigorously; every piece of additional equipment for the improvement of the training or for the comfort of the students was obtained only after overcoming the most strenuous opposition, or, as was more usually the case, was "wangled."

The fact that I, the *commandant*, was a "dug-out" of the deepest dye was, at times, a serious detriment to the school, but, in the long run, it was of inestimable value to "The Cause" (as Lindsay called it), since I was able to commit iniquities in Military Procedure, which would have been impossible for a serving soldier. On many occasions I took chances and perpetrated military crimes which, if discovered, or, perhaps rather, if brought officially to the notice of higher authority, must have ruined the career of a regular soldier. It is quite certain that G.H.Q. would not have had the least compunction in offering me up as a burnt-sacrifice, if it had seemed expedient. All these iniquities I committed with open eyes and I realised that no one would lift a finger to save me, but "The Cause" seemed to me to be of such paramount importance that, if it was not possible to accomplish something by legitimate means, then illegitimate means must be employed.

If my various proposals had been put forward by a serving soldier and a graduate of the Staff College, they would have been listened to and given serious consideration. Because I had not answered a prescribed set of examination papers and been awarded a certain number of marks, my opinion on any military subject was of no value. I did not even possess the melancholy distinction of having tried for the Staff College and been unsuccessful. If I had been able to write after my name "Failed P.S.C." in the same manner as the *babu* in India writes "Failed B.A." after his. It would have at least proved that my intentions had been good, even though my ability was moderate.

As a matter of fact, if I had been a Staff College graduate, it is extremely improbable that I should have ever concerned myself with such a trifling matter as machine guns.

The reader must remember that in 1914-15 the subject of machine guns in the British Army *was* trifling. It was only later that the High Command, by hard and bitter experience was forced to realise that no other single weapon of itself was capable of completely holding up an attack.

Artillery barrages might inflict heavy casualties on the attacking forces, but they did not annihilate them in the same way as machine guns did on a hundred different occasions.

The standard of musketry in the German Army was extremely moderate in comparison with that of the British Army in 1914, partly because the German was a conscript army and efficiency in shooting cannot be acquired in a short time, partly because they realised the enormous fire-power of the machine gun and pinned their faith to machinery rather than to brawn, both in attack and defence.

Although this fact was flagrantly and terribly patent to the soldier in the front line, who was called upon to face the enemy machine guns, the High Command was unable to realise the crucial importance of it, even after the Battle of the Somme, and it was only in the following year, during the ghastly and bloody fiasco known as the Third Battle of Ypres, that the full truth was forced upon them.

No doubt, if I had not had the good fortune to be the instrument of fate, someone else, in time, would have arisen to impress on the High Command the overwhelming importance of machine guns; but it would necessarily have been at a considerably later date, thereby deferring the advent of the additional guns, the lack of which must have entailed thousands more casualties.

Do not let it be thought that I wish to decry the value of a Staff College education. Far from it. Other things being equal, it is a most excellent and beneficial training, so long as the graduate preserves his sense of proportion and remembers that this training does not entitle him to adopt an air of omniscience and of superiority towards those who may not have been so fortunate.

3

The calling in of the Press to assist "The Cause" was a typical example of the unmilitary procedure which the situation demanded. I had endeavoured by every legitimate means in my power to overcome the opposition of G.H.Q. without success. Now the time had arrived when other methods must be brought to play.

I had already made the acquaintance of the four or five accredited representatives and, apart from their journalistic abilities, which were beyond question, there was no doubt concerning their whole-hearted patriotism and readiness to help in every possible way. The treatment which they received in the early stages of the war had been far from encouraging, to say the least of it, and at his time, the spring of 1915, every word they wrote was submitted to severe scrutiny and heavily censored.

With the ready co-operation of Valentine Williams (at that time correspondent of the *Daily Mail,* later an officer of the Irish Guards), I laid my plans.

First of all, I dined with the Press representatives in their billet—I nearly wrote prison—in St. Omer and poured into their ready ears the story of my machine-gun difficulties. They listened with the greatest interest, and it was easy to see how eagerly they appreciated the situation. Question after question was asked and answered. Before I left that night, they had a good grip of the problem. The next day, at my invitation, they arrived at the school, where they listened to lecture after lecture on machine guns generally and were furnished with, extracts from my original memorandum.

A few days later, The *Times, Morning Post, Telegraph,* and *Daily Mail* all appeared with heavily leaded articles on the machine-gun question on their main page. For one moment I was rather taken aback lest the noticeable similarity in phrasing, which recurred in all the papers, might be too obvious and awkward questions might be asked. However, nobody at G.H.Q. seemed to have detected it, except Charles Deedes (then Major, now Major-General C. E. Deedes, C.B., C.M.G.,

D.S.O.), who with a twinkle in his eye, asked me whether the views expressed met with my approval.

Valentine Williams had also written to Lord Northcliffe, who, replying to me direct, stated that he was in full sympathy with the movement and would be delighted to use all his power to forward it.

It is impossible to say to what extent "The Cause" was forwarded by the action of the Press, but, judging by the powerful influence it exercised in other matters it must have been very considerable.

Pressure from the fighting line was also beginning to make itself felt, and it was not long before we had the satisfaction of learning that sanction had, at last, been given to increase the number of machine guns per battalion from two to four.

Within twenty-four hours of hearing the news, I put forward a proposal to double this amended establishment. G.H.Q. was horrified.

"Look here, Baker," I was told indignantly. "We've given you two extra guns per battalion. You ought to be satisfied."

Vainly I pointed out that the additional guns were not a personal present to me, but a badly needed increase in the armament of the fighting troops. But it was useless to argue.

I returned to the school and we began to put into shape our long-cherished scheme for the formation of a Machine Gun Corps.

CHAPTER 7

The Conception of the Machine Gun
Corps

1

For several months past, Lindsay and I had been discussing the
formation of a Machine Gun Corps, whose personnel would be composed of selected men, whose training would be complete and uniform and whose employment in battle would not be at the whim of
a commanding officer, enthusiastic perhaps, but hopelessly inexperienced in the first principles of machine gun tactics.

The personnel of the existing Machine Gun Detachments, at this
time, was not always drawn from the pick of units. Company commanders, when asked for men, naturally, but at the same time short-
sightedly, were prone to send those with whom they could best dis-
pense, though others, realising how valuable machine guns were for
the general benefit, sent of their best.

Our basic idea in this respect was that the Machine Gun Corps
should be made a *Corps d'élite,* as in the German Army, and that the
personnel should be chosen from those who volunteered to join it. An
esprit de corps would thus be built up and a high standard of efficiency
and devotion ensured.

The question of uniformity of training was of prime importance.
As long as the school was able to cope with the ever-growing demand
of the divisions, the training was uniform; but, as the numbers of divisions in France increased, we were unable to allot all the vacancies
demanded. In consequence, several corps and divisions initiated supple-
mentary machine gun schools of their own, in which instruction was
given with the best intention, but too often totally at variance with the

established method.

It was, however, on the score of tactical handling that the formation of a corps appeared most essential. Gradually, after months of thought, experiment, and endless discussion with machine gun officers of experience in the line, we had evolved a definite scheme of tactics. This scheme was communicated to the classes in the shape of a series of lectures, after which officers and men were encouraged to make criticisms and offer suggestions.

When officers and N.C.O.s returned to their units, it sometimes happened that their commanding officer might hold quite different views from those which had been inculcated at the school. The Machine Gun officer was absolutely at the mercy of his C.O. and frequently found himself in hot water for putting into practice the basic principles which had been taught by us.

Many, many letters did I receive, marked "Private and Confidential," asking for help and advice, written by recent students at the school, who had been ordered to site their guns in absolute contravention of accepted principles.

In some cases, divisional commanders took a keen interest in their machine guns and, in laying out their line of defence, allotted a definite role to them. The commander of the next division, however, who took over the line, might hold entirely diametrically opposed views, with the result that all the previous work was torn down and a completely new system introduced. This, in its turn, would be demolished when the previous division took over the line again.

A scheme of indirect fire, with map and compass, by machine guns, searching roads and approaches at night, had been worked out at the school. It was a most efficient and disconcerting form of "Hate," if properly employed and regarded, mainly, as a side-show. Several brigadiers, and, at least, one divisional commander, became so enamoured of this type of "frightfulness" that many machine guns were permanently diverted from their proper uses and converted into "Pocket Howitzers." Under a Machine Gun Corps organisation this misuse would be impossible.

It was, furthermore, essential that a line of defence should be laid out on a comprehensive and co-operative system. Commanders at that time were too ready to consider their front, and their front only, forgetting that their flank on either side was of equal importance to them.

The greatest value is obtained from a machine gun when it enfilades its target, *i.e.* fires at it obliquely. Not one but dozens of machine gun emplacements did I see in the line which faced directly to their front, thereby reducing the value of the weapon by anything up to 90 *per cent.* The lie of the ground often was such that some particular portion of the line could be effectively swept only from a point in somebody else's area, two or three hundred yards away. Under existing conditions, it was expecting too much of battalion commanders to utilise their guns for the protection of someone else, who might be in another division or, even, in another army corps. The whole problem of Machine Defence required to be placed on a well-thought-out comprehensive basis, which could only be successfully accomplished by taking the guns out of "parochial" control.

All this and much more was worked out in detail by the staff of the school. Many days and many nights we spent in putting it into such shape as to soften the shock as much as possible for G.H.Q., when it was received. We knew full well that our proposals would be regarded almost in the light of open mutiny. Not only would they be character-ised as rank foolishness, but, also, as contrary to all established practice, a far more demanding offence to Military Mind.

Our scheme visualised a corps, consisting of selected men, trained on the same principles, working on the same tactical lines, free from inter-ference by well-meaning, but misguided, battalion commanders. Each brigade was to have its Machine Gun Company, under the general orders of the brigadier; each division (consisting in those days of three brigades) was to have its reserve Machine Gun Company, making a total of four companies, under the supervision of a divisional gun officer. Each corps and army was to have an officer on its staff to co-ordinate; finally, G.H.Q. was to appoint an officer to the General Staff to superintend the whole.

It was a beautiful scheme, worked out in every detail, down to the junior second lieutenant's batman and the last spare gun-part. When the orderly-room sergeant (still in actual fact, a private in the Artists, but dressed up in sergeant's costume) had made several copies of the completed document, I carried it in person to G.H.Q. and delivered it to the deputy chief of the General Staff.

2

It was obvious that such a far-reaching change of organisation would have to be approved by the Army Council and sanctioned by the Secretary of State for War himself, if, by any miracle, G.H.Q. expressed itself favourably, and, further, that it would take a long time before this could happen.

In order, therefore, to save many valuable weeks, possibly months, I decided once more to disregard "the usual channels" and I forwarded privately a copy of my proposals, with a long covering letter, to General Sir Archibald Murray, at that time Deputy Chief of the Imperial General Staff at the War Office. I knew that Sir Archibald had always taken a very keen interest in the subject and that I could rely on him to give the scheme a thorough and impartial consideration. Nor was I disappointed, as the subsequent history of events will show.

Meanwhile, my memorandum started on its weary round. Although I was not told so officially, I was given to understand by G.H.Q. that the whole thing was considered grotesque. They had, however, paid it the compliment of sending it out to army and corps commanders for their opinion.

Up till now, my chief support in all my schemes had come from the front line. On this occasion, however, I knew that the main opposition would be put up by the commanders of smaller units, such as brigades and battalions. They, at any rate, had awakened to the value of the machine gun and would strenuously resist any proposal to take it from their immediate control, even though, from the larger viewpoint, it might be generally advantageous. Somebody, however, will always be found to oppose any new project, and our efforts at propaganda were confined to assaults on the commanders of armies, corps, and divisions, who might be expected to support the scheme, inasmuch as it put under their direct control a vast weight of fire-power, previously withheld.

The opinions, which we were able to collect, ranged from enthusiastic support to uncompromising hostility. It was evident that considerable attention would be paid to the views of brigade and battalion commanders and these, we knew, would almost universally be unfavourable. The prospects did not appear good, but we never had expected that they would be. The only thing to do was to keep plugging on and await events.

CHAPTER 8

Visitors

1

The move from the squalid barrack-rooms, hidden away in a corner of St. Omer, to our spacious quarters in the imposing, conspicuous convent at Wisques not only exercised a beneficial effect on staff and student alike, but, also, tended to bring into greater prominence the actual existence of the school.

While we had been more or less tucked away out of sight in dingy quarters, there had been but little to attract the interest of visitors. The space had been much restricted and there had been few opportunities for practising drill and tactical exercises. The spectacle of two or three hundred men endeavouring to master the intricacies of the mechanism of a machine gun lock is not wildly exciting. In consequence, I had not gone out of my way to stimulate the presence of visitors.

Now, however, with the splendid accommodation at our disposal, it was quite a different matter. Not only did the instruction generally benefit from our much-improved circumstances, but the prestige, which the school acquired from its new habitat, was enormously enhanced. A shop in a backstreet may, and probably does, sell equally as good articles as a shop in Bond Street; but it is the shop in Bond Street that gets the name and attracts the customers. We had now moved from the back street into Bond Street and people began an interest in our shop-window, which we took care to dress to the best of our ability.

2

Almost every day, a visitor, distinguished or otherwise arrived at G.H.Q. In England, it must have been a thrilling moment when permission was granted to proceed to St. Omer and spend a few days "at the front." Anything more boring, in actual fact, could hardly be conceived.

Picture to yourself a small, provincial French town, consisting of one long, main street, a couple of *places,* two or three churches and a town-hall; people it with assorted French citizens, intersperse them with a few British officers and men, and you have before you G.H.Q.

The General Staff Office consisted of a number of officers in khaki uniform, garnished with red tabs, who sat at tables surrounded by files, on which they were busily writing, "Passed to You," etc., etc., etc. The offices of the adjutant-general and quartermaster-general were indistinguishable from that of the General Staff, except, perhaps, that the atmosphere of the latter was even more solemn.

After visits had been paid to the various departments and the "Brains of the Army" had been seen at work, there was extremely little left for the enterprising tourist to inspect.

Then, one day, somebody had a "brainwave."

"Send Sir William Blank out to the Machine Gun for the day!"

It was a brilliant idea. Not only might the visitor be amused and interested, but, better still, the task of entertaining him would be off the mind of G.H.Q. for several hours.

At first I was somewhat disturbed at the prospect of a stream of visitors, but soon I found that they were the most delightful people in the world to entertain and that, if they were allowed to loose off a machine gun their cup of happiness was completely full.

It is a great source of regret to me that I kept no Visitors' Book. We received visits from all sorts and conditions of men, of many nations, of every colour. His Majesty graciously paid us a visit later on and astonished us by his remarkable knowledge of all that was taking place in the machine gun world.

3

Almost the first of the really distinguished visitors was Mr. Asquith, at that time Prime Minister. I found him extraordinarily easy to entertain and seldom have I met with anyone who so rapidly comprehended a point, even on a subject of which he could have known little or nothing.

After showing him everything that could be of interest to him in the building, we spent some time on the parade-ground, where squads were busy at their outdoor work, dashing about doing drill, mounting and dismounting gun, etc., then down to our little range in a sandpit, where all the different patterns of guns, Vickers-Maxim, the light Vickers, Lewis, Colt, Hotchkiss, etc., were set up ready to fire at a moment's notice.

During our tour of inspection, I had endeavoured to impress upon Mr. Asquith the vast importance of the automatic weapon. He appeared fully to appreciate all that I said and I was much elated at having found an "easy mark" in a personage of his importance. Looking back, however, I have an uneasy feeling that I exaggerated in my mind the impression I had created on him and had forgotten that it was the *métier* of a politician to appear to be favourably disposed, even to a lowly and unimportant individual as myself. Perhaps, after all, I was only one of the babies whose face had been specially washed for the candidate to kiss!

However that may be, I was so much encouraged that I took the opportunity to pour into his seemingly interested ear my project for the formation of the Machine Gun Corps. He nodded appreciatively when I made my point about the saving of manpower. That what he *wanted* to hear, but when I went on to say that I should need thirty or forty thousand additional men, then he wasn't quite so pleased. *That* put a very different complexion on the proposal.

"But, sir," I greatly ventured to suggest, "it would be quite easy to find the men."

"How?"

"By Conscription, or Universal Service, if you don't like the word Conscription, sir."

"When my Military Adviser, Lord Kitchener," he replied coldly, "tells me that Universal Service is necessary, then Universal Service will be enforced. At present he informs me that it is *not*."

Shortly afterwards he took his departure, with many expressions of admiration for the work which the school was doing; but leaving me with an uneasy feeling in my mind that conscription, which everybody, including the politicians themselves, knew would have to come, was still very far in the dim future.

4

One of the many strange phenomena of the war was the extraordinary misconception by the politicians of the spirit of the British nation. From the very beginning they endeavoured to keep back bad news and fed the people on misleading "pap," as though they feared lest the truth might discourage them. The Retreat from Mons, for example, was camouflaged to such an extent that no one had the slightest conception of what was taking place, until the famous *Times* article "let the cat out of the bag" with a vengeance. Victories were grossly exaggerated and reverses minimised, till it seemed as though the campaign was to be a walk-over for us.

Not only were the politicians extremely indifferent psychologists, but they were, also, apparently unable even to appreciate facts. Recruiting was invariably stimulated by the news of a reverse and fell off after a success. The reason for this ebb and flow is not far to seek. There were hundreds of thousands of men who, for various reasons, were hesitating to take the plunge and enlist. When things seemed to be going well, they said to themselves, "They can get on all right without me," but, when the situation looked black, many of them threw away the last remnants of indecision and joined up. It is remarkable that Lord Kitchener, who, alone of those in high places, prophesied a war of three or more years' duration, should have failed to see that eventually some form of universal service would be essential. Great man that Kitchener was, there is no doubt but that towards the end his powers were waning. All his life he had ploughed a lonely furrow and, through his very self-reliance, had at last come to mistrust the opinion of others.

Up till the time of the Great War, Kitchener's tasks had always been a "one-man show." His mind was one eminently lacking in plasticity and, at the age of sixty-three, it was too late to expect any change to take place. Accustomed, as he was, to an unquestioning acceptance of his fiat, he was impatient of the views of others, though these, in many cases, might be in a far better position to form an accurate judgment. His conception of the duties of the Secretary of State for War was that everything in connection with the war fell within his province, including the disposition of the armies in the field. Hence the stormy interview with Sir John French in August 1914, when Kitchener appeared at G.H.Q. in field-marshal's uniform, and started to issue orders to the Commander-in-Chief of the Expeditionary Force.

In 1914 the name of Kitchener possessed an almost hypnotic effect on the great mass of the British people. His cold aloofness, his striking personality, his reputation for fanatical devotion to duty, all created in their minds an impression of infallibility. "Leave it to Kitchener" came to be the national expression of faith, to doubt the wisdom of which was regarded as a sin against the Holy Ghost.

In the beginning, the Press, with unanimous voice, daily sang a *paean* of praise in his honour. A man would have been more than human if he had been uninfluenced by this wave of adoration.

Such was the implicit faith of the country in Kitchener's judgment at this time that, if he had said, on accepting the post of Secretary of State for War, "This war will last three years. We shall need every man in order that we may emerge victorious. Conscription must be enacted forthwith," no one, except a few negligible cranks, would have opposed it. So great would have been the wave of enthusiasm that the "Wait-and-Sees," if they had dared to raise a voice in protest, would have been swept for ever and ever into outer darkness.

Everybody and everything conspired to imbue Kitchener with the sense of his own omnipotence. Every wall and hoarding was covered with invitations to join "Kitchener's Army," not "His Majesty's Army." Although machinery was already in existence, created under Lord Haldane's Territorial Army Scheme, whereby our military strength could be expanded to an almost unlimited degree, Kitchener saw fit to ignore it and built up a parallel organisation, to all intents and purposes in competition.

I often wonder if anybody ever had the courage to suggest to Kitchener that he might be wrong in this matter. If so, it would be extremely interesting to know what his reply was. In all likelihood, none whatever. The rash intruder probably crept from the room, wilted by one look from those steely, blue eyes.

The principle that the Secretary of State for War should be a civilian has much to commend it and is one from which another departure is improbable. In the Cabinet Lord Kitchener was a law unto himself. At the War Office he rode roughshod over his departmental chiefs until the arrival of Lieutenant-General (now Field-Marshal) Sir William Robertson, from France to take over the position of Chief of the Imperial General Staff, at the War Office.

Sir William, a man of indomitable determination, afraid of nothing and nobody on earth, had written down, beforehand on half a sheet of note-paper the duties which he conceived to be within the province of his post, though several of these duties had been usurped, quite incorrectly, by the Secretary of State. In effect, the new C.I.G.S. said to K., "This is my conception of my job. If I accept this post, this is what I intend to do. Take it or leave it. I never asked for the job."

This situation arose after the war had been in progress for some thirteen months and the nation's faith in Lord Kitchener's omniscience was waning. The idol's feet of clay were not yet visible, but ominous cracks were beginning to appear in the toes of his boots.

Very wisely, Lord Kitchener surrendered.

At the two interviews, which I had with Kitchener during the war, no one could have been more kind and considerate than he was.

The first occasion was during his visit to G.H.Q. in the early summer of 1915, when he spent several hours at the Machine Gun School. He expressed himself most appreciatively concerning the work we were doing and took a lively interest in our various activities.

It was during his inspection of the school that he made the remark concerning "dug-outs," which has often since appeared in print, usually incorrectly. What he actually said to me was this:

"If the war has done nothing else, it has produced two remarkable 'dug-outs,' you and myself."

Little did I realise at the time of what paramount importance to "The Cause" his visit was to prove. By this time I was so inured to stereotyped expressions of admiration from visitors (after all, they could hardly say it was a rotten show after having eaten my food and drunk my drink), that I largely discounted their sincerity, but, on this occasion, at any rate, the impression created must have been considerable, in view of the fact that he thought it worthwhile to send for me, three months later, to ask for my opinion and advice.

5

One of my most interesting visitors at this period was General Cadorna, then C.-in-C. of the Italian Army.

By this time we had evolved a regular "set-piece" for visitors, something on the lines of a "three-ring circus," *i.e.* squads learning mechanism, squads at drill in the open, squads firing on the range.

Cadorna's visit started badly. He was billed to arrive at nine-thirty a.m. After a final glance round at nine o'clock to assure myself that everything was ready for the curtain to go up punctually, I hurried from the school to my house for a little breakfast. I had hardly swallowed the first mouthful before a breathless orderly rushed down with the news that Cadorna had arrived and was awaiting me.

Hastily I ran back to the convent, where I found a large concourse assembled. I was presented to the C.-in-C, who spoke French fluently, but with an execrable accent, and made my apologies, which he accepted with perfect good humour.

Leading the way with a following of ten or fifteen satellites, I con-

General Cadorna

ducted him through the various classrooms where squads were working. He did not appear wildly interested, so, cutting this turn short, I escorted him outside on to the parade-ground where squads were engaged in drill. I had ordered one squad to stand by to perform any evolutions which the visitor might demand. The eight men were drawn up in a line, their gun on the ground in front of them. On the left of the squad stood a magnificent-looking private of the London Scottish.

Suddenly Cadorna stopped in front of the squad and turned to me, his face alight with interest. At last, I said to myself, he has found something worthy of his attention.

"*C'est vrai que les écossais ne portent pas de caleçons sous les jupes?*" he asked, pointing to the Highlander.

"*Oui, mon général,*" I replied. "*C'est bien vrai.*"

Cadorna approached the man, who stood rigidly to attention, looking straight to his front. Leaning down, Cadorna took the bottom edge of the kilt between his finger and thumb. Cautiously he raised it, while the wretched soldier grew more and more embarrassed.

With a quick movement Cadorna let the kilt fall and turned to me with a beaming smile.

"*Vous avez raison, mon vieux!*" he exclaimed.

6

In the Convent of Wisques, for ten days, I entertained a clandestine and most unofficial visitor. Even now, I do not know to what extent G.H.Q. was cognisant of my visitor, but I am quite sure that I should have been made the scapegoat, if anything had gone wrong.

At that time, the supply of machine guns was extremely poor. The increase in production had not yet materialised and the new K Divisions were being equipped with Lewis guns, until such time as the Vickers became available. Any satisfactory automatic weapon was worth its weight in gold and we were prepared to accept practically anything that was obtainable.

One day, Colonel Dick, one of the King's Messengers, came out to the school to see me. He had, by some means, got in touch with the representative of the Rexer rifle, an automatic weapon in use in the Danish Army. Apparently, this representative, whom we will call "Hansen," had approached the Home Authorities without success. He had, therefore, requested Dick to see if anything could be done in France.

It was manifestly useless to apply in England for a permit for Hansen to come to France officially and, at the same time, I could not very well recommend to G.H.Q. the adoption of a weapon without having carried out a series of trials, although I had some knowledge of the Rexer, which had been tested at Hythe while I was on the staff there. It had been "turned down," chiefly on the grounds of finance.

This was another of the occasions when the fact that I was a "dugout," and not a serving soldier, permitted me to do something not strictly in accordance with the usual Military Practice.

I arranged with Dick for him to bring the Rexer representative and his gun surreptitiously under his wing across the Channel to Boulogne. There I would meet them with my car and drive Hansen and his goods direct to the convent. Not a soul was to be informed and, at the end of the requisite time, Hansen would be spirited back to England in the same manner as he had come.

In due course Hansen arrived and was smuggled into a room in the convent, unseen by anybody. He was kept there out of sight and his meals were brought to him, the excuse given being that he was an officer who was seriously ill. As there were a hundred or more officers, drawn from every division in France, already assembled at the school, nobody's suspicions were aroused.

In the evenings Hansen, disguised in British officer's uniform, sallied forth with his gun and we fired a series of tests in a sandpit not far from the school. It was necessary to take my armourer-sergeant somewhat into my confidence but, as Hansen spoke perfect English, I did not need to inform the armourer-sergeant of the fact that the owner of the gun was in reality a Dane. All I told him was that we were carrying out some secret trials and that it was up to him to keep his mouth shut.

After we had satisfied ourselves as to the desirability of obtaining the weapon, the next step was to secure the approval of G.H.Q. for an order for five hundred guns, without being obliged to disclose my somewhat unmilitary procedure.

Having got Hansen safely back to England, I wrote a report on the Rexer and forwarded it with a strong recommendation that five hundred should be ordered forthwith.

For once there was no "havering." Sanction was given immediately; but an entirely unforeseen difficulty arose.

The Danes, already expecting at any moment to be swallowed up by Germany, steadfastly refused to accept an order from the British

Government for war material, which could be construed by Germany into an unfriendly act, with dire results to Denmark. It was, moreover, out of the question to manufacture the guns in England, where all existing machinery was needed for making our own patterns of weapons. It was hinted, however, that, if the order were given in the name of a private individual, the company would be prepared to manufacture in Denmark.

I, therefore, placed my own personal order with the Rexer Rifle Company for five hundred guns, involving a trifle of over a hundred thousand pounds.

Not till nearly a year later, did I hear the sequel and, then, from a most unexpected source. The Danish company, having manufactured the guns, found itself in a quandary as to how they were; to be delivered. As it did not dare to deliver direct to England or any of her Allies, the only method must be through a Neutral Power, favourable to the Allied Cause. Roumania was obviously indicated.

Forthwith the guns were dispatched, but, unfortunately for us, the route lay partly through Germany territory. At the frontier the packing-cases were opened for inspection.

"Just what we were wanting," said the German official and the guns were seized and issued to the German cavalry!

I often wonder who paid for those guns and whether Hansen ever received his commission on the deal.

7

The Commission inquiring into the so-called German atrocities spent several months in St. Omer and one of the members, whom I knew well, dined at our house on several occasions. Much capital was being made out of these alleged brutalities, though such propaganda had not yet come fully into its own. My friend related to us many stories, some tragic, some comic, others purely farcical, of which one in particular has remained in my memory.

The Commission was engaged in an inquiry into the alleged raping of several women in Bailleul.

"*C'est vrai que les allemands vous ont violée, Madame?*" gently asked the president of one of the witnesses.

"*Oui, Monsieur, plusieurs fois,*" replied the woman. "*Mais—mais pas brutalement!*"

Undoubtedly there were many cases of bestiality and wanton destruction, but against this must be set the impeccable behaviour of the

German troops in big cities such as Rheims, Amiens, Abbeville, and many others. Charges of cruelty and destruction have always been hurled against soldiers and always will be. It is whispered that even the British themselves were suspected of doing a little looting in China during the Boxer Rising and, during the Boer War, some of our Continental friends had no hesitation in charging us with the vilest treatment of innocent women and children in Concentration Camps.

8

In the spring of 1915 I was warned by G.H.Q. that, on the morrow, the Representative of Machine Guns at the Ministry of Munitions would come out to discuss with me the number of machine guns which would be needed. I inquired whether the General Staff had mentioned any provisional estimate and was informed that no figure as yet had been decided. This statement relieved my mind as it gave me more or less a free hand.

The next morning, there was ushered into my office a burly, genial, red-faced individual, who announced that he had come to discuss with me the question of the supply of machine guns. He admitted quite frankly that he knew nothing about them technically, and was only concerned with the manufacturing end of the business.

I had already made up my mind regarding the figure I intended to suggest, but, before doing so, I thought there would be no harm in impressing on him the value of the automatic weapon. He listened most carefully and I could see that he fully appreciated its importance.

"How many guns, then, do you think we ought to plan to manufacture?" he asked at length.

I took a long breath.

"Twenty thousand," I replied.

He never blinked an eyelid. He took out his little notebook and wrote in it my demand. He even smiled as he returned it to his pocket.

"Goodbye," he said, getting up. "I've enjoyed my talk with you very much. I'll do all I can to help you get the guns."

After he had gone, I sat in my office, wondering how long it would be before G.H.Q. would ring me up and tell me what they thought about the fantastic figure I had given. At that time there were less than three hundred machine guns in the whole British Army in France, and here was I calmly asking for twenty thousand.

Sure enough, in an hour's time, I was wanted by the General Staff on the telephone, but the voice I heard at the other end was not so fierce as I had expected. Apparently, my estimate was considered too ridiculous to be taken seriously and was regarded as a somewhat ill-timed attempt at humour. I was given to understand that steps would be taken to put the matter right, and a reasonable number of guns would be ordered.

As I laid down the receiver, without having said one word, I caught sight of the card which my visitor had left. I had not looked at it before, but I was interested to learn who this cheerful business-like person might be. He struck me as the type of man whom we badly needed.

"Mr. Eric Geddes," I read.

Not till eighteen months later did I again meet Geddes, by which time he had been made a major-general and a K.C.B., shortly to become an admiral and a member of the Cabinet.

Several of the senior officers of the Tank Corps were being sent to attend a comparative trial of British and French tanks at Marly-le-Roi. The rendezvous was the Ritz Hotel in Paris, from which we were to proceed by car to the trial-ground. As I stood waiting on the steps of the hotel, my late machine gun purveyor came up, and, shaking me warmly by the hand, invited me to drive down with him in his car. During the journey we discussed, among other things, machine guns, and he told me the story of the sequel to our interview.

On leaving the school, he had gone back to G.H.Q., where my demand for twenty thousand guns had been received with derision. Undeterred, he had, on his return to London, submitted this figure to Mr. Lloyd George, then Minister of Munitions, who promptly accepted it without comment.

At this period, Lord Kitchener, in common with almost all other soldiers in high position, failed to realise the importance of the automatic weapon. He had definitely laid down that two machine guns per battalion were a minimum, four per battalion a maximum, and anything in excess of four a luxury. When informed of Lord Kitchener's decision, Mr. Lloyd George, on his own initiative, laid down a figure of sixty-four per battalion and it was on this basis that orders for manufacture were placed. Thus are wars won.

"I don't mind telling you," Geddes concluded, "that you were one of the very few officers I met in France who really knew what he wanted, and wasn't afraid of big figures."

"I was wrong just the same," I replied. "I ought to have asked for a hundred and twenty thousand."

9

In October 1915, the late Lord Haldane paid a visit to G.H.Q. and spent several hours at Wisques. After he had seen everything and had exhausted his stock of conundrums, we adjourned to lunch, where the conversation turned from the particular to the general.

Only a few days previously I had had my second interview with Lord Kitchener on the subject of the Machine Gun Corps, when he had given me certain facts and figures, which were not generally publicly disclosed.

The question of Universal Service inevitably cropped up and I asked Lord Haldane why, in his opinion, so form of compulsion was not enforced.

"It is not necessary," he replied. "We can get the men without it."

"But, sir," I exclaimed, "our weekly wastage is well over thirty thousand."

"Yes," was his answer, "but recruiting is fairly satisfactory."

"Did we get enough men last week to make up the wastage?"

"Not quite. I don't remember exactly what the figure was."

"I can tell you, sir. It was fifteen thousand."

"How do you know that?" he asked quickly.

"Lord Kitchener told me, sir. If we go on at that rate, there'll have to be conscription of some sort."

"Impossible, impossible!" exclaimed Lord Haldane. "If the government were to attempt to enforce Universal Service, the country would break out into open revolt. There would be a general strike the next day!"

Within a month Universal Service was enacted amid the universal approbation of the Nation. "Thank God! now the decision has been taken out of our hands," was the general expression of feeling of those whose ties had prevented them from taking the plunge.

So much for the knowledge of the spirit of the people, possessed by politicians.

10

Lastly, we received the great honour of a visit from His Majesty, though actually this visit did not take place until the school was established in its final home near Etaples.

The knowledge which His Majesty possessed on machine gun matters was almost uncanny. He discussed the relative merits of each gun, as though he had had years of experience of them and fully appreciated how different types of weapons were suitable for different purposes. Much to my surprise, he was, also, completely informed concerning the Rexer rifle episode and it was he who first told me how the weapons had been seized by the Germans and used against us.

His Majesty must realise how great is the pleasure his visits give and, also, how his frankly expressed appreciation acts as an incentive to further efforts, but I should like to offer my humble tribute of thanks to him, on behalf of the staff of the school, whose work, arduous and unceasing though it was, provided but little opportunity of personal distinction and was, at times, apt to be lost sight of amid the greater glamour of the fighting line.

They also serve who train.

CHAPTER 9

I am Sent for by Lord Kitchener

1

We left the memorandum on the formation of the Machine Gun
Corps started on its way round the army.

Patiently we waited as best we could, though, in our hearts, we
were not too hopeful. All of us realised how revolutionary our scheme
must appear and how long it would take for the Military Mind to rec-
oncile itself to such a drastic change. It must be remembered that we
had been at war for less than a year and few people realised that more
than three years of blood and mud still lay before us. Many suggestions, which afterwards were adopted, were then disregarded on the
grounds that, by the time they materialised, the war would be over.

Much to my surprise, the opposition at G.H.Q. had perceptibly
decreased. No great enthusiasm, however, was apparent, though the
general principles were no longer regarded as rank heresy. A "Wait and
See" attitude had been adopted, which could be modified in either
direction if needful.

At long last, the reports from armies came in and were collated.
Although I did not see the reports from the smaller units, such as brigades and battalions, it was obvious from the comments of the Higher
Command that it was these reports which had turned the scale against
us. The opinions of the commanders of armies, corps, and divisions
were by no means unfavourable.

In spite of the result being along the lines we had anticipated, we
were all somewhat cast down by this definite refusal. We still hoped,
however, that the question might be reconsidered as the defects in the
existing system, which we had pointed out, became more apparent.
The one really satisfactory feature was that the War Office authorities

were distinctly (though, of necessity, unofficially) favourable to the scheme, which fact I had learned from a private source.

It was not the appropriate moment to return to the charge. Nothing is more calculated to stir up resentment and court a final and irrevocable "No," than to press for a reconsideration immediately after the first refusal has been recorded. It was necessary to bide our time and trust that events would aid in forcing our proposals to the front once more.

<h1 style="text-align:center">2</h1>

The new Kitchener Divisions were now beginning to arrive.

If my memory serves me aright, the 12th Division, under Major-General Wing, was the first to land in France. Each of the new divisions, as it arrived, was concentrated in the Wisques area to spend a week or ten days before being sent into the line.

It so happened that McGillycuddy, one of the members of my staff, met General Wing, who was a personal friend of his, in St. Omer and told him of all our machine gun activities. Wing was much interested and asked if he might be allowed to bring out his commanding officers, machine gunners and others for a day's instruction. On the proposal being put before me, I at once issued a cordial invitation to General Wing to bring as many of his officers as he liked. Fortunately, a break of four or five days between courses was in progress, with the result that the whole staff was available to give lectures, demonstrations, etc.

Two days later the divisional commander, accompanied by his brigadiers, battalion commanders, company commanders, and the whole of his machine gun personnel, arrived at Wisques at nine a.m. A full and busy day was spent, with only an hour's interval for lunch, which our visitors had brought with them. At six p.m. our friends took their departure, full of gratitude and information.

Unfortunately, General Wing was so carried away by his enthusiasm that he informed G.H.Q. that, so far the best instruction his division had received had been given at the Machine Gun School.

Once more I was "on the mat." Why hadn't I asked permission before inviting the division to the school, etc., etc.?

I gave *"the soft answer that turneth away wrath,"*; although I did not feel in the least contrite and fully, intended to do it again, as soon as opportunity arose. I was, however, saved any further trouble on this score as the next day G.H.Q. issued instructions that "all new divisions

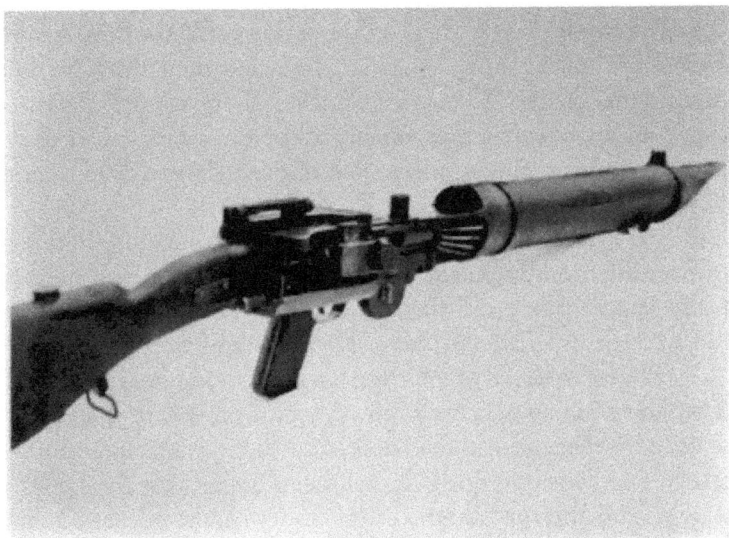

Lewis gun

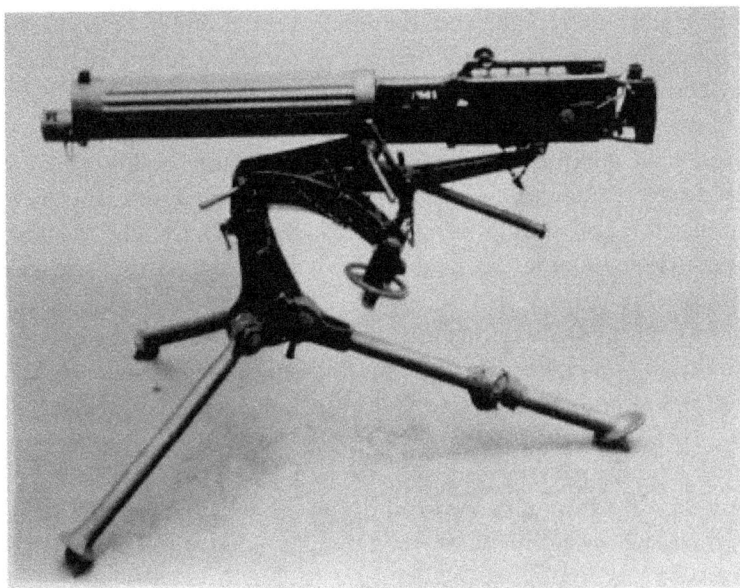

Vickers machine gun on MK IV tripod

will spend at least one day at the Machine Gun School. Commandant, M.G.S., please note." The *commandant* noted.

It was a real pleasure to do everything one could for these magnificent troops. Their keenness was incredible and their thirst for information unquenchable. When we had given them enough instruction to satiate an army corps, they merely asked for more and, at the end of the day, we were almost compelled to drive them off the premises with a club.

The first hundred thousand was the pick of the nation. In this case again, were demonstrated the defects of voluntary recruitment. The best and keenest were the first to join and thousands of men, who would have been invaluable later as officers and N.C.O.s, met their death as private soldiers. Magnificent perhaps, but certainly not war.

The later of these new divisions were equipped with the Lewis instead of the Vickers gun, as the latter was not yet available in sufficient numbers. The divisions, however, had been taught that the Lewis was a machine gun and the training of the crews had been carried out on these lines.

In actual fact, the Lewis gun possesses many attributes denied to the Vickers, but it is not a *machine gun,* in that it is not capable of prolonged, continuous, rapid fire, the first requisite of a machine gun. The Lewis is extremely light and, therefore, very mobile; it can be fired from the shoulder, if the fore-part is placed on a rest; it requires no fixed mounting and can be carried about safely, ready to fire.

It was necessary to explain all this to the new divisions, but it was a somewhat delicate task. The divisions must not be allowed to lose confidence in their only automatic weapon, but it was, also, necessary that the gun should not be used improperly, thereby destroying its efficiency. In order to lend colour to the legend that the Lewis was a machine gun, it had been provided in England with a machine gun mounting. You then had the grotesque picture of a twenty-seven pound gun perched on the top of a fifty-six pound tripod.

This was not an important matter so long as the commanders realised that the Lewis, as a gun of position, was only a *pis alley* until the genuine article was available. What I feared was that the Lewis would be called upon to perform duties for which it had never been designed and would inevitably fail, thereby undermining the faith of its crews.

Within a month this very thing occurred.

One day I received an urgent message from G.H.Q. The 18th Division had sent in the most damaging report on the Lewis gun, which, in their opinion, "was not only absolutely useless, but actually a source of danger, inasmuch as commanders had put faith in its reliability, which in fact did not exist. Would G.H.Q. kindly take immediate steps to abolish it at the earliest possible moment?" or words to that effect.

Duly I sallied forth and drove to a Brigade Headquarters near Albert, where I had asked all the complainants to assemble for the purpose of ventilating their grievances.

On my arrival, I found quite a large number of officers, including a brigadier and several battalion commanders. The atmosphere was distinctly chilly and I felt rather like the chairman of a board of directors about to confront a hostile meeting of shareholders.

The best thing was to let them talk and to see if I could sift out the cause of the trouble. One after another they got up and abused the gun, telling how, on this occasion and on that, they had been let down. I allowed them to meander on, as nothing relieves people more than talking. The greater part of their speeches was totally irrelevant. I was not concerned with the details of their experiences; what I wanted to get at was for what cause the gun had failed, as it obviously had.

Gradually, there emerged from this welter of words one definite fact: the piston-rod, which actuates the mechanism, always broke after firing a few hundred rounds. As soon as this became clear, my mind was completely set at rest. *That* little trouble could be settled in two minutes.

I let everybody "say their piece" and then I said mine:

Gentlemen, the cause of your trouble is perfectly clear. The return-spring against which the piston-rod works is set far too lightly, with the result that the rod bangs violently against the end of the cylinder at every discharge. The rod becomes crystallised and snaps. Set your return spring at thirteen pounds and I will undertake myself to replace every piston-rod that breaks during the next month.

My little speech was received in silence. They didn't believe one word of it and thought that I was giving them a plausible excuse in order to keep them quiet. As a matter of fact, I had known for some time past, that the instruction given in England by self-styled "experts" was most misleading.

The great majority of unskilled machine gunners consider that the machine gun is firing its best when it is firing its fastest. This, in fact, is the reverse of the truth. A machine gun or a Lewis gun is capable of firing at the rate of eight or nine rounds a second. In an attack, the object of a machine gun in defence is to kill as many of the attackers as possible. One or two bullets are ample to disable the average man; it is, therefore, waste of good ammunition to "kill the same man half a dozen times over," which would be the case if the gun fires at its maximum speed. In practice, generally speaking, the slower a gun fires, the better the result. The Germans were well aware of this and it was easy for any of us, who were familiar with machine guns, to distinguish between our guns and the enemy's by the great difference in the rate of fire.

It had been our policy not to interfere, unless called upon to do so, in any matters with reference to training given in England. This incident, however, was sufficiently serious to justify the taking of a definite step.

Leaving my audience to discuss matters amongst themselves, I drove to the headquarters of the Divisional Commander, Major-General (now Lieutenant-General Sir Ivor) Maxse, who did not suffer from the Military Mind and who, later on, was to prove one of the best friends the Tanks ever had. I knew him only slightly at this time, but I had seen enough of his methods to be able to speak quite frankly and openly. I told him what was the cause of the trouble and how it could be obviated in future. He at once saw the point and, cordially and in picturesquely lurid language, promised to see that my instructions were carried out. I then returned to G.H.Q. and reported.

Not one single demand did I ever receive from the 18th Division for a piston-rod, and any further trouble in this respect was eliminated by an instruction sent out to all units from the General Staff at G.H.Q. on the subject of return-springs.

The advent of the Lewis gun was to prove of supreme importance in the formation of the Machine Gun Corps.

As has been pointed out above, the deciding factor against its formation was the opposition of battalion commanders, who did not wish to lose control of the machine guns. It now struck us that this opposition would be rendered nugatory, if the machine guns of a battalion were replaced by four, and, later, eight, Lewis guns.

Already at the school, after weeks and weeks of heated argument with G.H.Q., we were teaching the classes that the machine gun and the Lewis gun possessed different virtues and should serve different purposes. The Lewis, we said, was a weapon eminently suited for in-

GENERAL IVOR MAXSE, G.O.C., XVIIITH CORPS, PRESENTING
MEDALS TO MEN OF THE 152ND BRIGADE

fantry and did not require special tactical training in the same way that a machine gun did. Any soldier of average intelligence could learn the mechanism, etc., of a Lewis gun in a few days. If four, with a promise of eight or, even, sixteen, Lewis guns were given to each battalion, the commander would have under his direct control a greater weight of fire-power than he had previously.

3

It is always interesting to reflect how important matters may hinge on the veriest trifles, and how the trend of events may be altered by a chance word. It is more than probable that the Machine Gun Corps would never have come into existence if I had not happened to be in the General Staff Office one morning when all the officers in that particular room were absent. Further, if the head clerk, a most intelligent and capable man, had not, for some reason, been favourably disposed towards me personally, I should never have known of something which would have, once and for all, destroyed all hope of reviving my scheme.

As I stood waiting, the head clerk pointed to a big, black, wooden case that lay beside his table.

"What's that?" I asked casually.

"All papers marked 'Of no further interest' are in there sir. They're being shipped to Havre today for safe custody."

"What about it?" I asked again.

"Your memorandum on the Machine Gun Corps is in there, sir."

"Great Scott!" I exclaimed. "I was just going to have another go at it."

The clerk looked around cautiously.

"I can get it out for you, sir, if you like," he said in an undertone. "Nobody'll ever know. I'll send it out to the Machine Gun School tomorrow, sir, if you wish."

I thanked him hastily, as one of the General Staff officers came into the room.

The next day the file arrived and, after going through the whole correspondence from beginning to end, I wrote another memorandum, which dealt chiefly with the opposition of battalion commanders and how these objections could be completely overcome by the issue of Lewis guns.

To this day I do not know whether G.H.Q. ever realised that the file had been disinterred and brought to life surreptitiously, but, if so, it was never officially noticed.

Out went the memorandum again, but this time only the Higher Commanders were consulted, it being considered that the objections of the commanders of smaller units had been fully met.

Within an incredibly short time, I was informed that everyone had expressed a favourable opinion, but I was warned that War Office sanction had still to be obtained and that this was very doubtful in view of the fact that, up to the present, they knew nothing whatever about it in London. I preserved a discreet silence.

The next day all the papers in connection with the scheme were forwarded to the Chief of the Imperial General Staff at the War Office, with G.H.Q.'s recommendation that it should be adopted.

Imagine the surprise and delight of the General Staff when an urgent message was received a week later from the War Office, asking that three officers from G.H.Q. should be sent to London immediately to settle details! Indeed, the War Office, the despicable and dilatory, had arrived at a rapid decision!

I managed to keep a perfectly straight face when I was told. Charles Deedes, who was in the General Staff Office at the time, undoubtedly had his suspicions of me, but not, I'm much afraid, having a really Military Mind, he contented himself with saying, with a little smile:

"Mails working satisfactorily with England, Baker?"

A few days later I was called up on the telephone from G.H.Q.

"It's all right, Baker," said a well-known voice at the other end. "Our Machine Gun Corps Scheme has gone through all right. The War Office has given its approval."

I nearly laughed into the receiver. *Our* Machine Gun Corps, forsooth! For six months or more, I had fought everybody at G.H.Q. to get my scheme through and, except from my own staff, I had never received one word of help or encouragement. I had been told that I was a visionary, a fanatic, a meddler with things that did not concern me, an insubordinate young "pup" and several other complimentary names. My scheme had been characterised as ridiculous, impossible, impracticable, subversive (whatever that might mean), and contrary to all accepted Military Practice.

To such an extent, however, had G.H.Q. taken over the scheme as its very own that, when the three officers from G.H.Q. were chosen to consult with the War Office about the details, no one even suggested that I should be one of them.

I am not by nature a vindictive person, but the calm assurance with which G.H.Q. had "pinched" my ideas and claimed them as their own after months of ridicule and abuse, did somewhat raise my ire. The next day, however, I was to have my revenge in full.

Again I was summoned to the telephone.

"The Secretary of State has refused to sanction the formation of the Machine Gun Corps until he has seen you. You are to proceed to London without a moment's delay," said the voice of yesterday.

This time I'm afraid I did laugh, but, before I could reply, I was cut off. Evidently, I was unpopular again. It must have been a terrible blow to the pundits of G.H.Q. to be ignored by Lord Kitchener in favour of the despised and rejected "dug-out."

On my way to Boulogne to catch the boat, I called in at the General Staff Office to ask if there were any further instructions; but I was informed, very tersely, that I had already been told all there was to know. Most decidedly, I was very unpopular.

The next morning I presented myself at the War Office. Not knowing quite how to approach the matter, I first went to the office of the Director of Military Training, whom I had never met before. My reception here was positively frigid.

"I understand that Lord Kitchener wishes to see me about the formation of the Machine Gun Corps" I began timidly.

"The Secretary of State has seen fit to disregard the advice of myself and the other Directors of the War Office, until he has consulted *Major* Baker-Carr. Good morning!"

I faded from the office. Nobody seemed to like me. The best thing I could do was to go straight to K.'s office.

There I was received most kindly by Mr. (now Sir Herbert) Creedy, K.'s secretary, who told me that Lord Kitchener was expecting me and that I was to be shown in as soon as I arrived. The Russian Ambassador was also waiting to see the Secretary of State, but I was to go in first. Things were indeed looking up.

In a few minutes I was ushered into the presence.

Lord Kitchener, in undress uniform, was sitting at his desk. He rose when I was announced and gave me a most cordial greeting. He pulled up a chair beside his desk and told me to sit down.

"Now then," he said in his most pleasant voice. "Tell me all about this Machine Gun Corps of yours. I've heard something about it, but I wanted to get information from you at first hand before I gave my sanction for its formation."

For over half an hour I talked. I explained the whole thing from beginning to end and set forth all the advantages which I hoped would ensue. When I had finished, he asked me a few questions, which I answered to the best of my ability.

"How many men will you want?" he inquired.

"About forty thousand to start with, sir."

"It's going to be a difficult job to find them."

From a drawer in his desk he produced a statement showing the shortage in each branch of the service, infantry, cavalry, etc. etc. Everybody seemed to be thousands and thousands under strength.

"Our wastage is over thirty thousand a week, he said at last. "The recruiting figures are dropping. There were only fifteen thousand last week."

"The Machine Gun Corps would be a great saving of manpower if used properly, sir," I ventured to suggest. "If only the High Command would substitute machinery for men, I think you would find that the wastage would be decreased."

K. sat in deep thought for a few moments.

"Very well, my boy, you shall have your men. Some of the other arms will have to go a bit short, but it can't be helped."

"Thank you, sir," I replied.

"I'll order a meeting of the Directors of the War Office at half-past two this afternoon to draw up the Army Order. You will attend. If anybody raises objections, you can tell them that I said it would be all right."

I got up and took my leave.

Throughout the interview, Lord Kitchener had been kindness and consideration itself. He had not evinced the least symptom of the harshness and hectoring from which all his subordinates suffered. I had entered his room more or less in fear and trembling. After a few minutes, he had put me completely at my ease and he had listened to my long dissertation on machine guns without a suspicion of impatience or boredom.

By good luck, Lindsay happened to be in London and was anxiously awaiting me outside. He was naturally delighted when I told him the result of the interview and readily agreed to attend the meeting with me, although he had not been invited. I felt that I might need some support and Lindsay was obviously the man to give it.

We felt that we were entitled to a good lunch, partly to celebrate our victory, partly to put us in good heart for the meeting.

At two-thirty p.m. we were shown into the Directors' Room. Already most of the directors were assembled, and we were introduced to any of those whom we did not know. We then sat down at a long table, the Chief of the Imperial General Staff, General Sir James Wolfe-Murray, in the chair. Lindsay and I sat on his right, while the eight or ten directors took their places on either side of the table.

The C.I.G.S. was already on the verge of a nervous breakdown; in fact, this meeting must have been the last at which he ever presided, for two days later he resigned and Sir William Robertson took his place.

With some little difficulty, the Army Order, calling the Machine Gun Corps into existence, was drawn up. When this had been settled, the C.I.G.S. turned to General Sir Henry Sclater, the adjutant-general, who was lolling back in his chair, gazing fixedly at the ceiling.

"Major Baker-Carr says he will want forty thousand men, Sir Henry."

"Can't be done," said the A.-G., without removing his eyes from the ceiling.

"Then I'm afraid I'm wasting your time, sir," I said. "I'd better tell Lord Kitchener. He said that I was to have the men."

"Did he say that?" asked the A.G., sitting up suddenly.

"Yes, sir," I replied. "He did."

"Well, I suppose you've got to have them then, though I don't know where the devil they're coming from."

"Who's going to train all these men?" asked the Director of Military Training, my cordial friend of the morning.

"I thought they could be trained, partly in England and partly in France, sir."

"Impossible. We've got all we can do to train the men we are getting now."

"Very good, sir," I replied. "I'll train them all in France at the Machine Gun School."

"Ridiculous nonsense!" exclaimed the D.M.T. "You can't train forty thousand men."

"We can, sir. All that we shall need is some more instructors, and those we'll train ourselves."

The D.M.T. appeared to be on the verge of an explosion, but Sir James Wolfe-Murray, who was becoming distinctly nervous, interposed with a suggestion that the problem of training should be deferred till a later date.

Nothing more remained to be discussed and Lindsay and I were permitted to take our leave.

On the whole, things had passed off a great deal more easily than I had anticipated. At any rate, an Army Order would be published in a few days calling the Machine Gun Corps into existence. The main difficulties had been overcome, though a tremendous amount of energy and administrative ability would still be needed to put the new corps on a sound basis.

4

It had been suggested to me by Sir Archibald Murray that the task of organising the Machine Gun Corps would naturally devolve on myself, and he said that he would use all his influence to further my claims. I was not sure that I was very anxious to take the post, which would be almost entirely one of administration and which would necessitate the severing of my connection with the work in France. I was, however, saved the difficulty of making a decision by the fact that I was not offered the post. Actually, the War Office suggested to G.H.Q. that it should be offered to me, but G.H.Q. refused to allow me to go. As things turned out later, I am extremely grateful, but it was a little galling not to be given the opportunity, in view of the fact that, officially, I had been responsible for the scheme from start to finish, although, of course, Lindsay and the others had done as much as I.

The appointment was given to Colonel Hill, an old colleague of mine at Hythe, than whom no one more suitable could have been found.

Often in France, with my extremely competent staff and smoothly running organisation, I used to think of Hill, battling with every sort of difficulty and tribulation. Things at Grantham, the home of the new corps, in the beginning were terribly chaotic, especially as battalion commanders thought this was a wonderful chance to get rid of all their "duds" by sending them to the Machine Gun Corps.

Although I personally was not sent to build up the organisation, the authorities had no hesitation whatever in stealing my chief instructor, Lindsay, McGillycuddy, and several other valuable members of my staff. I gladly let them go, though I knew how much I should miss them. It was all for the good of "The Cause" for which we all had striven for many depressing months. The Machine Gun Corps was an accomplished fact.

CHAPTER 10

The First Suggestion of the Tank

1

During the eighteen months of the existence of the Machine Gun School in St. Omer and at the Convent of Wisques, in addition to my work as *commandant* of the school, I was frequently called upon to perform many duties besides those connected directly with machine guns.

As soon as the war became stationary and the opposing armies "went to ground" permanently, endless devices were invented for the safety of our own troops or for the discomfiture of the enemy.

At first, no definite machinery existed for the consideration of these inventions, but later, when everybody in the army regarded himself as a budding Edison, an Inventions Committee was formed at G.H.Q., to which were submitted the results of the various "brainwaves." Of this committee I was appointed Technical Member and was called upon to deal with all problems connected even remotely with rifles or machine guns.

Before the committee came into being, however, the most far-reaching invention of the war had been put forward, the embryonic idea from which was evolved the tank.

At G.H.Q., since the first day of hostilities, there had dwelt and had his being a Colonel of Royal Engineers, whose real name was unknown to the general public, but whose journalistic efforts, signed "Eye Witness," must have been read and appreciated by the largest number of readers in the world, for he was the sole correspondent at G.H.Q. Under the *nom de plume* of "Ole Luk-oie," he had already achieved some little fame as a writer of short stories, but the name of Swinton would have conveyed but little to the average reader.

Hundreds of people have laid claim to be the inventor of the tank, but, in point of actual fact, the idea itself is thousands of years old.

After all, what is the purpose of a tank? It is to enable the attacker to come to grips with his enemy and destroy him, with the minimum of risk to himself. There is nothing new whatever in this idea. The Roman Legions were trained systematically to act as tanks. They did not call them "Tanks," they called them "*Testudo*," which means "tortoise-shell." On the command being given, the *legionaries* closed ranks and locked their shields together in front of and above them. Thus protected from the spears or arrows of the defenders, they advanced until they were able to fight hand-to-hand. The formation was also used to attack fortified places.

The knight in mediaeval times was merely a one-horse-power tank. The average man-at-arms in his leather jerkin was helpless against the knight, encased in an iron covering from which he was unable to emerge without the help of a page.

The two principal features that render possible the tank of today are the internal combustion engine, which gives enormous power in relation to its weight, and the caterpillar track, which enables it to cross ditches an trenches several feet in width.

One day early in 1915, Colonel (now Major-General Sir Ernest) Swinton came out to the school to discus with me the best means by which the enemy machine guns might be overcome. Even at this comparatively early date, it was obvious to some of us how great the Germans relied on their automatic weapons for defensive purposes, though, for some reason, the British still relied on brawn.

Swinton's original idea was to discover an antidote to the enemy's machine guns which he, almost before anyone else, recognised as being the most formidable arms possessed by the Germans.

When he first conceived the idea, within a few weeks of the commencement of hostilities, the battle was still a battle of movement, and trench warfare had not yet become the order of the day. Immediately, however, that the battle became stationary, he further developed his conception and included the crossing of trenches and the crushing of the enemy's wire-entanglements within its scope.

Many times did Swinton discuss with me this neutralisation of the German machine guns, and eventually he set forth his views in an extremely able and convincing paper.

This memorandum, the first ever written on a weapon which was destined to play such an important part in the war, was submitted to the pundits at G.H.Q. Nobody had a good word to say for it; in fact, most of the readers were inclined to regard it as a huge joke. It was left, however, to a technical officer of the highest standing to write, at the conclusion of his comments, what might easily have been the epitaph of this brilliant conception.

The summing up ran:

> If the writer of this paper would descend from the realms of fancy to the regions of hard fact, a great deal of valuable time and labour would be saved.

What a glorious example of the Military Mind! One can almost see the malicious joy of the writer, as he pens his peroration. One can almost hear him say to himself with gleeful satisfaction:

> I'll teach the blighter to interfere with my steady routine, hallowed by decades of tradition, by making me read his imaginative twaddle. Stuff and nonsense! The whole thing is most unmilitary. What's the army coming to when officers of the Royal Engineers, who, at least, should know better, put up this sort of thing for serious consideration?

Fortunately, however, fate ruled otherwise, Swinton was sent for by Mr. Asquith, in July 1915, to act as secretary of the War Committee and he was able to arouse in high places considerable interest in his idea, though, it must be admitted, he received no encouragement whatever from the military authorities.

In spite of every sort of rebuff, he still persisted until by chance be discovered that the Admiralty, under the administration of Winston Churchill, had already started working on somewhat similar lines. After endless difficulties, the War Office at last gave a grudging assent to certain experiments being carried out. The two services joined hands and, in due course, the tank was born.

Little did I dream, during my talks with Swinton, that his "armoured traction-engine" was destined to play such an important part in the winning of the war or that I, myself, would be fortunate enough to be amongst those who directed its operation.

2

An experiment, which was carried out before the formation of the Experiments Committee, has remained in my mind chiefly on account of its termination, which, but for the greatest of good luck, might have resulted in a catastrophe.

Early in 1915 all kinds of trench-mortars were being tested, one of which appeared to give satisfactory results. The projectile, which was fired from a short, stumpy mortar, had three fins or vanes, running longitudinally along its sides, for the purpose of keeping its nose in the right direction. It had been christened "The Flying Pig." A series of tests were carried out successfully with unloaded and, also, with loaded shells, with the result that the experimenters were fully satisfied.

A demonstration was arranged and everybody at G.H.Q., including the C.-in-C, C.G.S., A.G., etc., was invited to witness the show.

It was a fine afternoon and hundreds of officers, including all the "Big-Wigs," turned up on the flying-ground (late Rifle Range), half a mile from St. Omer.

The spectators were drawn up fifty yards behind the mortars, which, for safety, were fired from a deep trench. Targets had been set up; fully loaded shells were to be used; everything was ready for the performance to start.

Bang! Off went the first round. The projectile flew out of the mortar and could be seen proceeding leisurely on its way through the arc of a circle, up the range. It fell a few yards short of the target and burst with a dull roar, sending up a cloud of black smoke. Subdued cheers from the spectators.

Bang! went the second round. Even better this time, for the shell fell squarely on the target. More cheers.

Bang! went the third shell. Slowly it sailed away, but on rather a wobbly course. Suddenly it seemed to change its mind and, to our horror, it looped the loop and came slowly back towards us. We stood there, rooted to the spot. Where in Hades was the thing going to land? Slowly it passed over our heads, landed on the ground a hundred yards in rear and burst with a loud explosion. Mercifully no one was standing near to where it fell and there were no casualties.

But "The Flying Pig" had flown for the last time. Nobody wanted ever to see him fly again. "The Flying Pig" was pork.

3

The first "tracer" bullet, for use in aeroplanes, had just been invented and one evening, after dark, at Colonel (now Marshal of the Royal Air Force, Sir Hugh) Trenchard's request, I went with him to the range to see an experiment with it.

A machine gun was set up at a range of five hundred yards and laid on the target. Trenchard and I stood immediately behind the gun. As soon as everything was ready, the order was given to fire. *Pop—pop—pop*, chattered the gun and up the range flew little sparks of light, till they disappeared into the stop-butts behind the target. The eye seemed to be able to follow them throughout their journey with the greatest ease. We moved to a flank, but still the little sparks were visible.

The result of the tests appeared quite satisfactory and both Trenchard and myself were quite convinced that we had been able to watch the bullets for the whole distance. Both of us reported to this effect and we were dumbfounded when we heard, a few days later, that the quantity of magnesium in the base of the bullet was sufficient to burn only for about two hundred yards, whereas we both were absolutely certain that we had clearly seen it for five. This was proved beyond argument by photographs taken up the range at intervals of fifty yards.

Shortly afterwards, I was called upon to carry out an experiment of an entirely different nature with "tracers."

The Germans, as usual, made an accusation against us of using bullets which burned after they had penetrated into a man's body and inflicted cruel torture. It was an obviously absurd statement, but, in order to dispose of the accusation once and for all, I was ordered to fire a dozen "tracers" into a dead sheep.

The test took place one Sunday morning and I had quite a large audience as I lay down to fire. I was somewhat nervous lest I should miss the sheep altogether, but, fortunately, I managed to hit it every time. The sheep was then examined by several medical officers, who pronounced the wounds to be absolutely normal.

4

A serious and delicate situation arose during the summer of 1915 in connection with the armament of the Canadian Corps.

Rumours began to circulate in G.H.Q. that the rifle in use in the Canadian Corps was giving rise to much complaint. Eventually a report was called for, but the views given were so conflicting, that it was decided to appoint a committee and refer the matter to impartial consideration.

In order fully to appreciate the circumstances, it is necessary to go back several years. At Bisley each year the Mother-Country and teams from each of the Dominions take part in a competition for the Palma Trophy. This prize, which is much coveted, is shot for with the rifle in use in the military forces of the country.

A few years before the war, this trophy was won by Canada, whose team had used the Ross rifle. The prize was presented, but later it was discovered that the Ross rifle, though a most admirably accurate weapon, was not the recognised rifle of the Canadian Forces. There was a good deal of acrimonious discussion on the subject, but the decision of the Canadian Government to adopt the Ross rifle as its weapon completely put an end to the trouble. In consequence, the Canadian Corps arrived in France, armed with the Ross rifle.

The complaints were based on the grounds that, after a few shots had been fired rapidly, the action jammed and the breach could not be opened. The reason for this phenomenon was that the chamber, into which the cartridge was inserted, was made a very tight fit in order that the utmost benefit should be derived from the explosion of the powder charge. Consequently, there was no allowance whatever for the expansion of metal, due to heat. No difficulty was experienced as long as firing was deliberate and the chamber had a chance to cool between each shot. But, immediately that rapid firing commenced, the metal of the chamber became heated and the empty case of the fired round was jammed so firmly against the chamber that the bolt could not be rotated.

As in almost every situation in Canada, there entered into this a question of politics. In studying the reports from battalion commanders and others, it was possible to detect a man's political affiliations. If he abused the rifle, he belonged to one party; if he praised it, he belonged to the opposing camp.

Already I was fairly well posted in the main features of the case, as I frequently visited the Canadians on the subject of machine guns. Not being obsessed by the Military Mind, the commanders were only too willing to try any new suggestion and, if satisfactory, to adopt it. The head machine gun officer, Major Brutinel, was an extremely brilliant and able officer, who not only was eager to test any novel proposals, but in many cases put forward valuable suggestions of his own. Through him I had been able to obtain much useful information with reference to the Ross rifle.

It was a difficult problem for G.H.Q. to tackle. The Canadian Corps was a completely self-governing unit as regards its internal organisation and it was the policy of G.H.Q. not to interfere in any way, apart from general instructions. G.H.Q. was now faced with dissensions within the corps on a point which was of vital importance.

The reports received from the supporters of the Ross, stated that it was the best weapon in existence "and then some." The opposing party proclaimed equally emphatically that it was "the worst ever" and departed considerably from correct military parlance in their descriptions of it.

A committee of five officers was appointed, one officer of the General Staff, one from the Adjutant-General's Department, one from the Quartermaster-General's Department, one from the Ordnance Department, and myself, the technical member. It was an amusing collection of experts to decide on such an important and far-reaching question.

The first three members (all, of course, Staff College men) were far more qualified to write a *précis* of Napoleon's Campaigns, with special reference to his mistakes in strategy, than to give an opinion on the value of a rifle. The representative of the Ordnance Department, a most capable and highly trained officer, had not, in all probability, had anything whatever to do with what he, as an ex-gunner, would have designated a "hand-gun" for ten or fifteen years. Remained myself, whose only claim to serve on the committee was that ten years previously I had been on the Instructional Staff at Hythe.

The five of us, plus the secretary of the committee, assembled one morning in a sand-pit just outside St. Omer. An armourer-sergeant and one or two myrmidons of the Ordnance Department assisted, in case any mechanical aid might be needed. On a blanket lay six Ross rifles and a hundred rounds of ammunition.

Nobody seemed to have a very clear idea of what we were going to do or how we were going to do it. There appeared to be a general reluctance to take the initiative. It certainly was not for me, being junior to everybody else present, to make suggestions.

After some desultory discussion, the president of the committee asked me what I thought would be the best way to arrive at a definite conclusion.

"I think the best thing to do would be to fire rapid from each rifle and see how long it takes to jam," I replied.

This brilliant suggestion was passed with acclamation.

"Shall I do the shooting?" I asked.

This suggestion also being approved, I lay down and slipped ten cartridges into the magazine of one of the rifles.

"Ready," I said.

"All right. Fire away," replied the president.

As rapidly as I could, I fired five shots in succession. After the fifth round I was unable to work the bolt of the rifle. I got up, laid the rifle on the ground and kicked the bolt with my boot. Not a fraction of an inch did it budge. I handed the rifle in turn to each member of the committee. Not one of them could move the bolt. I lay down once more and fired the other five rifles in the same manner. The result was identical in each case, except that the number of rounds necessary to jam the mechanism varied from four to eight.

"It looks fairly conclusive," said one of the members.

The secretary of the committee, who had been keeping a record of the tests, stood by with pencil and paper to take down the opinions of the committee.

"Will you give your views first, Baker-Carr?" asked the president. "You're the technical member."

"Certainly," I replied.

The secretary wrote down my name, rank, etc.

"Right," he said.

"'In my opinion,'" I dictated, slowly and carefully, "'it is murder to send a man armed with the Ross rifle into the trenches.' That's all."

"I say!" exclaimed the president. "That's a bit thick, isn't it? Couldn't you modify the language a little?"

"No. That is my considered opinion. If people don't like it, that's their trouble."

After some little discussion, the other members of the committee registered their views, which, though fully in agreement with mine, were expressed in more correct military phrasing. We then returned to our various duties.

The report was accepted and orders issued for the rearmament of the Canadians with the British weapon, the Short Lee-Enfield.

When the requisition for the rifles, required for this rearmament, was received at G.H.Q. it was found to be greatly inferior to the number of men. In reply to an inquiry why this was the case, it was discovered that a large number of Canadians had already armed themselves with the British rifle, which they had collected off the killed and wounded of British units.

Further comment is needless.

5

It was extremely convenient for G.H.Q. to have at their beck and call an officer who possessed a little technical knowledge and whom they could immediately disavow, if his too frankly expressed views seemed likely to lead to trouble. The fact that I was a "dug-out" and was not a graduate of the Staff College would always have enabled them to disown any of my actions or recommendations which subsequently proved unpalatable. On the other hand, they could always take credit for my more successful ventures.

It is a curious fact that a body of men collectively will perform actions which individually each would scorn. Take half a dozen honest, kind-hearted gentlemen and call them a Board of Directors and they will, without the slightest compunction, pass resolutions that, as private citizens, they would characterise as coldblooded robbery. Similarly, all the individual members of G.H.Q. were the best of good fellows personally, but, as a body, they seemed to lose all sense of justice and fair play.

Another case in which all the responsibility for taking serious action fell on my shoulders was that of the American ammunition for rifles and machine guns.

Soon after this ammunition began to be issued to the fighting line, I commenced to receive a large number of complaints from machine gun officers. The carrying out of a few trials soon satisfied me that these complaints were well grounded.

In a machine gun, and, to a lesser extent, in a rifle, huge stresses are thrown on the case of a cartridge near the base, when it is fired. Unless the case is solid-drawn, *i.e.* made from a solid piece of brass, there is a likelihood of a fracture of the case, which leads to a stoppage of the mechanism. The American ammunition was supposed to be solid-drawn, but, in truth, it was not. As a result, some 50 *per cent*, of the cases split in half, on being fired, at the point where the junction of the two pieces occurred, with disastrous results.

At once I forwarded a strongly worded report to G.H.Q., recommending that, at any rate, as far as machine guns were concerned, the ammunition should be withdrawn.

At that time the supply of ammunition from England was still much short of our requirements, and the six or seven million rounds, arriving weekly from the United States, were certainly welcome. If, however, the cases were defective and liable to cause jams, they ceased to be a benefit and became a positive source of danger.

As a result of my report, I was instructed to carry our further tests and to make definite recommendations, in the event of these tests confirming the opinion I had already expressed.

The second trials fully confirmed my previous views, and I recommended that the American ammunition should be withdrawn. My advice was accepted and the ammunition was marked "For Practice purposes only." Millions upon millions of rounds of small arms ammunition, sent from America, were absolutely useless, as proved later also to be the case with a large proportion of the shells. I never heard, however, that the money paid for these munitions was ever refunded, although Mr. Coolidge recently told the world, in his farewell speech to Congress, how hard-hit financially the United States had been by the war.

6

On occasions there was in my work a lighter side where the comic element predominated.

There arrived one day at the school a parcel, weighing several pounds, accompanied by a bulky file of correspondence. I first read the various memos in order to find out what it was all about. It appeared that a steel cylinder, with a threaded tube running through its centre, had been discovered in a captured German machine gun emplacement. When found, "it was somewhat dirty and smelt strongly of cordite."

The General Staff requested me to examine the cylinder carefully and report, as it was considered likely to be some new "gadget" for use with a machine gun.

Greatly interested, I opened the parcel and took out the contents. I looked at it and looked at it again. Was G.H.Q. trying to "pull my leg"? I re-read the correspondence, particularly the memos of the chief engineer and chief ordnance officer, departments which never jest. No. Everybody was in deadly earnest and deeply intrigued.

I sent for McConnel, a most capable, energetic member of my staff, who had passed first in and out of Woolwich, before exchanging into the cavalry.

"James," I said, handing him the file of correspondence and the cylinder, "here's something that will interest you. G.H.Q. thinks it's a machine gun 'gadget.'"

McConnel's eye sparkled with enthusiasm. He took the correspondence and the cylinder and disappeared into the nether regions to consult with his friend, the armourer sergeant.

In an hour's time he was back in my office.

"I think it's a silencer for a machine gun, but I can't be sure yet," he said excitedly. "The thread of the screw fits the barrel of a Vickers perfectly. I'll go out and try it this evening on the range."

I left the thing on my desk, and during the day all my staff drifted in to look at the new "gadget." At five o'clock McConnel and the armourer sergeant appeared at the office to take away the cylinder to try it.

"James," I said, "I'm afraid you'll have to give up your experiment. We haven't so many guns to spare that we can afford to smash one up by screwing on to the barrel the bowl of a cream-separator!"

There was no reason, I suppose, why the chief engineer or the chief ordnance officer should be familiar with the working parts of a separator, but I did not see why the War Office should be deprived of expressing its views concerning it.

I therefore wrote a brief report in which I stated that, in my opinion, the cylinder was *not* connected with machine guns, but that I should prefer it to be submitted to experts at the War Office for examination. I could not refrain from mentioning that the thread of the cylinder fitted the muzzle of a Vickers gun and I also added that it appeared to smell strongly of cordite. This last statement was quite true and not surprising, in view of the fact that it had lain in the German machine gun emplacement for several weeks or, possibly, months. My recommendation was approved and the cylinder was dispatched to the War Office. As I never heard what happened subsequently, I can only assume that it remains to this day one of the deep and impenetrable mysteries of the war.

7

Although the Machine Gun School was a purely instructional establishment, on one occasion it nearly went into battle as a fighting unit.

I happened to be in the General Staff Office on the morning when the first gas attack took place. The situation was critical for the British, doubly so in that it was impossible to obtain any sort of reliable information. All that was known at G.H.Q. was that a large portion of our front line near Ypres had fallen into the enemy's hands, and that the French on our immediate flank had been obliged to retire.

In those days reserves were mostly conspicuous by their absence and nobody could say where any were to be found. Everybody in the General Staff Office was wondering what was going to happen next. Tentatively I made the suggestion that the Machine Gun School should be mobilised and go out to fill the gap with their machine guns until the situation was re-established. I pointed out that, in a couple of hours, I could have forty or fifty machine guns ready for action, with the finest crews that had ever been mobilised. All I should need was transport.

The proposal was accepted gratefully and I telephoned Atkinson, who acted as adjutant, to knock off work at once, fill every available machine gun ammunition belt and to have everybody ready to start at the earliest moment.

I then got into my car and went out to prospect.

There was an uncanny quietness in and about Ypres. Nobody seemed to know quite what had happened, and all sorts of rumours were afloat. I met dozens and dozens of men in various stages of gas poisoning, but they could tell me little, except that they had been forced to abandon their trenches. A faint smell of chlorine pervaded the atmosphere even a long way; behind the line, but not enough to cause any great inconvenience.

When I arrived back at Wisques, I found a long; string of motor buses drawn up, ready to move off at a moment's notice. The whole class had been told off into machine gun companies under the command of the officer instructors, hundreds of belts had been filled, and the guns and tripods were packed ready for transport.

G.H.Q. had telephoned, ordering us to stand by until further orders, but warned us to be prepared to start as soon as the order was given. All that evening we waited and late into the night, when I ordered the crews to turn in, but to sleep with their clothes on.

Late that night we received information from G.H.Q. that the situation was now restored and that we could demobilise. Glad as we were to hear that all was well again, I think we were all a little disappointed that we had not been called upon to help.

This was the second of the three occasions when Germany could have won the war. If, instead of using gas on a front of a few thousand yards, they had used it on a front of twenty miles and had realised how effectual would be the result, nothing on earth could have stopped them from walking straight through us. As it was, their patrols came down within a few hundred yards of Ypres and for many hours a gap existed in the Allied Front, through which they could have marched in fours.

The only explanation is, that the enemy did not have the least idea how terrifying and effective would be a first attack with gas. When, later on, gas was used against our troops, we were more or less prepared to meet it and, thereafter, any chance of forcing a definite decision by its use had disappeared for ever.

8

Many months later G.H.Q. was startled by reports from the front line that machine guns were useless during a gas attack in that they always jammed. I was at once ordered to go out and gather all the information that I could. It did not take me long to collect several machine gun officers upon whose statements I could confidently rely. There was no doubt that the guns had jammed several times during gas attacks, but nobody had any satisfactory explanation to put forward.

The only thing to do was to carry out tests for myself.

In a room of a brick-walled house, I piled up in one corner ten or twelve sand-bags to act as a bullet-stopper. In the other corner a machine gun was set up on its tripod, half a dozen boxes of ammunition in belts beside it. Meanwhile, the senior gas officer from G.H.Q., who had come out to assist, was rendering the room thoroughly gas-tight by plugging up the window, etc. When all was ready, we put on the old, primitive gas-helmets, which made one look like a member of the Inquisition. A cylinder of chlorine gas was brought in, the door of the room closed and the gas turned on. In a few seconds the room was saturated.

I sat myself down behind the gun and fired off a belt of two hundred and fifty rounds. The gun worked perfectly. I put in another belt, and, after half of it had been fired, the gun jammed. I signalled to the gas officer to open the door and we carried the gun out into the fresh air, where we could take off our masks and examine the gun at our ease.

It did not take long to find out the cause of the trouble.

As soon as the cartridges were exposed to the action of the gas, a tiny film was formed on the brass case and this film was deposited and left in the chamber by each succeeding round, with the result that, after two or three hundred cartridges had been fired through the gun, a hard ring was formed, which prevented the next cartridge from going fully home, thereby jamming the mechanism.

Having diagnosed the disease, the next thing was to discover the remedy.

In order to be quite sure of our ground, we laid several boxes, with the cartridges in the belts, open, inside the gas-filled room, and left them there for an hour. At the end of this time, we examined the cases and found them discoloured and covered with a thin film. On firing these belts, the mechanism of the gun very soon jammed.

After thoroughly cleaning the gun again, we fired with boxes of ammunition which had been kept outside and were only brought in at the last moment. The gun fired perfectly and no stoppages occurred.

Obviously the solution of the difficulty was to render the belt-boxes gas-proof. This was accomplished by nailing narrow strips of flannel along the lid of the box, where it met the sides when closed. Orders were at once sent out to all units to carry out this provision and no complaint was again received on the score of stoppages due to gas.

I was not sorry when the experiment was finished, as both the gas officer and myself were beginning to feel the effects of the gas. The original helmets were only partial protection and we had spent an hour or more in an air-tight room in a concentration of gas many times stronger than would have ever been encountered in the open. For a couple of days afterwards I had a most uncomfortable catch in the back of my throat and both food and tobacco tasted extremely nasty.

9

From one short lecture given almost unwillingly, to the second class that ever assembled after the formation of the school, there had been evolved a series of lectures, that had been collated and issued by G.H.Q. as the official hand-book. As the importance of the automatic weapon came to be realised, so did the necessity that every officer in the army should possess some knowledge of its use.

The first lecture which I gave outside the school was to a class of cadet officers, assembled at G.H.Q. It was a great success and, thereafter, the Machine Gun Lecture became a regular feature of the curriculum. It was extended later to all the various Officers' Schools of Instruction instituted in most armies and corps. In addition, Staff Courses were instituted for officers, selected as suitable for Staff employment, both in France and England, and a lecture on Machine Guns was laid down as part of the training. Almost all these lectures I was instructed by G.H.Q. to deliver personally and, by the middle of 1916, my average number of outside lectures exceeded two or three per week. For a long time the instructional work at the school had been running so smoothly that I was content to leave it in the hands of my extremely capable staff and devote myself almost entirely to the work outside.

By request, I paid a visit to the French Machine Gun School at Vincennes, and, after my inspection, I was surprised that the French machine gunners were as efficient as they were.

It has always been laid down in our machine gun instruction that eight men was the maximum number in a squad, and each squad possessed its own gun. At Vincennes the number of a squad, apparently, was anything from fifty to eighty, with the result that some of the less enthusiastic members could only have seen the gun occasionally in the course of their training, and then, at a distance of several yards. For some reason, also, the amount of ammunition per man was ludicrously inadequate and it often happened that a man returned to his unit as a trained machine gunner without having fired a single round.

I discussed with the *commandant* his system of tactical training, but there appeared to be practically none at all, this side of the instruction being confined to the inculcation of a few theoretical platitudes. It is a curious fact that the French, right up to the end of the war, never thoroughly appreciated the value of the machine gun and placed far more reliance on their field guns for the repelling of German attacks.

10

One of the duties with which I was charged was of a somewhat delicate nature, the inspection of Reserve Lines with reference to the machine gun arrangements. Whereby hangs a tale.

Early in 1915 I had, by chance, visited a new line that was being dug behind Ypres, to be used in the event of our being forced to retire. The machine gun arrangements were so utterly puerile that I felt it incumbent upon me to report, quite unofficially and confidentially, to the Deputy C.G.S., at that time Brigadier-General E. Percival. He was very grateful for the information and instructed me in future, when on my travels, to inspect any line I saw and to make a report on the machine gun dispositions.

"It's rather a difficult problem for me, sir," I said. "After all, I have no authority whatever to do so. I'm only *commandant* of the Machine Gun School."

"That's soon settled," he replied.

From his paper-rack he took a sheet of note-paper, and, with his own hand, wrote a short letter addressed to me, instructing me to make a confidential report in writing, if I came across any machine gun arrangements of which I did not approve. I put the letter in my pocket and took my departure.

Several reports on this matter were sent in by me during the next few months, making suggestions and criticisms. The scheme worked well and without any friction arising.

Later in the year, Lindsay, who had been visiting a portion of the front line, on his homeward journey spent some time looking over a new and important section of what was known as the G.H.Q. Line, the main line of defence in the event of a retirement. The disposition of the machine guns was even more futile than usual, and I instructed Lindsay to write a full report. He did so in his best, incisive style, and I forwarded it, marked "Private and Confidential," with a covering letter from myself to the D.C.G.S., G.H.Q., in the same manner as I had done previously.

Two days later, as I was changing into flannels at about five p.m., before going up to the school for a game of tennis, Atkinson came down to the house to tell me that I was wanted at G.H.Q. at once.

"I don't know what it's all about, but I'm afraid there's something serious up," he said gloomily. "Apparently you're in awful trouble. H., who spoke to me on the telephone, seems to think you're going to get the sack."

Hastily I changed back once more into uniform, hurriedly reviewing in my mind the more recent of the military iniquities that I had committed. I could think of nothing outstandingly reprehensible. In fact, the only possible cause of trouble could be Lindsay's report. I wondered if, by any chance, Whigham, the new Deputy Chief of the General Staff, did not approve of the action of his predecessor, Percival, who had lately been promoted to the command of a division.

As a precautionary measure, I slipped my letter from Percival into my pocket, and drove off to G.H.Q., where I reported at the General Staff Office.

Things were obviously extremely wrong, and my reception was decidedly chilly. I waited a few minutes till the D.C.G.S. was ready to see me and was ushered into his office. I had had a good deal to do with Whigham (then Brigadier, now General Sir R. Whigham, K.C.B., K.C.M.G., D.S.O. and had always found him most kind and considerate. I knew that, at any rate, I should get a square deal from him, but as I saluted him seated at his desk, I didn't like the hard look in his cold, grey eyes. In front of him on his desk lay Lindsay's report.

For five minutes I was treated to the most comprehensive and biting lecture on the subject of (1) Insubordination; (2) Interference in matters outside my scope; (3) The unforgivable offence of criticising my superior officers; and (4) the dire results to be expected therefrom. The matter would be reported to the C.G.S., and it was very doubtful whether I should be retained in my position, though, he courteously added, the work I had done up to the present had been extremely meritorious.

I waited until he had finished. Then, from my pocket, I produced my letter of instructions from General Percival, and silently laid it on the table before him.

I watched his face as he read it. He read it again. He even read it a third time.

"This, puts an entirely different complexion on the matter," he said, as he rang his bell. "I can only say how sorry I am for having spoken to you as I did. I hadn't the slightest knowledge of this letter. You were perfectly justified in what you did. You can go."

As I saluted and started to leave the room, H., who had for nearly a year been on the General Staff, entered.

"I should like to know why I haven't been informed about General Percival's letter to Major Baker-Carr?" began the D.C.G.S. in the same cold voice as he had used to me during the delivery of his homily. "Here I have been . . . . . ."

I closed the door softly behind me and left, without having spoken one single word. Probably it was not H.'s fault at all, but somebody had to "cop it" and I could not help experiencing a little glow of satisfaction that it was not myself. There flashed through my mind all the various crimes that I *had* committed, which had not been brought home to me, and I determined that, in the future, if I could not be good, I would be very, very careful.

11

One of the things I most desired, after I was satisfied that the instruction was as good as we could make it was to render the course at the school a pleasant interlude from the horror and squalor of the trenches. The sergeant instructors, in their spare time, had constructed a tennis court in the grounds of the convent and I had rented a level field in the vicinity, where we erected a couple of rugby goal posts.

In addition to these games, at the end of each class, a concert was held in the lecture-hall (late chapel) where eight or nine hundred persons could be accommodated in comfort.

We were extremely fortunate in having among the staff sergeants at the school one or two men who were not only Artists but also artists. There was one who was about to become a professional pianist when war broke out; another who was quite the best comedian I have ever seen off the stage, and a great deal better than most on it; and several other lesser lights.

Then, as the *pièce de rèsistance,* we always had Kennerley Rumford, who, incredibly generous, was ready to sing anywhere and at any time, travelling miles and miles in a car on cold, wet nights, to give pleasure to the men.

"I think you are perfectly wonderful," I said to him one day, "the way you go tearing about the country, singing in draughty barns."

"It's all I can do," he replied simply. "I'm too old to fight. I've got my ambulance work, but that isn't much, and if I can cheer up the men by singing to them, so much the better."

His appearance on the stage was always the signal for a storm of cheering. Twice each night his name appeared on the programme, but, usually, he was not allowed off the stage until he had sung five songs at each appearance.

Instrumental music was provided by the first violinist of the Paris Opera House, employed on some clerical work in St. Omer, who was always kind enough to play for us.

Another turn, always uproariously applauded, was that given by a real "old soldier" (the servant of an officer of the School Staff), who played the bones with anything, including knives, forks, and spoons, banging them on his head, feet, elbows, and knees. Of its kind, it was a really remarkable performance.

The remainder of the programme was made up of "turns" by officers and N.C.O.s of the class, among whom were always to be found some first-class artists, professional or amateur.

In particular, I shall never forget the terrific ovation that Dennis Neilson Terry received after his recital of Henry Vth's speech before the Battle of Agincourt. In my opinion, recitations should be made a criminal offence, but, occasionally, one hears a performance such as this and one feels perhaps that one's judgment has been too hasty.

The high-water mark of our concerts, which had become quite celebrated in the neighbourhood (even officers of the General Staff at G.H.Q. attended!), was that given in honour of the Guards Division, which was being concentrated, on its formation, in the Wisques area.

In addition to our usual "Star Turns," I borrowed the choir of the

Welsh Guards, who opened the concert with "Land of our Fathers." Above and at the back of the stage were two large balconies, on which the singers were stationed. The splendid voices, lifted up in the fine old hymn, provided one of the most stirring pieces of music I have ever heard.

Never before have so many officers of the Guards been assembled under one roof and probably never will again. H.R.H. the Prince of Wales attended, as did Lord Cavan, the divisional commander. Certainly not less than three hundred Guards officers were present, in addition to a large number of other distinguished guests.

A few days later I lent the messroom in the convent to the grenadiers for a dinner to celebrate the existence, for the first time in history, of three battalions. I was much honoured at receiving an invitation to this function, at which I was the only non-Guardsman present. Several ex-grenadiers attended, including Lord Derby, and it was one of the most cheerful parties at which I have ever assisted. Fortunately the floors of the building were of stone, as several "accidents" with lighted oil-lamps took place before the party broke up in the early hours of the morning.

The very next night the Scots Guards held a similar celebration, to which also I was invited, but I was forced to decline the honour on the perfectly truthful grounds of ill-health.

12

On the 20th November 1915, a dinner of the whole staff was held to celebrate the first birthday of the Machine Gun School. This, also, was a memorable occasion, and, as I sat at the head of the main table and looked down the long rows of sergeant instructors, I could hardly believe that it was only twelve months since the school had consisted of myself, twelve privates of the Artists' Rifles, and "Slushy" (also present at the dinner, but completely unrecognisable in his smart uniform).

From that tiny beginning had emerged, thanks to the loyalty and enthusiasm of the officers and sergeants of the staff, an institution that was training many hundreds of machine gunners every month; a complete system of the tactical handling of machine guns and Lewis guns had been evolved, sanctioned by G.H.Q. and issued as the official manual; several valuable inventions for use with the machine guns and Lewis guns had been worked out and adopted; finally the Machine Gun Corps, after many months of universal opposition, had received official blessing.

It had been a long and uphill task, which never could have been accomplished but for the devotion and keenness of every member of my staff; but, when I rose at the end of dinner to read the kind letter of congratulation from the commander-in-chief and to make a short speech, the reception accorded to me more than made up for the disappointments and difficulties encountered and overcome.

CHAPTER 11

Looking for a New Home

1

By the beginning of 1916, the school once more had outgrown its quarters. Division after division was pouring into France and greater and greater were the demands for vacancies at the school. The number of Lewis guns per unit was constantly being increased and trained men were sorely needed.

Knowing full well that, if I mentioned the subject of seeking more ample accommodation, I should be ordered not to do so, I decided to start off on a little, secret journey of exploration.

The classes had now attained enormous numbers, and it was becoming almost impossible for all of them to be sent by bus or lorry, on the day of assembly, from the distant parts of our ever-increasing front. It was, therefore, essential that our new home should be in the vicinity of the railway.

In addition, I needed a larger area of ground over which tactical exercises could be carried out and where better range accommodation would be available.

With these points in mind, I bethought myself of the coast, somewhere in the neighbourhood of Boulogne. On consulting a map, it seemed as though the Etaples district was the most likely to fulfil the conditions. It was to this part of the world I paid my first visit, hoping that I might there find something which could be rendered suitable.

In vain I searched the coast from Boulogne to Berck and was almost on the point of giving up, when my attention was drawn to a huge hotel, which stood on the seashore at the end of a private road from Camiers, the next station before Etaples. On making inquiries, I found that the hotel had been built a few years before the war by a German company and, on the outbreak of war, it had been closed and sequestrated by the authorities. This looked promising, so I drove down to the end of the little road and examined it from the outside.

It was a large, square, four-storied building, standing within a few yards of the sandy shore. Through the windows I could see huge bales of goods, and a peculiar and extremely unpleasant odour pervaded the atmosphere. Not far away stood a casino and several small houses and villas were dotted about.

I sought out the authorities and learned that the place, though still partly furnished, had been utilised as a store-house for the cargo of a wool-bearing ship from Australia, which had been wrecked near by a year previously. Yes, I was told, the place could be taken over at a price, but application must be made to the Custodian of Enemy Property.

Although the situation was ideal and the building itself entirely suitable, I was not completely satisfied, as the number of students was now so great that not one-half of them could be accommodated in the hotel itself.

For some time I had been considering the advisability of separating the instruction of the Lewis classes from that of the Vickers classes, and this seemed to be a good opportunity to effect the change.

In view of the fact that the Lewis classes were far larger numerically and were increasing every month and, also, the duration of the Lewis classes was considerably shorter, I decided to house the Vickers classes in the hotel, if I could obtain possession of it, and to find another home, perhaps of a less luxurious nature, for the Lewis classes elsewhere. It might be that, if all other means failed, I could erect a camp somewhere in the vicinity, capable of infinite expansion. After a long and thorough search, I came to the conclusion that a camp was the only solution. By the time that I obtained sanction for the proposed move to be made, spring would be coming and there would be no great hardship for men from the trenches to spend ten or twelve days under canvas.

I laid my proposals before G.H.Q. and, after the inevitable opposition had been overcome, I was told to go ahead.

The first thing to do was to inspect the hotel and learn the actual amount of accommodation available. After obtaining the key, Darwell, one of the members of my staff, and myself entered the building.

Two steps were enough. We fled into the open air gasping for breath.

Of all the appalling stinks I have ever encountered, I have never met one to be compared with that of rotting sheep-skins, steeped in sea water. There were thousands upon thousands of them in various stages of decomposition. They had been lying there for twelve months, gradually disintegrating.

We sat down on the far side of the road and wondered if anything would ever eliminate that stink. Even after several minutes in the fresh air, it still clung to our nostrils and a cigarette tasted like nothing on earth.

"Let's open all the doors and windows we can," suggested Darwell. "The place hasn't been aired for months. I'll have a try if you like."

He disappeared through the open door. Now and again I could hear doors and windows being flung open. In a couple of minutes he was back again, pale but smiling.

"It's only on the ground floor that they're stored," he managed to gasp faintly. "Let's give it an hour and then see what it's like."

At the end of this interval, we ventured in once more. The atmosphere was still absolutely nauseating, but we managed to make our way into every room and throw open all the windows. It was a great relief to find that only the ground floor had been utilised, though naturally the whole building was permeated with the smell.

"I wonder if it can ever be made habitable again," I said.

"We'll manage somehow," replied Darwell optimistically. "Let me have a good fatigue party and lots of soap. We'll fix it up all right."

The little casino stood about a quarter of a mile away. It was a ramshackle, though pretentious, building, but serviceable in every way. This would do admirably for a home for the staff sergeants. There were other buildings, belonging to the German company, all of which could be put to good use.

There were two first-class tennis courts; at the front door lay the sea and one of the finest stretches of sand in the north of France. A couple of miles away were Le Touquet golf links. A course at the Machine Gun School was going to be more sought after than ever.

Having decided (though I still was not quite happy, concerning the stink) that the hotel at Cécile-Plage could be rendered habitable, we drove to Le Touquet to prospect for a camping-ground.

At the back of the casino, where the Duchess of Westminster's hospital was housed, lay the golf links. There was not one camping-ground there, there were hundreds. The whole place was absolutely perfect. The ground was covered with short, green grass, smooth and level, surrounded by belts of fir trees. Water was laid on all over the course and there were roads and tracks, conveniently situated.

I was fortunate enough to find Mr. Stoneham, the owner of the property, in his house and no one could have been more helpful and considerate. Of course I could have all the ground I needed and he himself would lay a water supply to the selected spot.

We sallied forth together and discovered the most charming spot for a camp that could be imagined. It lay off the fairway of the course and would not interfere with anyone wishing to play. Mr. Stoneham absolutely refused to consider the suggestion of receiving any rent and was almost hurt when I proposed that any work in connection with the water supply should be carried out by the Royal Engineers.

I returned to G.H.Q. and reported.

2

By this time G.H.Q. had either gained a little confidence in my proposals or had given me up as a bad job (probably the latter) and, without further demur, I was told to go ahead. The only difficulty I encountered was when I demanded a fortnight's respite from classes in which to settle in to our new home. After a lot of argument, I was allowed ten days.

The most pressing and urgent problem was the removal of the Stink (I think it is fully entitled to a capital S).

First of all, I applied to the G.O.C. Etaples for a fatigue party. Not a man could I get. The only thing to do was to carry out the work ourselves. I knew the sergeant instructors would take on any job, no matter what it might be. I warned them what it would be like, but they refused to be daunted.

As soon as the last class at Wisques had departed, the sergeant instructors moved down to their new abode in the casino. The next day we started in to abolish the Stink.

All the doors and windows had been kept open night and day and the atmosphere was more tolerable, until we started to shift the sodden bales. Then the Stink showed what it really could do.

Holding their breath, four sergeant instructors seized a bale, carried it outside and dumped it on the far side of the road. They then retired to a secluded spot and were sick.

All day long they worked, until, at length, the bales had all been removed, but the Stink remained. The floors were saturated with it, even the floor of what had once been the dining-room seemed to have soaked it up, although it was made of tiles.

We rested from our labours the next day, while I obtained from the R.E., R.A.M.C, R.A.S.C., etc., every known form of soap and disinfectant. In Boulogne, also, I bought every sort of stink-extinguisher I could find. There was, of course, among the sergeant instructors a certificated sanitary engineer, who was placed in charge of the proceedings.

For days we wrestled and fought the Stink with soap, carbolic, and everything else. At times we were almost defeated, but we still carried on until, at the end of the fourth day, victory was in sight. The Stink was still putting up a strong rear-guard action, but it was definitely retreating. At the end of a week it had almost gone, but, for many months afterwards, its ghost still haunted the building.

3

The Lewis Gun School, situated on Le Touquet golf links in tents, was a complete success. A vast camp had arisen and, the weather growing warmer every day, the classes were comfortable and happy.

There had been the usual difficulty concerning messing arrangements for the officers, but Major Piggott, Moody and Major Tate, the two senior officers of the Lewis Gun School, had most generously put their hands into their pockets and, at very considerable expense, had fitted out the messes with every sort of equipment, reimbursing themselves, after many months, by a nominal subscription from each member of the classes. It is quite comprehensible that there can be no fund available, by the aid of which such messes can be equipped with the necessities of life, but, unless these philanthropists had been found, there would have been no alternative for the officers but to draw their rations and cook them in their mess-tins, as recommended by G.H.Q.

The golfing enthusiasts who attended a Lewis gun course were able to take advantage of the excellent links, the freedom of which had been kindly given to the school. Not only had Mr. Stoneham been kind enough to allow officers to play without payment of any sort, but he actually put at our disposal fifteen or twenty sets of clubs for the use of anyone who wished to play.

An amusing incident occurred in connection with this.

One of my staff, a very good player, noticed an officer in a Scottish cap wandering about in the vicinity of the shed in which the golf clubs were kept. The officer instructor, whom we will call T——, was looking for someone to play with. He, therefore, accosted the Scottish officer, who accepted the invitation gratefully.

T—— was in good practice, while the other, playing with borrowed clubs, showed excellent form, though obviously he had not played for some time. At the end of the round, T—— had won by three up and two to play.

"You'd play quite a decent game, if you practised," said T——, as they walked back to the camp, "What's your handicap?"

"What should you think?"

"Four?"

"No."

"Two ?"

"No."

"Scratch?"

"No."

"What the devil is it then?"

"Plus four."

"Who are you?"

"My name is Jenkins. I won the Amateur Championship in 1914."

4

Early in the summer of 1916 I was asked by G.H.Q. if I would take fifty or a hundred officers and N.C.O.s of the Anzacs for a course of instruction at the school. It was impressed upon me that I was under no obligation to do so and it was hinted that a refusal would not be misunderstood. Fine fighting men as they were, the Australians were not the most tractable soldiers in back-areas, and at Etaples had recently displayed their resentment against what they considered unjust treatment of some of their comrades by forcibly releasing them from confinement and burning down the guardroom.

It seemed a pity not to help in any way one could, so I agreed that they should be sent on the condition that I was at liberty to return them at any time to their unit, without any reference to higher authority, if I saw fit.

The request was granted and a week later my first Australian squads assembled. I had them all up on parade and gave them a short address, ending up by telling them that the whole lot would be sent straight back to their unit, if a single complaint was made concerning them.

The days went by and the sergeant instructors reported that their "Aussies" were the best behaved and the most intelligent men they had ever had to deal with. At the end of the course, the class departed after their spokesman had come to me and thanked me on behalf of his comrades, not only for the instruction given, but also for the jolly good time they had had. It was the first of many Australian classes and not one single "crime," serious or trifling, did they ever commit during the whole of their stay.

Outside, however, in their reinforcement depot they did not behave in quite such an irreproachable manner.

Soon after their arrival from Havre, whence they had been sent at the request of the Municipal Authorities, who needed a little rest, a party of them thought they would like to pay a visit to Paris-Plage. At the bridge, which leads to the town, were posted two military policemen, whose duty it was to prevent soldiers without a special pass from crossing. Naturally the Australians possessed no such pass, but a little thing like that was not going to stop them. They took the two policemen, gently dropped them over the bridge into the river, and went on their way rejoicing.

5

During the first stages of the Battle of the Somme, I received a request from Colonel Trenchard of the R.F.C. to come to his headquarters and discuss with him machine gun matters. It appeared that he was by no means satisfied that the pilots and observers possessed a requisite knowledge of their weapons. He, therefore, wished me to pay an unofficial visit to some of the squadrons and discover for myself how much the airmen knew about their guns.

I visited two or three squadrons in the vicinity and it did not take me long to find out that neither pilots nor observers had the remotest idea of the mechanism of the weapon on which their lives depended. With few exceptions, the extent of their knowledge was confined solely to the loosing off of the Vickers or Lewis gun. Not once, but half a dozen times, I was told stories of air-fights that had to be broken off on account of the stoppage of their weapons and, in several cases, because the man behind the gun had not known how to reload when the belt of the Vickers or the drum of the Lewis: was exhausted.

Trenchard was naturally much perturbed by the; result of my visit and was very grateful when I suggested that thirty or forty selected officers should be sent at once for a short course in the mechanism and remedy of stoppages in the Vickers and Lewis guns.

Within a few days, a special R.F.C. class was assembled at the Machine Gun School and, until the corps had its own instructors, these classes were continued.

6

Preparations for the Battle of the Somme were already beginning. At last the supply of shells was such that the offensive, on that score at least, would not be held up. Hopes were running high of creating a gap through which the cavalry could gallop, bringing panic and devastation in its train.

It seemed possible that open warfare might again become the order of the day. This possibility had raised in the minds of many officers the question as to what extent the troops under their command were capable of fighting in the open.

The proportion of officers and men who had had experience of this type of warfare was negligible. Ninety *per cent*, or more had fought only in trench warfare, where everybody was a specialist. There were specialists in machine guns, Lewis guns, bombs, trench mortars, rifle grenades, etc., etc., but the rifle, the first weapon of the soldier, had become a purely secondary consideration.

For some time past commanders had been much exercised in their minds concerning the appalling lack of skill in rifle shooting prevalent in the army.

Sir Charles Munro, who, before being sent to Gallipoli to report on the situation there, had been in command of the First Army, was one of those to whom it was most obvious. Few people realise to what an extent the musketry efficiency of the British Army was due to Sir Charles, who was *commandant* at Hythe from 1902 to 1907. During his tenure of that appointment, the whole programme of the annual musketry course was revolutionised and the short Lee-Enfield rifle, the best military rifle in the world, was introduced in face of the strenuous opposition of all the old "pot-hunting" experts.

Although rifle-shooting lay entirely outside the scope of my duties, Sir Charles asked me one day to witness an exhibition of rifle practice in his army.

I stood beside him, as man after man lay down and competed in a rapid-firing contest.

The winner of this contest was a sergeant in a Guards Battalion who, if I remember rightly, managed to fire off twelve rounds in sixty seconds.

In 1914 almost every man in the British Army had been able to

147

fire fifteen aimed rounds a minute, and experts, such as the Experimental Staff at Hythe, had been able to fire well over thirty rounds a minute.

At the end of the contest, Sir Charles turned to me and stated in a few and forceful phrases exactly what he thought about it. He then suggested that I might add yet another department to the school by starting a rifle class, but, ready as I was to do anything I could for my former chief, it was out of the question, seeing that I had already bitten off as much as I could chew, perhaps even a little more. All I could do was, at the close of my lectures on machine guns and Lewis guns, to give a short lecture on the essential part played by the rifle in open warfare and impress upon my audience the absolute necessity of training their men in musketry on every possible occasion.

7

At Audricq, a small town, not far from Calais, thousands upon thousands of shells were being collected for use on the Somme battlefield. This fact soon became known to the enemy and steps were taken to put it out of action as soon as possible.

One night a German aeroplane, guided, it is said, by a traitor within our lines, flew over Audricq and dropped half a dozen bombs. The explosion which resulted must be one of the greatest on record. Windows in Boulogne, nearly twenty miles away, were shattered and the shaking of the ground, resembling an earthquake, was felt for many miles beyond.

The next morning I drove to Audricq to see the damage that had been done. If I had not seen the devastation with my own eyes, I would not have believed it possible.

In one place a whole train-load of shells had been struck as it lay in a siding. Nothing remained save a huge hole in the ground, forty or fifty yards wide and twenty feet deep, in which could be seen twisted fragments of iron and some charred wood.

All around were smaller craters, marking the site where huge stacks of shells had been piled. Every building within a radius of a quarter of a mile had been flattened.

The whole surface of the ground was covered with millions upon millions of rifle bullets from cartridges that had been exploded, probably by the tremendous heat engendered. It was as though there had been a terrific hail-storm of lead.

Already parties were out collecting shells from the surrounding neighbourhood. Mercifully, a shell, until the fuse is inserted, is a fairly safe thing, if handled carefully, and, unless it is subjected to great heat, is not liable to explode. The casualties, therefore, were negligible (except for the small guard of half a dozen men which was posted on the entrance gate and was never seen again), though eight- and twelve-inch shells had been hurled into the air and were found two or three miles distant from the scene of the disaster.

It speaks well for the supply of munitions that, in spite of this immense destruction, no battery suffered from a shortage of shells for even a single day.

I remember being told, a short time previously, by the officer of the General Staff, Operations Branch, who was responsible for such matters, that the "bottle-neck" of artillery supplies was transport across the Channel. The manufacture of guns was actually in excess of demand; the replacement of casualties amongst the personnel was being carried out without difficulty. The controlling factor in the weight of our artillery fire was the amount of accommodation on ships that could be allocated to the transport of material for the guns.

The meagre measure of success, therefore, achieved during the Somme Battle cannot be attributed to lack of either guns or shells.

Many factors contributed to the lack of success, but, generally speaking, the entire absence of the element of surprise was the most important of all.

Although the preparations for this battle were, in theory, a deadly secret, it was a "*secret de Polichinelle.*" Everybody knew about the coming offensive, though everybody pretended he didn't. Further, the vast preliminaries for a full-dress offensive, such as the Somme Battle, cannot possibly be carried out without the enemy's knowledge, if the cutting of the defenders' wire entanglements is to be effected by shell fire (in those days the only known method) and if reliance is placed on an overwhelming weight of artillery fire in order to enable the infantry to advance.

We shall see how every single offensive, staged by either side after the deadlock on the Western Front had commenced, failed completely when the element of surprise was lacking. We shall see, also, how every offensive where surprise and rapidity of movement were the predominating features succeeded, even though the High Command on both sides failed to exploit the first and paralysing blow delivered.

The Battle of the Somme and the Third Battle of Ypres, the French assault on the Chemin des Dames, on the Allied side, and the Battle of Verdun on the German side, are notable examples of full-dress offensives that failed. The first gas attack by the Germans at Ypres in 1915, the Cambrai Tank Battle in 1917, the German offensive in 1918, and the British offensive, which culminated in the final defeat of the enemy, were all based on the element of surprise. All were successful, though the advantage gained at the outset, except on the last occasion, was never pushed fully home.

Even after the Cambrai Tank Battle and the German reply thereto (both of which actions were based entirely on the element of surprise), the British High Command still failed to appreciate the fact that only by entirely novel methods could the deadlock on the Western Front be broken.

CHAPTER 12

The Somme Battle

1

High hopes were entertained that the coming battle would prove, if not decisive, at least a sufficiently serious blow to compel the enemy to fall back and to inflict on him heavy losses.

The Russians, at this time, though still deficient in almost every conceivable respect as regards warlike equipment, were occupying the attention of large enemy forces, which it would be impossible to reduce below a fixed minimum.

The new Kitchener Divisions were arriving in France in ever-increasing numbers and the supply of munitions, especially that of high explosive shells, was satisfactory. The French were mounting a big offensive in the south towards Rheims and they were extremely optimistic as to the result. It may be said with truth that the British attack on the Somme was subservient to that of our Allies.

The question of co-operation between allied forces in the field is, and always will be, one of considerable difficulty. Although the British commander-in-chief was still in supreme and sole command of the Expeditionary Force, it was incumbent upon him to conform to the strategical and tactical dispositions of the French *generalissimo*. At the time of the Battle of the Somme, the British Armies in France were numerically much inferior to the French and inevitably any operations by them were compelled to play a subsidiary role, with the result that much "donkey-work" fell to our lot. Further, even at this period, the French did not entertain a very high opinion of the abilities of the British commanders, and, especially during the short *régime* of General Nivelle, did not consider that the British were capable of staging a big offensive alone.

The basic idea of the Somme offensive rested on the ability of a heavy concentration of artillery to blast away the barbed-wire entanglements, the trenches and holders thereof, thus allowing the infantry, protected by our barrage, to capture the enemy positions with a minimum of loss.

This plan, if it had been possible, would, in all probability, have proved successful twelve months previously; but, unfortunately for us, the Germans had learnt their lesson and had constructed huge, deep dugouts in their lines in which the defenders could remain in safety till the artillery storm was past and then man their defences against the attackers. Further, the system of a preliminary bombardment, lasting for a week or ten days before the delivery of the assault, gave unmistakable warning as to the point to be attacked and precluded any semblance of surprise.

In respect of hard work in the preparation of a line of defence, the Germans were infinitely superior to any other of the combatants on either side. It may have been that the British and the French were imbued with a Micawber-like hope that *"something would very shortly turn up"* which would render elaborate digging a waste of labour; but the fact remains that the enemy protection of their defenders was immeasurably better than ours. Everybody who saw them marvelled at the elaborate and comfortable dugouts in which the enemy lived, replete with every home-comfort, absolutely proof against the heaviest shell fire, frequently lit by electricity and warmed by stoves. In these comfortable and safe refuges the defenders remained until our barrage was past, when they hastened to their posts and, with the aid of innumerable machine guns, endeavoured to beat off the oncoming attack.

In spite of the most meticulous preparation, it is utterly impossible to prevent an attacking force from capturing a considerable portion of the first, second, or even third, line of defence, provided always that the assailant has at his command an adequate force of artillery and is ready to face heavy casualties. If, however, the defence has been prepared in depth, the attack, after the first initial success, will gradually spend itself until it is finally brought to a complete standstill. Further advance can only then be made at almost prohibitive loss.

Every new method in warfare, every new improvement in offensive or defensive armament, automatically produces its antidote. The first ships provided with armour-plating called forth the armour-piercing shell, the armour-piercing shell called forth the steel plating, which gradually became thicker and more resistant as shells acquired greater penetrative power. Then came the submarine, to which the answer was nets, depth-charges, and aircraft. In some cases the only reply to a weapon is an improvement on the existing pattern, as was, and is still, the case as regards aeroplanes. Nothing stands still in the world, and evolution continues in peace-time as in war-time, though such evolution is speeded up in war-time when financial considerations are, for the time being, of secondary importance.

Fortunate is the nation which is capable of producing, and producing rapidly and secretly, some new weapon which the enemy, either through inability to appreciate its true value or through lack of time, is unable to find the antidote.

Such a weapon the British were able to invent, produce, and put into action, the tank.

I do not wish to convey to my readers that the tank *won* the war, as many people are prone to think, but what I wish to convey is that the tank enabled the infantry to win the war, a very different matter.

In the beginning, when tanks were used for the first time in history, during the Somme offensive, their very moderate success undoubtedly tended to imbue the enemy with the idea that they were of relatively small value. The Battle of Arras, seven months later, demonstrated that they were a more dangerous weapon than anticipated, but their almost complete impotence in the Third Battle of Ypres revived the impression that such a weapon could obtain only local results and could have no decisive bearing on the main conflict. It was only after the Battle of Cambrai, where the whole method of attack was subordinated to the tanks, that the tank aroused grave apprehensions in the minds of the German High Command as to the results that might be expected from the intelligent use of them. The British High Command, however, as we shall see, utterly failed, even then, to appreciate their full potentialities.

3

Endless arguments, to which finality is impossible, have raged concerning the advisability of putting tanks into action before a sufficient number was available to obtain a decisive result from their use.

It was mainly the armchair critic who protested against what he called the "premature disclosure" of the new weapon. He can never, heaven be praised! find himself in a position to put his theories into practice. He deals almost exclusively in *post-mortem* discussions and lays down the law as to what he would have done in Jellicoe's place, Haig's, or Allenby's. Unfortunately, the public may be misled by the outpourings of some important personage whose opinion, if confined to its proper sphere, may be of paramount importance, but, if outside of his range of first-hand knowledge, may be not only misleading, but, actually, dangerous.

Only a very few people, confined to those whose duty it was to direct the tank in battle, are capable of giving an answer to the question whether we were justified in the "premature disclosure" of the existence of this new arm.

In my opinion, there are exactly two people to whose views it is worth while listening—those of Hugh Elles (now Major-General Sir H. Elles, K.C.M.G., C.B., D.S.O.), the first commander of the Tank Corps, and Colonel J. C. Fuller, D.S.O., the first Chief General Staff Officer of the Tank Corps and probably the most brilliant thinker in the British Army today, (1929). These two officers, both of whom had to deal not only with the Germans but with (a far more difficult business) the British, were definitely convinced that the benefits derived from the lessons learnt in battle more than compensated for the obvious disadvantage of "premature disclosure."

The very secrecy, which was essential during the embryo period, militated against the highest standard of mechanical and personal efficiency. Everybody was groping more or less in the dark. Even Swinton, who in England was the moving spirit and performed a service which has never been adequately recognised, was of necessity unfamiliar with the actual battlefields on which the tanks would be called upon to fight.

When the essential requirements of a tank were laid down, previous to the commencement of manufacture, the battlefield of Loos was taken as a model on which to work. Nobody at that time possessed the remotest idea of the future developments of artillery fire, and by the time the first tanks went into action in France, the whole face of things had undergone a complete transformation. Not only were far heavier guns utilised in the artillery preparation for the Somme offensive, thereby creating much larger craters, but the amount of ammunition expended was far in excess of the most extravagant forecasts; more shells, for example, being fired in a day or two on the Somme than were fired during the whole of the Loos Battle.

Nothing in the world has yet been produced in the full flower of its efficiency. The motorcar of today, (1929), after thirty years of use and improvement, is still in a constant state of development. The aeroplane, after twenty-five years, is still in its veriest infancy, though progress was made in four years of war which, in normal times, would have occupied fifteen or twenty.

How, then, could it be expected that a more or less perfect tank could be produced which would fill requirements, constantly changing and beyond the experience of those responsible for the design, far from the field of battle?

Only by actual use in war was it possible to find out in what respects the machines "filled the bill" and in what respects they failed.

A combination of engineering brains with practical knowledge of battle conditions was needed and, after many days, this combination was assured with the happiest results, thanks to the "team-work" which later became the hallmark of the Tank Corps.

4

The actual *début* of the tanks, for various reasons, was in many respects disappointing.

To me, personally, although at the time I had no idea whatever that I should take part in the future organisation, their comparative failure was a considerable blow.

Ever since I had been instructed to help in any way I could, I had taken much interest in their activities and had gradually become as enthusiastic about their possibilities as those who had been connected with them throughout. It may be, too, that I felt that I had played some infinitesimal part in Swinton's original conception.

A few days before the tanks went into action on the 15th September 1916, for the first time, I had been doing all I could, but, necessarily having no official capacity, I was able to make only tentative suggestions.

The first thing that struck me was the appalling lack of knowledge concerning battle-conditions. Few, if any, of the officers had had experience in France and that probably was completely out of date. Most of the officers and crews had been suddenly pitchforked from the calm, almost academic, atmosphere of a training camp in England into the ear-splitting, nerve-racking tornado of the front line. Operation orders by divisions and brigades, simple and easy of comprehension by the initiated, were unintelligible to the newcomer from England. Even the spoken jargon of war required explanation and amplification, to the detriment of the young tank commander, already over-awed at finding himself in conversation with a major-general. It is amusing to think how, a year or eighteen months later, this same young officer was to lay down the law to division and brigade commanders, but, before this came about, much blood was to be soaked into the ground.

It must be remembered, too, that a tank, once it has joined battle, is completely cut off from the world and must rely entirely on itself to find its way. Later on, a Reconnaissance Department was organised within the Tank Corps and was, without doubt, the most efficient in the British Army. This department was not only necessary, it was a matter of life and death. The view from a tank under peace conditions is extremely limited, but in battle, when loop-holes, upon which the enemy fire is concentrated, are closed, it is immeasurably decreased. It is, therefore, essential that the crew of a machine (N.C.O.s and men as well as the officer) should be familiar with the lie of the country generally and with outstanding landmarks, if such indeed exist, in particular.

Before the 15th of September, a few of the commanding officers of infantry battalions, with which the tanks were to co-operate, had seen the machines going through various evolutions. The majority of these commanders had been mildly amused, but not greatly impressed. Perhaps this was fortunate in that they did not allocate to the tanks any important duty which, through mechanical breakdown, loss of direction, etc., they might have failed to accomplish, thereby creating in yet another mind the impression that "the tanks were no damned good."

The opinions of the corps and divisional commanders, with whom I discussed how the new weapon could be used to the best advantage, were, of necessity, very varied. Some, quite frankly, disliked the whole idea and would have preferred to be without its embarrassing help; in fact, they were inclined to treat it much in the same way as they had been wont to treat the machine gun in happy, pre-war days—"Take the damned things to a flank and hide them!"

Some, on the other hand, had formed an exaggerated idea regarding the mobility of the new machines placed at their disposal and were apt to allot to them a multitudinous succession of tasks, completely ignoring the limitations imposed by time and space.

The company and section commanders of the tanks, already harassed almost beyond endurance by their domestic troubles of packing equipment, ammunition, food, water, blankets and a hundred other items into a space already overcrowded with machinery and human beings, were called upon to answer at a moment's notice a hundred conundrums which were suddenly hurled at them. Not only were they given orders which they did not fully comprehend, but these orders were constantly being modified or even completely changed. Maps, which had been carefully studied, had to be discarded at the last moment, and an entirely new set was issued in their place.

Up till midnight on the 14th of September, the eve of the battle, several tank commanders were not quite clear in their minds as to what they were to do or, even, at what hour they were to start.

Most of that night I spent in my car, going from section to section to find out if there was anything I could do. Once or twice I was able to be of some service, in one case, in particular, when I found that the tanks had no petrol whatever, and did not know where they could get any.

Taking everything into consideration, it is remarkable that the tanks succeeded even in reaching their "jumping-off" places and were able to take any part at all in the battle.

5

For once, the weather was not unfavourable.

Of the fifty tanks, which had been ordered to co-operate with the infantry, more than half reached their starting-point; the remainder, owing to mechanical troubles, becoming ditched in shell holes, loss of direction, etc., failed to put in an appearance.

Of the twenty-five or thirty machines that did arrive at the appointed place and time, ten or twelve did excellent work, either in the advance with the infantry or, as happened in several cases, clearing up "pockets" of the enemy which had been passed by.

One or two machines, partly by good luck and partly by good management, played more spectacular parts in the proceedings and served to draw attention to the great possibilities of the new arm under favourable conditions. One tank, for instance, led the infantry through the village of Flers, "with the British Army cheering behind it," as the well-known aeroplane message, reporting the incident, ran. Another machine was chiefly instrumental in the capture of three hundred prisoners, while several others gave much help in silencing machine guns.

On the whole, it is not unfair to say that the first appearance of the tank was, superficially, not such as to warrant any great enthusiasm. Two facts emerge, however, from the long tale of mishaps and misadventures which had taken place.

The first, and one which was completely ignored by the British High Command—was the moral effect on the Germans.

This moral effect was, even in those days, very considerable, though not to be compared with the consternation caused by them at a later date and against which Ludendorff himself issued a special warning to the troops.

The German morale at this time was excellent, in spite of the weekly statements to the contrary issued by the Intelligence Department at G.H.Q. We were constantly being told that "the enemy morale is breaking down under the continuous pressure of our attacks," etc., etc., but there were no symptoms of it in the splendid defence which was put up. Whether these statements were issued in order to inspire our men with confidence, I do not know, but they had no foundation in fact, neither at the time of the Battle of the Somme nor, a year later, during the Third Battle of Ypres, when we were informed almost daily, that "the breaking-point had been reached."

Anything, therefore, which might tend to destroy the morale of the enemy was, in itself, of incalculable value. Not only did captured officers and men admit that they felt absolutely helpless when attacked by tanks, but the German official Press lost no time in proclaiming to the world the inhumanity of the British in employing "these cruel and barbarous weapons." Our friends, the enemy, always "squealed" when frightened, but the reason for this particular paroxysm of righteous indignation appears to have been overlooked by G.H.Q.

The second fact which strikes the observer is that, if one or two of the new machines were capable of achieving a great success, there should be no reason why, given good organisation and favourable conditions, the large majority should not achieve equally good results.

It seemed quite obvious to me, after having collected every scrap of information that I could, that the chief cause of the comparative failure was the lack of organisation and proper preparations.

No one is to blame in any way and every credit is due to all concerned for the results that were obtained. The conditions, under which the first battle-test was made, were such that it is a wonder that anything at all was achieved. When one considers the meticulous care bestowed on the preparation for subsequent tank engagements, one can only gasp with astonishment at how much was actually accomplished.

In the report which I was instructed to make, I drew special attention to this fact. I cited every occasion on which a tank had proved of value and endeavoured to give reasons why others had failed. Although much disappointed that the first appearance had failed to fulfil all my hopes, I felt quite convinced that the moderate success, if closely analysed, demonstrated that there was nothing inherently wrong and that, given more reliable and less complicated machines, the tank, under favourable conditions and with suitable organisation, would prove to be of inestimable assistance in breaking the dead-lock on the Western Front.

When my report was read, I was told, of course, that I was an optimist and a visionary, but I had become so inured to these charges during the past two years that I did not take them too seriously.

Officially, tanks were given a good "chit" in dispatches, while the Press, especially the French, waxed lyrical over the new invention. It must have been a perfect Godsend to the writers of war news to be able to let themselves go for once. For weeks past they had been confined to writing solely of "the roar of the barrage," "the calm heroism of our gallant men," the mud and the ruined villages. This sort of stuff is all very well two or three times, but, after a while, it begins to pall. The joy of the correspondents can well be imagined when they were allowed to spread themselves on reams and reams of foolscap of descriptive writing.

To the personnel of the tanks, this fulsome *paean* of praise was most unwelcome, especially as they felt that the results achieved fell far short of their expectations.

6

For the next two months tanks were employed in twos and threes and met with qualified success. The weather steadily grew worse and the ground over which they were called upon to operate became one vast quagmire.

My work as Machine Gun Officer on the General Staff at G.H.Q. was extremely light, and I spent much of my time with the tanks, which, at this period, formed part of the Machine Gun Corps.

Early in November I was asked by Burnett-Stuart (then Brigadier-General, now Major-General Sir J. Burnett-Stuart, K.B.E., C.B., D.S.O.), who was my chief at G.H.Q., if I would like to go and take command of one of the new battalions of tanks which it had been decided to raise. I was delighted at being given the opportunity, especially now that the Machine Gun Corps was in satisfactory working

Flanders mud

order and there was little left for me to do.

In a few days' time I was instructed to report to the newly formed headquarters of the tanks and to hand over my machine gun work to my successor at G.H.Q.

I was much amused, a week later, to learn that the new incumbent of my post had at once been given the rank of brigadier-general. I had suggested, on one or two occasions, that it was not quite correct for my subordinates in armies and corps to hold superior rank to myself, but I was told it did not really matter.

My successor at G.H.Q. was a serving soldier and a graduate of the Staff College.

CHAPTER 13

Preparation for the Battle of Arras

1

It was not until the latter part of November 1916 that the tanks were finally withdrawn from the fighting area and the arduous task of creating four new battalions from the nucleus of the four original companies was commenced.

The action of Beaumont-Hamel was the last phase of the Somme Battle, which gradually flickered out in torrents of rain and a sea of mud.

Several tanks took part in this fighting but, with the exception of one or two minor exploits, played an unimportant role.

The winter had definitely set in and visual communication became almost impossible in the low-lying, misty valleys.

Much reliance was placed on the use of carrier-pigeons to get news back to corps and divisional headquarters, and each tank was provided with two of these birds. The infantry, also, carried pigeons which were to be released when certain definite points had been reached.

Many pigeons were lost through various causes, but they proved not only the most reliable source of information, but, later, the carrier-pigeons released from tanks were found to be the most rapid means of communication from the battle.

The proportion of pigeons returning to their abode from the tanks was far higher than in any other branch of the service, with the result that the O.C. Pigeons was most amiably disposed towards them. It was a difficult and uphill task to keep a good supply of pigeons on hand, especially in view of the fact that a distinguished colonial corps made a regular practice of having roast pigeon for supper on the night before a battle.

An amusing incident, for the truth of which I can vouch, occurred during the closing stages of the Beaumont-Hamel attack.

All day, news of the battle had been anxiously awaited, but on account of the low visibility and mist, no information whatever had come to hand. Towards evening, the corps commander, Lieutenant-General Sir Walter Congreve, V.C., K.C.B., walked up to the pigeon-cote, in the hope that some news might yet come in.

Soon after he arrived there, a pigeon was seen flying around the cote, but apparently unwilling to alight. A gun was sent for and the pigeon shot. Hastily the message, tied to the pigeon's leg, was torn off and handed to the corps commander. He opened it with eager hands and read the contents.

The writing ran:

I'm just about fed up with carrying this perishing bird. It can bleeding well go home.   Signed   John Brown, Pte.

2

At last orders were given for the tanks to be withdrawn and concentrated for expansion and reorganisation in the designated area between St. Pol and Hesdin. A large, unoccupied *château* at Bermicourt was taken over as Tank Corps Headquarters, while the battalions were each allotted a village in which the men were to be billeted.

My battalion, C Battalion, was especially fortunate in being allotted the village of Erin, where ample accommodation for officers and men existed and a comfortable *château,* belonging to the Marquis du Hays, whose family was still in residence, became the headquarters of the unit.

At this time, although I was not told till long afterwards, Elles, who had been appointed to command the new corps, twice approached Sir Douglas Haig with the request that I should be given command of the tanks, and that he (Elles) should be appointed my chief staff officer. This request had been refused, not on the grounds that I was unfitted for the post, but on the grounds that I was not a serving soldier, and not a graduate of the Staff College.

It was an extremely generous act on the part of Elles, but, from every point of view, it is as well that his suggestion was not acted upon.

In the first place, he was far more competent to carry out the difficult task of organisation and, further, his demands and recommendations would carry far more weight at G.H.Q. than mine would have, especially in view of the somewhat "buccaneering" reputation which I had acquired during my machine gun days. In spite of the fact that every important proposal I had put forward during the past two years had, in the end, been adopted, I was still regarded at G.H.Q. as a dangerous character and any new and far-reaching suggestions put forward by me would at once have been suspect.

Secondly, one of the main duties which would fall to the G.O.C. Tank Corps would be the working out of the various essential requirements of the machines (in conjunction with the Home Authorities) and this work Elles was far more capable of carrying out than I.

Thirdly, and probably of most importance, the Tank Corps would have been deprived of the services of Fuller, the first officer to hold the appointment of Senior General Staff Officer of the Tank Corps.

It is impossible to overestimate the service which Fuller rendered in connection with tanks, first in France and later at the War Office.

His grasp of essential factors and disregard of tradition, in conjunction with an almost uncanny foresight, proved of paramount importance in working out the best methods of employing tanks in battle.

Though a graduate of the Staff College, he was always ready to listen to other people's ideas and see if there was any merit in them. On the other hand, he was inclined to be intolerant of stupidity and possessed a biting and sarcastic tongue, which made enemies for him in high places. If, however, he remains in the army, there can be no doubt but that his brilliant ability will carry him to the very top, provided that, in the meanwhile, he does not, by reason of his cleverness, fall foul of those in whose hands promotion lies. Since the war he has done splendid work in the mechanisation of the army, but I am quite sure that, in fact, the results he has so far achieved fall far short of his recommendations.

As far as I, personally, am concerned, I am extremely glad that I was not given command of the Tank Corps. What little ability I possess lies in the direction of improvisation and rapid decision. The slow, laborious and systematic work of building up a permanent organisation has never been a congenial task to me and I was far more suited to the command of a unit in the field.

The work I had accomplished in connection with machine guns and the creation of the Machine Gun Corps was of a character entirely different from that of organising the Tank Corps.

I had built up from absolutely nothing a vast training establishment, but there was nothing permanent about it and it was merely an improvisation to meet immediate and urgent needs. The Machine Gun Corps, which, with Lindsay's invaluable aid, was my conception, had little in common with the Tank Corps, inasmuch as the former consisted of hundreds of small units, under the orders of infantry commanders, whereas the latter was a complete, self-contained body under the direct command of its own G.O.C.

The Tank Corps was indeed fortunate in its first commander. Nobody, except a very few who were closely associated with Elles, realises the enormous difficulties he had to overcome. As he often used to say to me, "Fighting the Germans is a joke compared with fighting the British." I, myself, had had a little experience of fighting the British, but it was mere child's play compared with Elles's battles. The fighting of the Germans, to a very great extent, he left in the hands of his brigade commanders, although, of course, he, with Fuller's invaluable help, laid down certain basic, tactical principles for us to follow.

For two years he had to strive with the tank authorities in England, mainly on questions of design and delivery.

The chief difficulty as regards design was that the Tank Committee in London steadfastly believed that it knew better than we in France what was required of a tank in battle. In the end, things eventually adjusted themselves, but only after much and, at times, extremely acrimonious discussion.

The question of deliveries of machines was a problem of supreme difficulty. It was necessary in those days that plans for a full-dress offensive should be made many months in advance, and Elles was called upon by the C.-in-C. to state how many tanks of certain patterns would be available on the appointed day. Naturally the only figure that he could give was that given to him by those in England responsible for manufacture. For various reasons (often quite beyond the control of the Home Authorities) these forecasts of deliveries invariably proved fallacious and Elles found himself in the unenviable position of having to revise his estimates, sometimes almost at the last moment.

It is not too much to say that the last two years of the war aged Elles by ten years. In 1916, when, at the age of thirty-six, he took over command of the tanks, he was almost a boy. By November 1918 he had become a grave, middle-aged man.

In spite of all his preoccupations, he found time to come out to the fighting line on every possible occasion and indulge in his favourite pastime of getting shot at.

Whether the fact of belonging to the Tank Corps inspired the personnel with additional courage I am unable to say, but the standard of bravery throughout was extraordinarily high. The example of Elles, Hotblack (the head of the Intelligence and Reconnaissance Branch), and Martel (assistant to Fuller on the General Staff) without doubt exercised a most beneficial influence throughout the corps. One often heard complaints among the infantry in the front line that they seldom saw the senior commanders, but, in the Tank Corps, the commanders and staffs never incurred this criticism and on many occasions took risks which were by far too great. Fortunately, however, the only casualty was Hotblack, who was badly wounded during the last few weeks of the war, while performing an even more gallant feat than usual.

3

The nucleus personnel, from which I was to form a battalion, consisted of a heterogeneous collection of men, not only from every branch of the army, but also from the Royal Navy. The officers, including one regular officer of the R.A. and two regular infantry officers, were a wonderful body of enthusiasts. They were, however, but a small lump of leaven wherewith to leaven the large mass of raw material which was needed to bring the battalion up to full strength.

A memorandum had been sent out to all units in the infantry and cavalry inviting officers and men to volunteer for service in the Tank Corps and we were overwhelmed with applications. In consequence, we found ourselves in the happy position of being able to pick and choose, with the result that a high standard of efficiency was established at the very start and never thereafter departed from.

My Battalion Staff, to whom I can never be sufficiently grateful for their loyal support during a most difficult period, was a strange collection of men.

My adjutant came from a box-factory in Wallasey near Liverpool; my Equipment Officer (the most efficient and outrageous collector of unconsidered trifles in France) was a Welshman and the best-known bee-keeper in Wales; my Reconnaissance Officer was a London lawyer; my Engineer Officer came from the Hillman Car Company of Birmingham; my Medical Officer from the South Pole, where he had been for the past two years with Shackleton; and my spiritual adviser from a remote parish in the depths of the country.

Whatever they lacked in knowledge and military experience they more than made up by their keenness. Their methods would have horrified the strict upholder of correct military etiquette, but having, myself, outraged all the canons of procedure, I found no fault so long as the results were satisfactory.

A very high standard of discipline and smartness was enforced in the very beginning, the first stone in the foundation of a successful organisation. I also did my utmost to carry out my old maxim that *a happy show is a good show* and made the men as comfortable and contented as was possible. I had my reward a few months later, when Fuller came down to give a lecture and, before beginning, told the assembled battalion that "he had not seen a surly face or a dirty cap-badge in the battalion, a sure sign of a well-run unit."

Not until the middle of December was it possible to start serious training. Instructors for the new recruits had to be found and manufactured from the ranks of the "old hands" and the supply of machines for training was far below requirements. For a long time we were dependent on machines salved from the Somme Battle, for instructional purposes, and most of these needed considerable overhaul and repairs.

Christmas Day was duly celebrated and a rugby football match between "C" and "D" Battalions was arranged. Many first-class players on each side took part in the presence of the entire corps. Great enthusiasm was displayed by the on-lookers throughout the game, but the applause was deafening when the commanding officer of "C" Battalion, playing wing three-quarter, was heavily tackled and brought down in a pool of muddy water a foot deep.

Soon after the New Year a hard frost suddenly descended and great difficulty was experienced in keeping the engines of the tanks from freezing up at night. The Engineer Officer of "C" Battalion, however, devised a scheme whereby this was prevented, by placing a coke brazier inside each tank. No other battalion apparently thought of this simple expedient and my drivers got themselves considerably disliked by going in their machines to call on their friends in other units whose engines were frozen solid.

Rumours of an early offensive were already in the air and we wondered what part, if any, the tanks were destined to play. The battalions were at full strength as regards personnel, but the supply of machines still fell far short of requirements, despite the many promises made.

4

Many were the visitors who came to see the tanks at work, some prompted by curiosity, others by a vague feeling that, perhaps, this new engine of war might really possess the great value which was claimed for it by a few enthusiasts.

The vast majority of these visitors were soldiers, it being considered inexpedient to encourage the presence of civilians, who might be interested enough to draw unnecessary attention to our activities.

One of the very rare exceptions to this rule was a visit paid to us by Mr. Bernard Shaw, who was spending a few days in France and had expressed a particular wish to see the tanks at work.

It was my great pleasure and privilege to give G. B. S. his first, and probably his last, ride in a tank.

With boy-like glee he watched the machines ascending and descending steep banks, going over their "jumps," and generally being put through their paces. He eagerly accepted my invitation to be a passenger and he sat on the improvised seat with a smile of perfect happiness on his face, while the tank jolted and bumped over the hard, uneven ground. After the ride was finished, he descended and was, with some difficulty, discouraged from pressing a Treasury note on the driver of the tank.

As we walked back to lunch, from which, out of deference to his vegetarian principles, "dead bodies," as he termed meat and fish, had been carefully excluded, he told me of his interview with Sir Roger Casement, which had taken place shortly before the latter's trial and subsequent execution for high treason.

You must picture to yourself the long, lean figure of the great man, sometimes walking rapidly along the road with quick strides, sometimes stopping abruptly and vehemently gesticulating with his hands to force home his point. The keen, sardonic face portrayed every passing thought and the eyes were bright with a burning intensity.

I told Casement that he was as good as dead already. 'Roger,' I said, 'they mean to hang you. They'll dig up some statute dating from the time of William the Conqueror, if necessary; but hang you they will. Now, look here. Don't go wasting your money on expensive lawyers. The result is a foregone conclusion. Plead guilty and then, when you are asked to say what you have to urge in mitigation of punishment, read out this speech, which I have specially written for you on the subject of Ireland and her wrongs. It is the best thing ever written and would cause a tremendous sensation.'

Shaw stopped suddenly in his stride and laid his hand on my arm.

"Would you believe it?" he exclaimed indignantly. "Casement flatly refused and lost the greatest chance in history. They hanged him, as I told him they would, in spite of all his costly lawyers."

I duly expressed my astonishment at Casement's crass stupidity and appalling selfishness, with a mental reservation that nobody in the world, except perhaps G. B. S. himself, would have dreamt of acting in any other way.

5

In February 1917 I was sent for, one day, to go to Tank Corps Headquarters at Bermicourt, where Elles took me into his office.

"There's going to be an attack by the Third Army in front of Arras about the ninth or tenth of April," he began. "You mustn't say anything about it yet, though."

I waited for further enlightenment.

"Your brigade will be employed," he continued.

"My which?" I asked.

"Your brigade. 'C' and 'D' Battalions will be brigaded under your command. You'd better start making your preparations."

It was the first time that I had heard of a brigade being formed and I was naturally delighted at being chosen as the First Brigade Commander, though I could not help being sorry that the battalion, which I had raised and commanded from its inception, was to go into action for the first time under someone else.

Shortly afterwards, orders for the formation of the First Brigade Headquarters were received. All the members of my new staff had already been chosen and, a few days later, I bade farewell to my battalion and moved into another house, not far from my late abode.

Almost until the end of the war, two members of my new staff were to remain with me: Tapper, my Staff Captain, and Williams-Ellis, my Reconnaissance Officer. Both of them, curiously enough, were architects, but I doubt if either of them, in their civilian occupation, was more efficient than in their military one.

To the Staff Captain fell all duties in respect of discipline and supplies. The former entailed a very considerable amount of work, but the latter, in the days before Supply Tanks existed, was almost overwhelming. Not only had provision to be made for the ordinary requirements of officers and men, but, also, when active operations were in contemplation or proceeding, thousands of gallons of petrol, thousands of pounds of oil, grease, ammunition, and tank stores generally had to be collected, and carried forward by hand to the selected "dumps." As the First Brigade was the first independent unit to go into action, there were no previous precedents to follow and everything had to be evolved out of our own brain. Later on, when we had all gained experience and a recognised system had been established, the question of supplies became comparatively simple, but, at the time of the Arras Battle, everything was experimental and all Tapper's energy and ability were needed to handle the task. The best proof of the splendid work he did is that on no single occasion did man or tank ever fail to obtain the necessary supplies.

The Reconnaissance Officer was responsible for everything in connection with the collection of information regarding the ground, obstacles to be expected and the best routes, not only on the field of battle, but, also, for the approach-march.

The comparative failure of the tanks on the 15th of September in the Battle of the Somme was very largely due to the entire absence of this reconnaissance work. As we gained experience, more and more attention was paid to this department until, in the end, it became almost the most important branch of all. In fact, the actual fighting of the tank was a simple matter in comparison with getting it into the position where it could fight.

Williams-Ellis had had a considerable experience of serving in the trenches as an officer of the Welch Guards and he brought to bear on his new duties an unparalleled keenness and enthusiasm. He was also no mean artist and, by the aid of boldly drawn sketches, was able to present to his audience a very clear idea of the country to be traversed, laying special stress on outstanding landmarks.

Like other members of the Tank Corps, he was possessed of an absolute disregard of danger.

It is interesting here to note the diverse forms of courage shown by different individuals.

General Elles actually seemed to enjoy getting into tight corners; Hotblack, apparently, was entirely without fear of any sort and completely ignored the enemy; Martel possessed a fine cunning, which enabled him to arrive at the desired spot, usually in extreme proximity to the Germans, with a minimum of risk; Williams-Ellis, on the other hand, became so absorbed in the task which he had in hand, that he entirely forgot that such a thing as an enemy existed. For example, during the reconnaissance work before the Cambrai Battle, he calmly led my brigade major and myself into No-Man's-Land and we only realised the situation when several shots were fired at us from the German lines and we saw a row of grinning, British soldiers, peeping from a trench fifty yards in rear.

Good reconnaissance work was the foundation of all success and much of the results achieved by the First Brigade must be put down to the credit of Williams-Ellis. In the Third Battle of Ypres, the Cambrai Battle, and, later, when in September 1918 we tackled the Canal du Nord, which everybody said was impassable by tanks, he carried out the most daring, personal reconnaissances, on which all my plans were based.

My first brigade major was Cox of the Gloucester Regiment, a most excellent and capable officer who, after being with me for only a few months, was taken away to help in the formation of the Third Brigade. He was succeeded by Thorp of the K.O.Y.L.I., who remained with the brigade until within a few months of the Armistice.

6

It soon became apparent that my new task was not to be an easy one. I had vainly hoped that commanders of corps and divisions would welcome the new weapon, placed at their disposal, with open arms. I found, instead, that the majority regarded the tank with a good deal of suspicion. This attitude, on being analysed, was not difficult to explain.

Several of them had had tanks allotted to them during the Somme Battle and, in many cases, the machines had failed even to reach their starting-points. Since the Somme Battle, they had heard little of the improvements in material and personnel and were prone to assess the future prospect in the light of past experience.

A few kept a perfectly open mind on the subject, but preferred to proceed with their plans on the assumption that little reliance could be placed on this auxiliary weapon.

It was an anxious moment when I took my seat at the first Conference held by General Allenby, commanding the Third Army, in whose area the main battle was to take place.

Of all the commanders in the field who occupied high positions in the British Army during the war, General Allenby must be regarded as the greatest.

Not only was he a born leader of men, with a most determined and resolute character, but he possessed an extremely imaginative and far-seeing mind and was not afraid to depart from the stereotyped meth-

GENERAL ALLENBY

ods of warfare. This was proved time after time in Palestine, where his brilliant and audacious tactics brought about the complete downfall of the Turks in an incredibly short time and considerably hastened the termination of hostilities.

I already had the pleasure of knowing General Allenby, but never before had I been called upon to serve under him officially. He was reputed to be outspoken in the highest degree, to put it mildly, and woe betide anyone who was unable to give a concise and satisfactory answer when questioned by him.

It was, therefore, not without some inward qualms that I took my place at the Conference table in company with his senior staff officers and the G.O.C.s Army Corps.

From the outset there was only one person in the room and that person was Allenby. He completely dominated.

With the utmost clearness and a minimum expenditure of words, he outlined his plans. He put a few queries to various members of the Conference and noted their replies. I was asked one or two questions concerning my proposed co-operation, which, fortunately, I was able to answer without hesitation.

It seemed as though the meeting was to pass off without a breath to ruffle the even tenor of the proceedings, but, just before we adjourned, Allenby turned to one of his principal staff officers, a major-general, and asked him whether a certain order had been carried out.

"I think so, sir," replied the staff officer.

"What the deuce do you mean by that?" burst forth Allenby, turning on the unfortunate man. "You're not paid to think. You've got to know. Find out at once and report to me immediately."

Inwardly I congratulated myself that I had been able to answer my questions without qualification, and I determined that, in future, a definite answer should be forthcoming in all circumstances.

After the conference was over, Allenby detained me for a few moments and told me how confident he felt that the tanks would prove of great value and assured me that he, personally, would give all the help he could and would watch the activities of the new arm with the keenest interest.

It was a most thoughtful and encouraging gesture and served to spur us on to further efforts towards success, if that indeed were possible. It is small things such as these which distinguish the great man from the lesser and ensure a loyalty and devotion which go far to bring about the best results.

At one time or another, I served under most of the senior commanders in France during the war, but I never met one under whom I would serve so gladly again as under General Allenby.

7

From the time when I was first given my general instructions by Elles, it was evident that the number of machines at my disposal would be ludicrously inadequate for the vast expanse of front over which we were to operate.

Deliveries from England had fallen far below the mildest expectations and it had been found necessary to refurbish tanks salved from the Somme Battle and others which had been intended solely for training purposes. It had been confidently hoped that at least fifty of the new Mark IV, a great improvement on the original Mark I, would be forthcoming, bringing up my total number of machines to over a hundred. In actual fact, only sixty tanks in all were available, all of which were Mark I, and most of these had already undergone considerable wear and tear.

It was a great disappointment, especially as we all felt that the tank was now definitely on trial for the first time under conditions where ample time and thought had been given for preparation. We had preached the Gospel of the Tank and had not hesitated, when giving lectures or demonstrations, to assure senior commanders that, granted a real opportunity, it should prove to be of invaluable assistance. One thing on which we could rely without a qualm of apprehension was the enthusiasm and courage of the crews. Everything that hard work and hard thinking could accomplish was done. The rest lay on the knees of the gods.

In addition to our domestic troubles, the enemy, thoroughly aware of the intended attack, decided to withdraw a considerable distance, thereby completely upsetting all arrangements and rendering necessary and almost entirely fresh set of plans. This move was particularly unwelcome to the tanks, as it necessitated the scrapping of many laborious days of reconnaissance work and the determination of new routes and objectives.

The small number of machines at my disposal were to be employed mainly on the Third Army Front, but a few, if conditions permitted, were to take part in the attack on the Vimy Ridge, which lay within the sphere of the First Army to the north, and a slightly larger number was allotted to the Fifth Army, which was to attack at Bullecourt,

MK I Tank going into action Chimpanzee Valley,
15th September 1916

MK IV Tank

some twelve miles south of Arras.

As it was quite impossible effectively to superintend this wide extent of front, I sent Hardress Lloyd, commanding "D" Battalion, with twelve of his machines, to Gough's Fifth Army with a practically free hand to do as seemed to him most advantageous, and concentrated my efforts on the front where the large majority of tanks were to be employed.

Even before any definite plans were made, it seemed to us that the ground, over which the Canadians were to attack the Vimy Ridge, was almost impassable by tanks. In spite of our fears, however, eight tanks were allotted to this task in response to urgent request for their presence. A *proviso* was entered that, if much rain fell, the machines could be withdrawn and dispatched to the south to join the detachment of "D" Battalion, to which they belonged, in the Fifth Army area.

To the Third Army, in whose area the "going" for tanks was more favourable, were allotted forty machines, less than half the number really needed for such an extent of front. There were many strong points, on which the Germans had lavished great labour and ingenuity, and it was against these that comparatively strong detachments of tanks were ordered to operate.

Once again, the British offensive was regarded as secondary and chiefly destined to serve as a decoy, in order to draw away supports and reserves from the front near Rheims, where our Allies were to set in motion a large attack a few days later. This attack, it may here be noted, was a complete and ghastly failure, partly owing to bad preparations and partly owing to the total inability of the French to keep a secret. For weeks previously, all Paris had known the exact spot where the attack was to be made, the date and the actual zero hour. If anyone had doubts concerning some point and desired more precise information, all he had to do was to ask a waiter or one of the fair *habituées* of the Café Maxim in order to obtain it. The French may pride themselves on being a military nation, but, in one particular, the despised "nation of shopkeepers" is immeasurably their superior, *viz.* its ability to keep its mouth tightly closed.

Many were the unexpected difficulties that I encountered, when conferring with divisional, commanders concerning the best methods of co-operation. Several seemed to think that tanks could travel at twenty miles an hour and, starting a long way behind the infantry, could catch them up before reaching the first objective, probably four or five hundred yards distant. One of them steadfastly refused to allow a tank to come within a thousand yards of his front line until after zero hour, in case the Germans might hear it (amid the roar of the thousand guns, be it remembered) and suspect that an attack was about to be made. After much argument I agreed to his *dictum*, but owing to a "misunderstanding" on my part, the tanks allotted to this division actually crossed our front line at the moment when the infantry went over the top. As I heard nothing on this subject later and received a most cordial letter of thanks from this commander, I can only think that either my "mistake" had passed unnoticed or had been condoned by him.

At last everything was in readiness, routes of approach had been marked out, objectives clearly defined, and advanced supply-dumps formed. There was nothing left to do but to hope for the best and to pray for good fortune.

8

Our prayers evidently were either of insufficient fervour or ignored.

In the first place, the weather, as usual, took a turn the worse.

Not only did the rain come down in torrents but, in the next few days, there was a heavy fall of snow, a rare occurrence in mid-April.

The first effect of the downpour was that the tanks, which had been concealed in the ditch of the old citadel of Arras, became hopelessly bogged whilst moving up to their "jumping-off" places. Preparations had been made against this possibility, but the material, ordered for the making of a causeway, failed to put in an appearance, in spite of almost superhuman efforts to extricate them, several machines were too late to take part in the task allotted to them.

Fortunately for my sanity, I was unaware of this *contretemps*, as I was tied to the end of the telephone in my extemporised office at Montenescourt. For days and nights on end, my staff and myself had worked without cessation. Anxious though I was actually to see the tanks move into battle, I felt that my proper place was in my office where I could be found, but all my staff, on that night before the battle, were absent on their "lawful occasions" and I was left alone in my glory.

For hours I sat there, wondering anxiously how things were going. Every few minutes the telephone bell rang and I was asked some question or told of some minor alteration in plan. A year or more later, these conversations would not have caused me one moment's uneasiness, but, at that time, realising how much was at stake, I was greatly disturbed. In addition, the telephone took the opportunity of behaving at its very worst. In the middle of a sentence there would be a sudden buzz and a crack, followed by a dead silence. Half an hour of blasphemous vituperation followed, and, when at last I got through once more to my late interlocutor, it was to find that he had gone out and would not be back for several hours. Nobody can realise, who has not found himself in the same position, the maddening difficulty of trying to keep in touch, by means of a hastily laid field-telephone, with two armies, five corps and a dozen divisions, as well as with the headquarters of one's own units.

In the small hours of the morning, Elles and Fuller arrived with the appalling news that most of the tanks had got stuck while leaving their "lying-up" place. I do not know if I wept, but I felt like it. It seemed so cruel after all the thought and care that we had lavished on our preparations.

Elles said that he would take my place at the telephone and ordered me to go to bed. I think he was afraid that I was going to have a nervous breakdown.

I lay down for an hour or more, but it was no good; and I got up again, without having slept, to find out from my returning staff what had taken place.

On the whole, things were not so bad as they might have been, and the first messages from the fighting line, which soon began to filter through, were quite encouraging. As the morning wore on, news of definite successes commenced to arrive. Two strong points, which had been expected to prove hard nuts to crack, had, according to the reports received from Corps Headquarters, been captured with small loss, "thanks to the magnificent work of the tanks."

The news from the north, where the Canadians were assaulting the strong Vimy Ridge (attacked by the French without success twice previously), was, from the general point of view, exceedingly satisfactory, but we knew that the heavy rain, which had fallen on the night before the attack, would, in all probability, have rendered the ground totally impassable for tanks. This presumption was fully borne out and not one single machine was of any assistance. Naturally we were disappointed at this failure, but I had, on several occasions, warned the Canadian corps commander that little help could be relied on.

The tanks which had been "bogged" on their way up to the line from the citadel, had all been extricated in the morning and, none the worse for their mishap, had joined the infantry, to which they gave invaluable help in clearing up strong points and machine gun "nests."

By evening, it became certain that a very complete victory had been won and that the tanks, in spite of their small numbers and unpropitious start, had played a very useful part. The result, on the whole, was as good as we had dared to hope and, in some respects, far better than we had really expected.

9

For the next two days, on the Third Army Front, several minor engagements took place and tanks were reported by the infantry to have given much assistance.

Gough's attack on the left of the Fifth Army against Bullecourt was launched as arranged, the Australians being selected to lead the van.

Unfortunately, the weather proved even more vile than usual and a heavy snowstorm blinded not only the tanks, but also the infantry whom they were supposed to protect. Some local successes were achieved, but these only led to disastrous results. Small salients were formed in the German line and, owing to their flanks being unprotected, the attacking force of infantry and tanks was cut off, surrounded, and taken prisoner.

It was a most unfortunate incident and one for which nobody can in any way be blamed, but it created an extremely bad impression among the Australians, who, for a year or more afterwards, gravely mistrusted tanks and actually refused their co-operation. In the end, however, the Anzac Corps became one of our most enthusiastic supporters and placed an almost childlike faith in their capabilities.

After a few days devoted to refitting, half of the original force of tanks, allotted to the Third Army, again took part in an organised attack. The result was, once more, very successful and every report received from infantry commanders was highly complimentary.

An attack was made on a village, Monchy-le-Preux, that stood in a commanding position on the top of a ridge. By some mistake, two of the tanks passed through our own barrage and arrived in the village a long way ahead of the infantry. When the latter arrived on the scene, the Germans in the village had surrendered and the place was "captured" by the infantry without loss. An hour later, the cavalry made a dashing, mounted attack and the village was again "captured." It surely must be the first time in military annals that a position has been captured by different arms of the service on three separate occasions in

Tank in action on the Western Front, 1917

the space of a couple of hours.

Another successful action was that of the chemical works at Roeux. Here the tanks fought for the first time in co-operation with the 51st Highland Territorial Division (commanded by my old friend and enemy of early machine gun days, Major-General Sir M. Harper), which at this time was beginning to win the great imputation it acquired later and fully deserved.

It was a hard-fought little battle and the infantry commanders were unable to speak too highly of the valuable assistance they received from the tanks. These reports were so eulogistic that I was much amused when the divisional commander in his report gave the entire credit of the successful action to the infantry and barely mentioned the fact that a tank had even been present. It was not any lack of generosity that prompted this omission, but "Uncle" adored his "Harper's Duds," and took good care that every single iota of praise should be bestowed upon them.

A few more disconnected actions were fought in the latter part of April, rather in the nature of clearing up than of further attempts to advance, but the Battle of Arras was finished. It had succeeded in its task completely and everybody concerned was fully satisfied with the result.

It was a great pleasure to myself and all ranks to receive the complimentary messages of thanks from every unit with which we had co-operated.

Not only did General Allenby issue a special Army Order commending the work of the tanks and allotting to them a generous measure of the success, but he also invited me to his headquarters to thank me in person for the splendid work which he said we had accomplished.

Corps and divisional commanders were all equally outspoken in their gratitude, especially Lieutenant-General Sir Aylmer Haldane, who commanded the corps in which our main successes had been achieved.

A few days before the brigade was finally withdrawn to the back area for refitting and training of "new hands," a conference was held in Arras for the purpose of eliciting the views of commanders as to the result that might be expected from the co-operation of tanks and the methods whereby the best results could be obtained.

There was no hesitation displayed in the prophecies of how important a part the tanks in the future would play, but considerable divergence of opinion was evident as to how this might be accomplished.

It was most interesting to listen to the various views, expressed, but one, in particular, which I was to recall vividly, eighteen months later, was that of Major-General Sir B. de Lisle, who stated that he definitely disapproved of tanks. When called upon to give his reasons for this unexpected remark, he stated that, in his opinion, if infantry once became used to having tanks to help them they would refuse to fight without them.

An almost uncanny prescience underlay this statement and, although it was not taken seriously at the time, it proved to be, as we shall see later, an accurate forecast of subsequent events.

A few days later, the bits and pieces were collected and the First Brigade, happy in the knowledge that it had, in spite of every sort of handicap, more than fulfilled expectations, moved back to Wailly, there to be rearmed and refitted against the time when its services would be required once more.

CHAPTER 14

The Attack

1

Before the First Brigade was withdrawn from the Arras Front, I had already been informed that a general offensive in the Ypres district had been planned and would take place some time in July.

To anyone familiar with the terrain in Flanders it was almost inconceivable that this part of the line should have been selected. If a careful search had been made from the English Channel to Switzerland, no more unsuitable spot could have been discovered.

To those of my readers who are unfamiliar with Flanders it must be pointed out that a large portion of it lies at, or just above, sea-level. Ypres itself at one time had been a seaport, and the drainage system, which had been instituted in order to render the land in the vicinity cultivable, had to be regulated with the utmost care. Every farmer was responsible for the efficient state of repair of his drainage ditches and was liable to a heavy fine if he neglected them.

For over two years this drainage system had, of necessity, been untended and, in addition to natural decay, had been largely destroyed by shell fire. The result was that many square miles of land consisted merely of a thin crust of soil, beneath which lay a bottomless sea of mud and water. Bad as it was in ordinary times, we knew that it would be a thousand-fold worse after the terrific preliminary bombardment which was now regarded as the indispensable forerunner of an attack.

To put it mildly, we were absolutely astounded at the decision to attack at this point.

We were told, of course, that policy rather than strategy had dictated it and that the C.-in-C. had been compelled, against his better

183

judgment, to accede to the desires of our civilian rulers.

It is true that at this time the submarine menace was assuming most dangerous proportions and that the Channel Ports of Ostend and Zeebrugge, which were in the hands of the Germans and used as submarine bases, constituted a grave threat to our supremacy at sea, a supremacy vital not only to ourselves, but, also, to our Allies.

Nothing is easier than to be wise after the event, but, in this case, the large majority of people who were familiar with the conditions was wise before the event. During the whole of the preliminary preparations, I never met one single soul who anticipated success, with the exception of G.H.Q., who, either through ignorance of the true state of affairs or for other reasons, endeavoured to inspire us with confidence concerning the result.

Policy must usually dominate strategy, but on occasions circumstances will arise that render political desiderata impossible of attainment.

If there had ever been the most remote chance of achieving our ultimate purpose, *viz.* the capture of the ports used as submarine bases, no sacrifice would have been too great. But this remote chance never existed, even at the very commencement.

It is difficult to believe that even the most confirmed optimist could have dreamt that there was the slightest hope of success, and yet, not only before the battle started, but, also, after it had been in slow and bloody progress for weeks, certain highly placed commanders talked and planned as though a breakthrough were imminent.

The total net result of more than four hundred thousand casualties and the expenditure of hundreds of millions of pounds of money was the capture of a few thousand acres of Godforsaken, uninhabitable, swampy desolation.

Much of a commander's plans must be based on the reports he receives regarding the state of the enemy morale. On this score, most misleading information was supplied. Optimism, within reasonable limits, is a great asset, but when, as in this case, it exceeds the most extravagant hopes, it becomes an inconceivable danger, bringing dire disaster in its train.

Not once but many times, at the Fifth Army Conferences, General Sir Hubert Gough, the Army Commander, opened the proceedings with a statement to this effect:

Gentlemen, I have just come from an interview with the com-

Working party going up at night over flooded ground, Wieltje, 11th January, 1918

mander-in-chief and he tells me that everything points to a complete breakdown of the enemy morale and that one more hard thrust will crumple up his defences.

There is no possible doubt but that General Gough implicitly believed in what he told us, but there was not one other single member of the conference who did not know how grotesquely inaccurate this statement was in fact.

Many writers have hinted that the conditions were such as to render success improbable, but, as far as I know, no one has yet told the plain, unvarnished truth.

In the first place, the Germans held all the high ground such as it was, and looked down on the morass over which we should be compelled to attack. Having fully appreciated the lessons of the previous year during the Somme Battle, they had prepared their defence in great depth. The reinforced concrete "pill-boxes," against which any but the most powerful guns were impotent, bristled with machine guns, most cunningly sited so as to sweep with their fire all the intervening ground, which was covered with barbed wire.

Unless one has actually traversed the ground on which the attack took place, it is absolutely impossible to form any conception of its condition.

After our preliminary bombardment, which lasted for sixteen days with ever-growing intensity, and the German retaliation thereto, the whole surface of the ground consisted of nothing but a series of overlapping shell craters, half full of yellow, slimy water. Through falling into these ponds, hundreds upon hundreds of unwounded men, while advancing to the attack, lost their lives by drowning. The mere act of walking over this tortured swamp, unencumbered by the sixty pounds weight which the soldier carries in action, was one that entailed considerable effort, though one was able to move at one's own pace and choose the easiest routes. The original roads had almost ceased to exist and, in order to enable wheel traffic to move at all, even in the area behind the line, it was necessary to lay down corduroy tracks which were constantly destroyed by shell fire.

Furthermore, at this period, the Germans had established a definite superiority in the air and these tracks and the "duck-board" walks were daily machine-gunned by low-flying aeroplanes. Every yard of ground had been carefully "registered" by the enemy's guns and a peculiarly effective form of gas-shell, containing "mustard-gas," had been evolved. For months past the Germans had been preparing against our coming offensive and had decided upon a method of defence, admirably suited to the circumstances.

Under the most favourable conditions, an attack against such a position as confronted us would have been a task of great difficulty and risk. As things actually were, it was nothing but rank folly.

2

If conditions were so hopelessly unpropitious for the infantry, how then would it be possible to employ tanks to any real advantage?

Already we had had a foretaste of bad ground during the Somme Battle and the abortive attempts to co-operate with the Canadians in their assault on the Vimy Ridge, but we, who were familiar with the Salient, knew that the difficulties to be faced there would be infinitely greater.

It was obviously worse than useless to make any protest and the only thing to do was to make the best of an extremely bad job.

Although the tanks had been of definite and acknowledged assistance in the Arras Battle and, as far as circumstances permitted, in the Messines Battle a month later, they were still regarded as a "stunt," rather than as an established and permanent auxiliary arm.

Their hold on existence was still precarious. In the struggle for priority of manufacture, they ranked far down on the list of precedence, occupying a place even below that of motor lorries. These were the days, too, when the whole faith of the High Command was pinned to artillery, and any weapon which might detract from the output of guns and shells was regarded with disfavour. All of us, from General Elles downwards, feared lest a disastrous failure on the part of the tanks might be the prelude to their complete disappearance.

The British mind, and especially the British military mind, is essentially conservative. If a thing has existed for hundreds of years and is hallowed by tradition, its position is unassailable, even though progress has entirely destroyed its original value. On the other hand, anything new is always suspect and its detractors are constantly seeking for some joint in its armour in order to destroy it.

The cavalry, for instance (magnificent body of men though it was), in its normal, mounted capacity might, when trench warfare began, just as well have been in China. It proved of supreme value in the early days as a splendid *dismounted* force and filled gaps in our line with unsurpassed courage. But, when acting as a body of mounted troops, they merely blocked the roads, badly needed for other arms during an offensive, and wasted precious tonnage of ships in order to feed thousands upon thousands of horses, that were absolutely valueless in battle.

3

The tanks, then, were still on trial and much would depend on how they functioned during the coming offensive. It was not difficult to perceive how greatly Elles and Fuller were perturbed in their minds, though both of them maintained the most correct of attitudes and never for one moment displayed the apprehension which, without doubt, assailed them.

The Tank Corps had now been organised into three brigades, each at present consisting of two battalions, with the prospect of a third battalion when such was forthcoming from the training centre in England.

The Second Brigade under Colonel Courage had already been formed and had co-operated in the successful Battle of Messines, though the part played by the tanks therein was relatively small, owing to the limited scope of the action and the meticulous care expended on its preparation. For once, the offensive had, in fact, pursued its intended course, "in accordance with plan," a phrase usually made use of by both sides to explain away an abortive attack or an enforced and unexpected retirement.

The Second Brigade, more fortunate than the First, had gone into action armed throughout with the new Mark IV machines, a great improvement on the old Mark I, which we had been compelled to use at Arras. The arrangements made by Courage and his staff were exemplary and it was unfortunate that the tanks did not have greater scope for displaying their capabilities, although we all naturally rejoiced in the small casualties suffered by the infantry.

The Third Brigade was formed under the command of Hardress Lloyd, lately commanding "D" Battalion in my brigade, by the conjunction of my old "C" Battalion with "F" Battalion, the first of the new units, trained in England, to arrive in France. Much as I disliked the separation from my old battalion, I realised how necessary it was that an experienced unit should be included in a new formation and "G" Battalion, which was allotted to me in place of "C," proved to be one of the very best in the whole Tank Corps. In spite of various readjustments, rendered necessary from time to time as the corps was doubled and redoubled in strength, "G" Battalion remained as an integral portion of the First Brigade, until the "Cease Fire" was blown, and no commander was ever better served.

Many were the Conferences at Bermicourt under General Elles concerning the coming operations. Several important lessons had been learned at Arras and Messines fund all of us were animated by an almost indignant "will to conquer," in spite of the appalling conditions with which we were faced.

The reconnaissance reports brought back from the Salient by Hotblack, Williams-Ellis and others were not encouraging, to say the least of it. If conditions were so unpromising at this early stage of the proceedings, what would the ground be like after tens of thousands of heavy shells had pounded it into a further state of disintegration?

Elles had already allotted tank brigades to their respective infantry formations and I found myself placed at the disposal of the Fifth Army and instructed to co-operate with the XVIIIth Corps in particular.

This, it must be remembered, was during the height of the "Gough tradition," and Sir Hubert had been specially selected to direct the offensive on account of his audacity and dash—save the mark!

It would be farcical, were it not so tragic, to speak of "dash" in connection with the Salient. Vast preparations for putting the cavalry through the gap were made; maps of the country ten, fifteen, even twenty miles within the German lines were issued.

At the end of nearly four months of slaughter and superhuman endurance, an advance of a few thousand yards had been made, and the cavalry, silently and sorrowfully, returned to the place whence it had come.

4

The Headquarters of the Fifth Army were established in Lovie Château, not far distant from Ypres. All sorts of rumours were current regarding its inexplicable immunity from shell fire, but the fact remains that, until the great German offensive in March 1918, the house remained unmolested and intact. Probably some simple explanation exists for this remarkable phenomenon, but I have never heard it.

The first Army Conference, which I attended, filled me with disquiet. It seemed to me (and I found out subsequently that my fears had been shared by others), that the whole plan of operations was grotesquely optimistic and based on false premises. The anticipated rate of advance would have been, if attained, surprisingly good under ordinary battle conditions, in the mud and the slime of the Salient, it was unthinkable. Frequently references were made to the action of cavalry and the important role they were destined to play in the breakthrough. Little or no attention was paid by General Gough, in the beginning, to the co-operation of tanks and he had no hesitation in saying that, in his opinion, they were far too slow to keep up even with the infantry. The commander of the XVIIIth Corps was General Maxse. I had already gained a little of his confidence, when he was commanding the 18th Division, in the matter of the alleged failure of the Lewis guns. During the next few months I was to know him intimately, and to conceive for him a very real admiration and affection. To General Maxse belongs the credit for the foresight and courage to plan the first attack in which everything was subordinated to the use of tanks.

It may seem, in these days, when tanks are regarded as part and parcel of the recognised arms of the Service, that this was no great thing; but, when he actually made his decision, the tank was an almost entirely discredited weapon and it required great moral courage on his part to allow me, a junior officer of no particular standing, to stage an offensive in which the infantry were to play a subordinate part and the artillery almost none at all.

The other corps commanders of the Fifth Army were Lord Cavan (who succeeded the late Sir Henry Wilson as C.I.G.S.) and Lieutenant-General Sir H. Smith. In the first attack, however, my activities were confined to the XVIIIth Corps and it was only later that some of my desperate efforts were made in other corps areas.

The date of the offensive had originally been fixed for mid-July, but, for various reasons, it was postponed till the last day of the month. The whole essence of the plan was based on a rapid decision, and we could ill afford to lose even twenty-four hours. The weather, on which so much depended, was liable to break at any moment, and, if it did, the hardiest optimists realised that our task would prove impossible.

Among the four divisions of the XIIIth Corps, we found our friends of the Chemical Works fight, the 51st Division. General Harper was much in evidence at the Corps Conferences and, although he was inclined to belittle the value of the tanks, he did not fail to put in a claim for a far greater number of machines than that to which he was justly entitled.

It had been decided to keep half the total number of the First Brigade, *viz*. seventy-two, in reserve, in order that any successes might be exploited without delay. This proved, in the outcome, to be a wise precaution and they were able to give much assistance later in clearing up strong points and repelling enemy counterattacks. More important still was the fact that I had at my disposal fresh crews and serviceable machines for the St. Julien attack.

The more one saw of the ground to be traversed, the more hopeless it appeared.

As it was impossible to obtain any general view of the terrain, owing to its flatness and the absence of any vantage point, I obtained special permission to fly over the German lines. There was a rigid order in the Royal Flying Corps, as it was called in those days, that no one other than an officer of the corps was allowed to cross our front line in an aeroplane. With some difficulty and only after having stated that I accepted entire responsibility, I was at length allowed to go.

It was the first time I had ever been up in an aeroplane and this, combined with the prospect of looking down into the German lines, filled me with a peculiar feeling of exhilaration.

The machine placed at my disposal was an R.E.8, a very slow but reliable type, chiefly used for photography and for "spotting" for the artillery. The pilot, whose name was Allgood, was an extremely capable officer, but I do not think he really enjoyed this particular job and he had been specially warned to take no risks.

I told him exactly where I wished to go and off we started. In a few minutes we got our height and headed in the direction of St. Julien and Poelcapelle. As soon as I had become accustomed to the novel sensation of being in the air for the first time, I leant over the side of the fuselage and carefully studied the ground, five or six thousand feet below.

It was an extraordinary sight. The whole country-appeared as though seen through the wrong end of a telescope. Curiously enough, I had no difficulty in recognising different landmarks, and, with Allgood's help, I could make out exactly how and where the enemy's lines ran. Everywhere the ground was churned up by shell fire and had the semblance of a face badly pitted by smallpox. All the craters were half-filled with water and it looked as though there was as much water as there was land.

As we drew near the German lines, my pilot, who kept gazing anxiously into the sky, let go completely of his controls and, standing with one foot on each side of the fuselage and grasping the upper wing of the machine with both hands, kept careful watch in the heavens, while the machine looked after itself. This seemed to me far more dangerous than the possibility of being attacked by enemy aeroplanes, but it was not my affair, and I continued my survey. We flew on, down the Valley of the Steenbeek, a nasty, marshy stream, that was to prove a serious obstacle later, and turned once more towards Houthoulst Forest.

Suddenly Allgood pointed at five tiny specks in the sky, apparently many miles away.

"Boche," he framed with his lips.

I suppose he was right, but, however that may be, he turned the machine's head homewards and, tilting her nose down at what seemed to be an angle of forty-five degrees, opened out the engine to its fullest capacity. The wind tore past the struts and every wire hummed with the vibration. The ground rushed up to meet us and, for an instant, I wondered if the machine were out of control. A glimpse of Allgood's calm and composed face reassured me and my momentary apprehension vanished. I kept swallowing every second or two to clear the buzzing noise in my ears, due to the rapid change in altitude. In a few minutes we were circling over the aerodrome and, after a couple of steep "banks," landed smoothly and gently on *terra firma*.

We had been absent for less than an hour, but it seemed to me far, far longer. It had been a most enjoyable journey, as well as most useful. Many times have I flown since, but that first flight will always remain a treasured memory.

A few days before the battle, the weather took a turn for the worse. A wind, bringing mist and fine rain, blew steadily from the west. It was the last piece of ill-luck required to complete the tale of our misfortunes.

One almost felt that the *Kaiser* was justified in his assumption that "*Unser Gott*" was an important member of his personal staff and had once again justified the appointment.

5

Meanwhile, we had not been entirely free from domestic troubles.

The machines of the First Brigade had been detrained at a special siding at Oesthoek Wood, where they were to lie hidden until required. The crews were accommodated in huts near by and everything seemed well.

A few days later, however, some peculiarly well-directed shelling appeared to indicate that the Germans had gleaned information that the wood was harbouring something worthy of their attention. At nights, also, a large number of bombs were dropped in the vicinity, with the result that the crews, who were busy all day in getting their machines into the highest state of efficiency, were deprived of their much-needed rest. I, therefore, withdrew the personnel and installed them in a camp within a few hundred yards of my own headquarters near Lovie Château.

It was subsequently discovered that complete and accurate information concerning the position of the tanks had been given to the enemy by a captured infantry soldier. Fortunately the actual results of this treachery were negligible, though they might have been exceedingly serious. The name of the betrayer and his regiment became a byword in the First Brigade, and a large number of men proposed to call on him after the war was over and explain to him, with vigorous action, exactly what they thought of him.

Almost daily, commanders and staffs of the First Brigade were out on the far side of the canal, selecting routes and sites for advance supply-dumps, Williams-Ellis, accompanied by the battalion reconnaissance officers, spending most of his time crawling about in the mud in close proximity to the German lines.

To the best of our ability, we feigned to be hopeful, but we knew full well that we were engaged in a hopeless enterprise. It was a heart-breaking task to order into faction the splendid, well-trained crews and their highly efficient machines, when one felt that most, if not all, of the effort would be wasted. The actual machines, valuable though they were, did not weigh so heavily on my mind; it was the personnel, who might, and probably would be, destroyed to no real purpose, which caused me so much uneasiness.

Already the inspiring doctrine that the principal duty of the tanks was to *save life* had been firmly fixed in the minds of the crews and was fostered on every possible occasion. It was impressed on officers and men alike that the only real heroes of the war were the foot-soldiers, who went into battle with nothing but a coat and shirt to protect them. The lucky people, we told them, were those who had an inch or two of armour-plating between them and the enemy's bullets. This teaching was inculcated until the last day of the war, and it speaks highly for the prevailing spirit of the corps that heads were never turned by the, at times, almost fulsome praise that later was lavished on the work of the tanks.

Battles cannot be won without lives being lost any more than omelettes can be made without breaking eggs; but the good cook does not break a dozen eggs in order to make use of four. A heavy responsibility rests on a commander carefully to guard the lives of those under his orders, but it is just as necessary, when circumstances demand it, to send men to almost certain death as it is to preserve them if no valuable purpose can be served.

On General Elles and the brigade commanders of the Tank Corps a heavy weight of responsibility fell during the last six months of the war and in their hands rested decisions on which the lives of thousands of men might hang.

6

A causeway of sand-bags had been constructed to enable the tanks to cross the Ypres-Commines Canal *en route* for their "jumping-off" places. The hour for crossing had been fixed for midnight on the 30th July, the eve of the battle.

At eleven o'clock General Elles, Hotblack, Thorp; (my new brigade major) and myself sallied forth to see the machines safely across the first obstacle.

It was a dark, muggy night and a fine rain was falling. The whole sky was obscured by dark clouds and the climatic conditions were as unpropitious as could be imagined. The only light visible was the dull-red glare of the guns, now firing at their maximum intensity, and the cold, white radiance of Very lights that blazed for a few moments in the sky and were gone.

Slowly we made our way down muddy tracks and across swampy meadows till we reached the banks of the canal and came to the causeway. We had not seen a single tank on our walk and the causeway stood deserted and empty.

"It's only a quarter to twelve," remarked Elles, as he looked at his watch, "perhaps they've been held up."

"No, sir," called back Hotblack, who was examining the approaches to the crossing. "I can see their tracks in the mud."

As the last words left his mouth, there was a *crash* and a *bang*, followed by others in quick succession.

"Gas!" yelled Hotblack. "Put on your masks."

As quickly as we could, we adjusted our gas-masks, but not before all of us had swallowed a strong whiff or two. The target of the shelling, a mixture of gas and high explosive, was evidently the causeway, of which the enemy, of course, was fully aware and whose purpose it was not difficult to guess. It was impossible for them to know the exact hour fixed for the crossing, but midnight was a probable moment.

In those days the box-respirator and "goggles" were all made in one, with the result that the eye-pieces could not be removed for visual purposes without letting in the gas. Immediately the gas-mask was in position, moisture began to collect on the glass of the eye-pieces and, on a dark night such as this, the wearer was completely blinded.

In the excitement of the moment I knocked off my "tin-hat" into the nearest ditch and had to grope for it with my stick; Thorp walked briskly in the direction of the canal and was only saved from an involuntary bath by Hotblack, who, by the greatest of good luck, had provided himself with a sample of the new pattern of gas-mask, the glasses of which were separate from the actual respirator.

The tanks were safely past and there was nothing to be gained by lingering in this unhealthy spot.

By gestures Hotblack explained what he proposed to do and the little party slowly started off. Hotblack walked in front, occasionally lifting his goggles to see the way; Elles followed, holding the tail of Hotblack's coat; then myself with a firm grip of Elles' coat, with Thorp, holding on to my coat, bringing up the rear.

It must have been a comical little procession, if there had been anyone to see it; but the humour of the situation did not strike us at the moment. Personally, I felt like a child in a thick fog (which, in fact, the gas had formed) who has lost his nurse. It took us several minutes (it seemed like hours) before we were clear and could take off our respirators for a breath of fresh air. Immediately, Elles and I lit cigarettes, but, after the first whiff, we threw them away in disgust. The taste, due to the effect of the gas, was absolutely nauseating and it was two or three days before we were rid of it completely.

7

Zero had been fixed for an unusually early hour and it was still dark and thick with fine rain when our barrage came down and the infantry went over the top.

The first objective on the entire front of six or seven miles was captured at once, and after a pause, the troops moved forward to the assault of the second objective. Here the resistance stiffened, but a large portion of it fell into our hands. On the front of the XVIIIth Corps, with which I was mainly concerned, practically all objectives in the third line also were captured, though farther to the south the attack had not been so successful.

The assault having come to a standstill, the Germans, in accordance with their new method of defence, everywhere hurled in strong counter-attacks and, in many cases, succeeded in driving out the captors.

The rain was falling in sheets and the whole position became more and more obscure, literally and metaphorically. Much ground was lost during the night but much was retained, though the inevitable, optimistic dispatch claimed a far more sweeping victory than actually had been gained.

How had the tanks fared in the battle? Had they completely failed, or had they, by some miracle, been able to justify their existence in some small way?

Such were the questions that were constantly present in our minds while waiting anxiously for news.

The first pigeon messages from the tanks seemed to indicate that the worst had happened.

"Hopelessly ditched behind our own front line." "Direct hit on tank by field gun. One killed, two wounded." "Ditched in German front line. Being heavily shelled."

Such were the dispiriting reports received in the early stages, but, as time passed, other information of a less depressing character began to drift in. Tanks were reported by aeroplanes to be in action in comparatively advanced positions and, later, pigeon messages from tank commanders, telling what they had accomplished, revived our drooping spirits. It was not, however, until late evening that we were able to summarise, from the infantry reports, the results achieved by the tanks.

On the whole, taking the appalling conditions into consideration, the tanks had been more successful than we had any right to expect. Several of the infantry units were loud in their praise of the help received from them, not only in the assault, but also in beating off enemy counter-attacks. General Maxse, with his usual generosity, gave us a full share in what success had been won.

It had been intended that blow should follow blow in almost daily succession; but these optimistic plans were doomed to failure.

The weather, which had now definitely turned to "wet and stormy," would alone, in conjunction with the deadly swamp, have been sufficient to stop further progress, but, in addition, we were now "up against" the real enemy line of defence and the "pill-box," which was

A DERELICT TANK, EAST OF ZILLEBEKE, 22ND SEPTEMBER, 1917

to take such heavy toll of the attackers, was proving its invulnerability to the orthodox methods of assault.

Another general offensive had been set down for the second day, the 1st of August, but, owing to the weather and the successful enemy counter-attacks, it had been postponed.

In actual fact this offensive never took place and, for many weary and bloody weeks, spasmodic attacks were mounted, but, of necessity, the limits of the proposed advance were much curtailed, in spite of the persistent optimism of G.H.Q. and the commander of the Fifth Army.

8

Some ten days after the opening of the offensive, I was called upon to give a lecture on tanks to the Staff College Course at G.H.Q. After the lecture had been given, I went to lunch with an old friend, Colonel Tandy, of the Operations Branch of the General Staff. I was naturally plied with questions concerning the progress of the battle and I expressed my views with considerable candour and in vigorous language.

It was evident that my remarks called forth surprise and incredulous disapprobation. It was more than hinted that my opinions were prejudiced by the failure of the tanks. To this I replied that it was not a question of tanks being unable to fight, but a question of anybody being able to fight under such conditions. I wound up by definitely stating that, in my opinion, the battle was "as dead as mutton," and had been so since the second day.

My statement was received in silence and shortly afterwards the five or six members of the mess returned to their respective offices. I went with Tandy to his room and gave him the further information that he asked for. While I sat there, an orderly came in and told me that Brigadier-General Davidson (at that time Director of Operations, afterwards Major-General Sir John Davidson, K.C.B., D.S.O.) would like to see me before I left.

On entering Davidson's office, I found him seated at his table, his head in his hands.

"Sit down," he said. "I want to talk to you."

I sat down and waited.

"I am very upset by what you said at lunch, Baker," he began. "If it had been some junior officer, it wouldn't have mattered so much, but a man of your knowledge and experience has no right to speak like you did."

"You asked me how things really were and I told you frankly."

"But what you say is impossible."

"It isn't. Nobody has any idea of the conditions up there."

"But they can't be as bad as you make out."

"Have you been there yourself?"

"No."

"Has anybody in O.A. (Operations Branch) been there?"

"No."

"Well then, if you don't believe me, it would be as well to send someone up to find out. I'm sorry I've upset you, but you asked me what I thought and I told you."

I took my leave and returned to my headquarters with an uneasy feeling in the back of my mind that I, personally, was responsible for the rain and the mud.

There is no doubt but that G.H.Q. was prone to live in a little world of its own, far removed from the turmoil and filth of battle. It is essential that the planning of manoeuvres should be carried out in an atmosphere of calm and quiet, but it is equally essential that these plans should be made with a full and complete knowledge of the conditions in which they will be put into effect.

I am absolutely convinced that the department responsible for the staging of the Ypres offensive had not the remotest conception of the state of affairs existing and, accordingly, formulated their plans on a hopelessly incorrect basis. Undoubtedly, the optimistic Intelligence reports and General Gough's own views encouraged the belief that success was possible, if not assured, and little heed was paid to the "croakers," if any, who dared to prophesy evil.

Whether G.H.Q. persisted in the ostrich-like attitude of hiding its head in the sand or whether someone was sent up to make a reliable and first-hand report on conditions, I am unaware, but, however that may be, the bloody fiasco of the Third Battle of Ypres still went on.

It may be true that the British never know when they are beaten, but there comes a time when banging one's head against a stone wall, however praiseworthy from the theoretical standpoint, becomes insensate folly.

The British Army for the last hundred years had been used to comparatively easy victories, with a "butcher's bill" of slight dimensions, though sufficient to justify references to "the gallantry of our brave troops," etc., etc.

The Battles of Loos and the Somme had been unpleasant shocks, but we had consoled ourselves with the thought that we were helping our Allies in their offensives, and that we were "killing Germans."

The Third Battle of Ypres, the first full-dress attack by the British to serve their own undivided purpose, will ever remain an example of British stubbornness and British stupidity. The very lack of success seemed to urge the High Command to more and more vigorous efforts. The Intelligence reports waxed more and more eloquent concerning the hecatombs of enemy dead and confidently prophesied an imminent *debacle.*

Our French Allies, before an offensive, were equally, if not more, optimistic about their success and had no hesitation in telling the world about it: but, being a hard-headed and logical nation, they did not have the slightest compunction in abruptly terminating an attack when it became obvious that the result anticipated was incapable of attainment.

If the Third Battle of Ypres had been abandoned early in August, when the *raison d'être* of the offensive, the capture of Ostend and Zeebrugge, was patently impossible, no great loss of prestige would have been incurred and a quarter of a million needless casualties would have been avoided. We did "kill Germans," but for every German dead two, if not three, British soldiers died.

From that time onwards the standard, in every particular, fell. The ranks were filled with conscripted men, the untrained, the unfit, the unwilling.

The British Army was dead.

CHAPTER 15

The Cambrai Battle is Planned

1

In the meantime, conditions in the Salient became steadily worse. The wind blew from the west and rain descended almost continuously. All three brigades of tanks had made every effort to assist in the various actions that took place, but, with few exceptions, most of these attempts proved abortive.

The situation eventually became so hopeless that General Elles called a meeting of brigade commanders and told us that the tanks could be withdrawn into Army Reserve, and remain inactive till conditions improved.

Although this was undoubtedly the most logical plan to adopt, it was fraught with dangerous and far-reaching possibilities.

Already it was being stated in high quarters that "tanks were no good." The Fifth Army Commander had reported on them unfavourably and, though the actual report was not sent in till much later, all of us were well aware of its contents. The general feeling at G.H.Q., based on information received, was decidedly hostile and there was apparently no one, except a few people in the fighting line, who had a good word to say for us.

It was probably the greatest crisis in the history of the tanks and, without doubt, the very existence of the weapon trembled on the brink of destruction.

It seemed almost certain to my mind that, if we retired from the contest and said that it was impossible, owing to the unfavourable conditions, to take any further part in the fighting, the disappearance of the tanks, probably for ever, was inevitable.

On the other hand, further failures could not much damage our already damaged cause, and it was conceivable that, by some extraordinary stroke of luck, we might accomplish something to redeem ourselves in the eyes of the army. There could be no possible harm in trying and I knew that I could rely on the most loyal support from all my tank crews, of which many had not yet had the opportunity of going into action.

All this and more I pointed out to General Elles and the decision whether or not my brigade should take part in further actions was left entirely to my discretion.

On the 16th of August, I made a desperate effort to send a dozen or more tanks to assist in an attack near St. Julien, but, in spite of the most determined and gallant efforts of the crews, not a single tank managed even to reach our own front line. The infantry attacked without them, but the assault was driven back with heavy loss through the inability to capture a line of concrete "pill-boxes."

The tanks had not been allowed during their approach-march to use the corduroy roads and had been compelled to make their way across the sea of intervening mud. If only I could obtain permission to use these roads, it seemed possible that the tanks might get into action and, once there, might do good service.

Of the very few friends of the tanks at that time, General Maxse was the greatest. On one occasion during the Somme Battle, at the capture of Thiepval, a tank had proved of great assistance and, during the first day of the Ypres Battle, several machines had played an important part. With a keenness of vision, as rare as it was welcome, he argued that, given reasonable conditions, the new weapon would be of incalculable value.

He was not in the least disturbed by our ghastly failure of the 16th of August and when I proposed, not without some trepidation, what, in reality, was a tank battle, he at once gave it his most earnest consideration.

The plan which I laid before him was briefly as follows :

The line of "pill-boxes," which had held up the infantry, in spite of the most determined and gallant attacks, and which were apparently impervious to shell-fire, lay on the far side of the Steenbeek, with the St. Julien-Poelcapelle road running parallel behind them. If it were possible to move tanks along this road, they would be able to attack the "pill-boxes" from the rear, and the solid foundations of the road itself would allow the tanks to approach their objectives from a comparatively short distance.

AMMUNITION TRANSPORT ON THE ST. JULIEN ROAD, NEAR YPRES, 17TH OCTOBER, 1917

I explained that surprise was the essence of the attack and that all I required from the artillery was a smoke-barrage to blind the enemy's guns. I also pointed out that the only work demanded of the infantry would be to take over the "pill-boxes," when captured, and I that, if the tanks failed in their mission, the small number of infantry to be employed would be able to return to their trenches without becoming engaged.

After some consideration, he agreed to the attempt being made.

First of all, he and I went to call upon the divisional commanders concerned. Both of these had actually prepared plans for another infantry and artillery attack, but neither was very confident of the result. Their estimate of probable casualties varied from six hundred to a thousand.

General Maxse listened carefully to their proposed plan of operations; then, turning to me, ordered me to outline my scheme.

It was received with contemptuous silence, but General Maxse, having made up his mind, was not to be deterred. He told the divisional commanders that this was "Baker-Carr's battle" and that any demands I made were to be met. He further pointed out that the number of infantry to be employed was considerably less than half their estimate of probable casualties.

Sanction now having been given, I started my preparations.

A composite company of twelve tanks, under the command of Major Broome of "G" Battalion, was made up from specially selected crews and careful plans were drawn up with the invaluable help of my reconnaissance officer, Williams-Ellis.

The tanks were to move up on the night of the 17th-18th, lie up in the ruins of St. Julien under their camouflage nets during the day of the eighteenth and, before dawn on the nineteenth, were to move up the Poelcapelle road, a pair of tanks being allotted to attack each of the five strong points, while two were kept in reserve. The infantry had been ordered to send forward one platoon for each objective and to remain inactive in position, until a flag was waved through the manhole in the top of the tank, as a signal that all was well; they were then to advance and occupy the captured "pill-box."

The tanks reached St. Julien village in safety, thanks to being allowed to use the corduroy road, and lay there throughout the 18th undetected.

At five a.m. on the 19th, the artillery, as directed, put down a smoke barrage on the strong points, and the tanks in pairs moved slowly up the Poelcapelle road in the growing dawn.

Early that morning I was at General Maxse's Headquarters and we anxiously awaited the news which was to be dispatched from the tanks by pigeon. We had not long to wait.

Soon after seven o'clock, the first message arrived, announcing the capture of the first strong point, the Gun Pits, without opposition. This message was shortly followed by another, telling of the taking of Hillock Farm, most of the garrison of which had beaten a hasty retreat on finding tanks behind them.

Shortly afterwards a further message arrived, stating that the Mont de Hibou had been captured, after being heavily shelled by the tank six-pounder through the backdoor. Several machine guns and forty or fifty prisoners had been taken, in addition to thirty dead being counted.

Our spirits were rising rapidly and soon we were further encouraged by the news of the capture of Triangle Farm, the defenders of which had put up a good fight, most of them being killed.

There was a short lull in the arrival of news, but after a while we learnt that the Cockcroft, the last of our objectives, had fallen, though the tank (its mate having got ditched on the way up) had become stuck in the mud fifty yards away. The firing of a few rounds from its six-pounder, however, had the desired effect, for the defenders ran away and most of them were accounted for by the fire of the Lewis guns.

Our success was now complete.

General Maxse was almost as delighted as myself, not only at the outcome of our venture, but, also, at the astoundingly small casualties. The infantry had had fifteen men wounded, the tanks two killed and twelve wounded, a total of twenty-nine in place of the expected "six hundred to a thousand."

No time was lost by General Maxse in writing out a telegram, informing G.H.Q. that the line on the front of the XVIIIth Corps "had been advanced on a front of over a thousand yards to a depth of five hundred yards, including the capture of five strong points. Total casualties, twenty-nine."

Within a very short time, an inquiry arrived from G.H.Q. demanding to know how this astonishing feat had been accomplished. To this General Maxse laconically replied: "Tanks." In an hour, the chief of the General Staff was on his way out to discover what had happened, and I was instructed to write a full report of the action.

Concrete pill-box in a trench at Gommecourt, March 1917

To General Maxse and to the tank crews, who carried out their orders so splendidly, all the credit for this success is due.

In no other corps of the British Army at that time would such a scheme have been allowed to be attempted. The lie of the roads, so placed as to render the plan feasible, good reconnaissance work by Williams-Ellis, and excellent arrangements by Major Broome (who deservedly received a D.S.O.) were responsible for the rest.

The little battle occasioned very considerable stir and undoubtedly contributed in a large degree to the planning of the Tank Battle of Cambrai.

Without the St. Julien Battle, the Cambrai Battle might never have been fought. If the Cambrai Battle had not been fought, it is certain that tanks, if not actually abolished, could never have played such an important part in the final stages of the war, when tens of thousands of valuable lives, by their aid, were mercifully preserved.

2

Many efforts were made, at various times, to co-operate with the infantry in attacks made during September and early October.

Whenever tanks actually got into action they did good work, but the conditions were such that, of those that started, a bare 10 *per cent*, arrived. All three brigades took part in these spasmodic battles with varying success, the only constant factors being the vile weather and the courage of the crews.

Our reward, however, was soon to come and the ceaseless toil and disappointment of the past three months were to be wiped completely from our minds by the overwhelming success of a battle fought under favourable conditions.

For us the Third Battle of Ypres was finished.

From a tank point of view, except for the action of the 19th of August, it had been a ghastly failure; but the tanks had failed in common with all other arms.

It would have been as logical to abolish the infantry, cavalry, and artillery, as to have abolished the tanks for their lack of success at Ypres.

The tanks failed through being employed in hopelessly unsuitable conditions. If the first submarine had been tested on Salisbury Plain, the results would not have been encouraging.

The infantry failed, not through any lack of leadership, courage, or determination, but merely through being faced by insuperable difficulties. The cavalry did not even have the melancholy satisfaction of failing, yet no one suggested that it should be abolished. Even the artillery failed, inasmuch as it was unable to blast a hole in the enemy's defences, as had been confidently expected.

But it needed foresight, imagination, and courage to visualise the true value of the new weapon, and these qualities were noticeably lacking in high places.

3

For many weeks, unbeknownst to all but a very few, General Elles had been working out a plan with General Byng (now Viscount Byng of Vimy), General Allenby's successor in command of the Third Army. In this scheme the element of surprise, which had been conspicuous by its absence since long past, was to be an important factor and the leading part in the proceedings was to be played by the tanks.

A battle of this nature had always been in our thoughts, but it had seemed to be beyond any hope of attainment, especially after the adverse reports during the Ypres offensive.

Not only was General Elles lucky enough to find a courageous commander, unprejudiced by the shortsighted opinions of others, but he also found, within this commander's area, a stretch of country, adapted in every way to the novel type of battle proposed.

There was to be no artillery preparation whatever to disclose our intentions. This, in itself, constituted an entirely new departure, all previous battles having been marked by an ever-increasing volume and intensity of shelling before the assault took place. The crushing of the wire, formerly the task of the guns and often only partially successful, was to be the duty of the tanks, which were to lead the infantry in place of following.

The terrain, over which these operations were to eventuate, consisted of rolling chalky downs, untouched by shell fire and providing magnificent "going" for the tanks. The Germans had expended enormous labour on this part of their defensive line and regarded it as unassailable. An attack upon it, therefore, would be entirely unsuspected and, if the utmost secrecy were preserved, we should fall on them like a bolt from the blue.

To us of the Tank Corps, who, through constant and daily association, were well aware of what the tanks could do, given a fair field, the proposed plan appeared to be not only practicable, but, actually, certain of fulfilment. It needed, however, great courage on the part of an infantry commander, whose knowledge was primarily based on official reports of a distinctly unfavourable nature, to undertake the responsibility of putting such a scheme into operation. Any failure would necessarily be laid to his account, aggravated by a chorus of "I told you so."

Having been convinced by Elles that the plan was feasible, the next thing for General Byng was to obtain permission from G.H.Q. to put it into effect.

The first answer was an uncompromising negative. Every available man was needed for the Ypres Battle which still obscured the vision of our High Command.

General Byng, however, was not to be so easily discouraged and returned to the charge once more. This time he received a grudging assent, coupled with the warning that he must accept the full responsibility in the event of failure.

G.H.Q.'s evident disapproval of the whole concern was clearly shown in the allocation of troops placed at General Byng's disposition, namely, five divisions which had suffered so severely in the Ypres Battle that they had been withdrawn from the line to refit. The Canadian Corps was also detailed to take part, but, before preparations were complete, it was taken away and sent into the "blood-bath" of the Salient, where, with magnificent gallantry and at appalling loss, it captured the Passchendaele Ridge. We shall see later how the lack of fresh troops prevented the exploitation of our success to limits of an incalculable extent.

The truth of the whole matter is that G.H.Q. had no confidence whatever in the proposed plan.

There were two factors essential to success, secrecy and absolutely reliable reconnaissance work.

In order to achieve the first, no one was told of the plan until the last moment that it was needful for him to know. Those of us who were, of necessity, informed in the early stages, went about disguised as officers of any unit other than the Tank Corps and were compelled to lie, freely and circumstantially, concerning our presence in compromising situations.

General Elles, Hotblack, Martel, Williams-Ellis and others were able to indulge to the fullest extent their predilection for crawling about in unhealthy spots. Masses and masses of material were collected, hundreds of aeroplane photographs taken, and every source of information tapped.

From an analysis of all this material, one fact of paramount importance emerged, in addition to many others of lesser moment. The trenches, which we were to attack, were anything up to fifteen or sixteen feet in width, a broader span than any tank could cross.

The never-failing ingenuity of Central Workshops at Tank Headquarters quickly and effectually disposed of this problem.

Each tank was provided with a huge fascine, composed of brushwood, tightly compressed and bound by iron chains. This fascine was to be carried on the roof of each machine and, when the trench was reached, released by means of a clever contrivance inside the tank. The fascine then rolled to the bottom of the trench and served as a stepping-stone on which the tank could tread and climb out safely on the other side. Each fascine, having once been dropped, could not be used again and, as there were three lines of trenches to be crossed, it was necessary that only one-third of the tanks should deposit their fascines at each of the three lines. It was, therefore, definitely laid down at which trench each machine should drop its fascine, the spot to be marked with a flag as a guide to the others.

Apart from the difficulty of crossing the trench lines, no serious obstacle appeared to exist, though, for a long time, the First Brigade was much exercised in its mind by a watercourse, marked on every map and grandiloquently entitled *"le grand ravin."* Aeroplane photographs failed to disclose anything very alarming and *"le grand ravin"* was subsequently discovered to be the main drain, about three feet wide.

A complete system of tank and infantry co-operation was worked out by Fuller and, whenever occasion offered, was practised with the infantry which was to take part. Company and section commanders were instructed to make friends with their "opposite numbers" of the Foot, with whom they were to work, and to do everything they could to gain their confidence. One of my battalions went so far as to celebrate in anticipation the victory by inviting their infantry coadjutors to dinner, at which eternal friendship was sworn with ardent and alcoholic enthusiasm.

Tank Corps Headquarters, under the camouflage of "The Tank Training Centre," were established in Albert, while Brigade Headquarters were housed in Nissen huts in the vicinity of the corps with which they were respectively operating.

The First Brigade had been allotted to the IIIrd Corps, commanded by Lieutenant-General Sir Charles Woollcombe, K.C.B., K.C.M.G., one of whose two divisions was our old friend, the 51st Highland Territorial, under Major-General Harper, while the other was the 62nd Division, under Major-General (now General Sir Walter) Braithwaite. The 62nd Division at this time was to us an unknown quantity, but on no part of the front was a greater success achieved on the day of battle than on theirs, thanks to their commander's whole-hearted support and the splendid behaviour of the men.

The first conference held at IIIrd Corps Headquarters could not, by any stretch of the imagination, be described as enthusiastic. If the corps commander and his chief staff officer were full of confidence, they did not betray it.

General Braithwaite had never before co-operated with tanks and was prejudiced neither in their favour nor against them; but "Uncle" Harper plainly demonstrated by his attitude that he thoroughly mistrusted the entire plan. He actually said little during the meeting, but after it was over, he took me on one side and described the whole conception as "a fantastic and most unmilitary scheme." Up to the very last moment he was completely lukewarm and, as I learned years later, had not hesitated to communicate his apprehensions to his brigade commanders.

It was not long before General Braithwaite became a confirmed tank enthusiast. He visited all the demonstrations given to the infantry to inspire confidence and was delighted when the tanks, without the least difficulty, negotiated the trench-system and barbed-wire entanglements which the infantry had been invited to construct in the most formidable manner possible.

His faith was reflected throughout the division and the Tank Units co-operating were loud in their praise of the whole-hearted support given.

The troops, holding the front line, were to take no part in the initial attack for fear lest the essential secrecy might be destroyed. In the event this precaution proved to be of paramount importance, the enemy raiding our lines and capturing one or two prisoners. This mishap caused us considerable anxiety, as it was impossible to know to what extent the troops holding the line suspected that an attack was to take place and whether the prisoners, under skilful cross-examination, would be able to conceal any knowledge they did possess.

A concentration of a thousand guns had been collected along the front of about ten thousand yards. Stacks upon stacks of shells were piled alongside the guns, but no "registration" of new guns was permitted; in fact, every precaution was taken to adhere rigidly to the conditions that had previously obtained.

For once, the weather was on our side. There was little or no rain (not, however, that this was of great import in that undisturbed, grassy chalk-land) and low clouds and mist aided to impede observation of the movement of lorries and transport, necessary for bringing up stores.

All movement of tanks was to take place at night, either by road or rail. If, through breakdown or other causes, a tank found itself surprised by dawn, it was ordered to conceal itself immediately beneath its camouflage nets and wait for darkness before proceeding on its way.

A very notable feat was performed by the Railway Staff of the Third Army. On it devolved the task of transporting more than four hundred tanks from the concentration-point at Plateau, near Albert, to the rail-head, where special detraining ramps had been constructed. Only a single line of track existed and the whole move had to be completed in three nights, the last train on each night arriving at such an hour as to allow the tanks to reach their place of concealment, five or six miles distant, before the dawn.

This railway journey was postponed, for reasons of secrecy, till the very last moment, and a schedule was framed which had to be carried out with clockwork precision. The minimum time only was allowed for detraining the tanks and everything depended on meticulous punctuality. We shall see how nearly the whole plan was wrecked by one small, thoughtless act.

4

The First Brigade was to co-operate with the infantry on the extreme left of the attack, with the Canal du Nord, which we were to encounter ten months later from a completely different direction, guarding and running parallel to our left flank.

Our lying-up place was in the extensive woods of Havrincourt, facing the ruined *château* and grounds of the same name across a gently sloping valley, through which ran the celebrated "*grand ravin.*" This valley constituted a no-man's-land of three or four hundred yards in width.

Behind and beyond, lay the wooded heights of Bourlon Wood and Village (the Mecca of the First Brigade), which from its commanding position looked down on the surrounding country and into the

important city of Cambrai, some eight miles distant. Between us and Bourlon lay the villages of Graincourt and Anneux, but we knew that, once the three lines of trenches were safely passed, there was no obstacle of any sort for many miles. If only we could capture the Bourlon Heights, the way to Cambrai lay open before us. The original plan had been to push the Canadian Corps through in motor buses and lorries, but, the Canadian Corps having been withdrawn a fortnight before the battle, we were, except for the cavalry, entirely lacking in troops of exploitation.

Never before had such terrific barbed-wire entanglements been encountered. A peculiarly heavy type of wire had been employed and there were several rows of entanglements of a thickness hitherto undreamt of. If artillery had been called upon to destroy it, it would have taken many weeks and would have cost millions upon millions of money. All element of surprise would have been eliminated and the ground rendered almost impassable. In place of this costly, tedious, and secrecy-destroying method, the tanks were to make passages in their stride, as it were, for the infantry and pass on to their serious work. Special wire-pulling tanks were detailed for clearing the wire for the cavalry, which, at long last, in actual fact were to be provided with a "gap," after waiting in vain for two weary years.

At length every preparation that thought and ingenuity could devise was complete and the first crucial move, by train, was begun.

It was a splendid picture to see train-load after train-load of fourteen machines, each with its fascine in place, waiting for darkness to fall before starting on its journey. This was what every one of us had been dreaming of for many long months past and there was not one man in the Tank Corps who would not gladly have laid down his life if, by so doing, success would have been more assured.

Never before in history has a more whole-hearted, single-minded body of men gone into battle. Our sole thought was for the victorious achievement of our hopes, hopes that by our aid the long and bloody struggle might be shortened, hopes that we might be the means of saving the lives of thousands of our gallant comrades of the infantry.

5

At the rail-head Thorp and I waited anxiously, watch in hand, for the arrival of the first train-load of our tanks.

On the very minute, the train came into view and halted, while the engine was uncoupled and moved back to the rear of the line of

2ND BRIGADE TANKS ON RAILWAY WAGONS AT FINS, CAMBRAI BATTLE, 1917

trucks. This manoeuvre was necessary in order to allow the tanks an uninterrupted passage along the train to the end-on ramp.

The signal was given and slowly the train was pushed towards its ultimate destination. Everybody was so intent on watching the train that an A.S.C. lorry-driver, anxious to proceed on his journey, was allowed to drive his vehicle across the metals in front of the approaching train.

There was a crash, followed by several heavy thuds and a rending of wood and iron. The train stopped with a jerk.

Hastily we ran to the spot.

The first truck, which had hit the lorry, had been completely overturned and the tank on it had fallen and was lying on its side against a low bank. The remains of the lorry, smashed to atoms, lay beneath it. There was no sign whatever of the driver and we found him later, completely flattened out and crushed into the solid earth.

The next three trucks were derailed, though the machines on them remained upright, but the whole permanent-way was torn up and the rails were twisted into fantastic shapes.

It looked a most hopeless mess and there were not a few of the onlookers who stated that, in their opinion, "the whole show was off."

Already much of the time allotted for detrainment had passed. Something desperate had to be done.

Calling for the company commander, I demanded the most efficient tank driver under his command.

A sergeant was produced and he was ordered to start up the engine of the tank on the truck next to the overturned machine, and swing the tank very cautiously until it stood at right angles to the truck, instead of lengthwise. This was successfully accomplished. The driver was then instructed to move the tank forward inch by inch, till its nose gently tilted downwards and rested on the earthen bank by the side of the track; slowly and carefully the machine crept forward till, at length, with a dull splintering of the side of the platform of the truck, it came to rest wholly on *terra firma*.

As quickly as we dared, the tanks on the other two, derailed tracks were unloaded in a similar manner. The remainder of the train was uncoupled and shunted into the second siding prepared. Another trainload for this siding was due shortly, but signalmen were dispatched to hold it up till we were ready for it.

Most of the railway personnel at this rail-head was drawn from an American Railway Company and it was amusing to listen to their comments on the tanks, which they were now seeing for the first time. They were splendid fellows and knew their job thoroughly, but they were firmly convinced that the mess could not be cleared up for an hour or more.

But they did not know the tanks.

One machine was sent off at once to pull his fallen brother on to his feet. A couple of machines were hitched on to the derailed trucks with wire hawsers and pulled them to one side. The hawsers were then attached to the twisted metals, which were pulled clear of the damaged track. In five minutes, the permanent-way was clear; in ten, new metals had been laid and a messenger hastily sent off to bring in the second train load, which was at once unloaded with marvellous rapidity. The third train was delayed by only four minutes; the fourth and subsequent trains arrived absolutely on time.

As I stood watching the railway gang complete the repairs to the track, I felt a hand laid on my shoulder. I turned and found the captain of the American Railway Company standing at my side.

"Say, boss," he said gravely. "Can them tanks of yours *sing*?"

6

The evening and night before the battle were filled with anxious activity.

In order to ensure that no mistakes might arise in moving up to the exact spot where the co-operating infantry were in waiting, a wide tape was laid along the track that each machine was to follow. Tens of thousands of yards were laid by tank commanders, under the supervision of the reconnaissance officers, and the result fully justified the time and labour expended. Each tank commander knew that at the end of his tape was standing the platoon commander, with whom he had already trained and made friends.

My staff and myself had planned to go down to the front-line trenches at three a.m., but, after a midnight meal, we started off and arrived in the line soon after one a.m. My old friend and helper of machine gun days, Lindsay (at that time Machine Gun Officer of the First Army), was paying me a visit in order to see the show.

Slowly we made our way down towards the trenches. The night was overcast and still. There was hardly a sound, except for the occasional boom of a gun, in accordance with the decision that everything should appear normal to the enemy.

Safely arrived at the spot, specially selected for us by Williams-Ellis, we spent our time peering out over the parapet into the gloom. We sat on the fire-step and wondered and wondered if anything had been left undone which might have been done. We discussed General Elles' decision to lead the attack in a tank and asked ourselves whether it was wise or not. All of us were very anxious, as his loss would have been irreplaceable and we knew that, once in action, he would fling all precaution to the winds. I, personally, also felt slightly resentful as I had, on more than one occasion, suggested to him that I might go into battle in a tank and was promptly threatened with every sort of pain and penalty if I did so. Elles was wise enough not to disclose his plan, till it was too late for his superiors to object.

Suddenly, at about half-past four, an hour and a half before zero, a heavy barrage was put down on the trenches in which we were peacefully seated. We hastily retired to a convenient dugout and sat anxiously wondering whether our plans had been betrayed. For half an hour the shelling continued; then, as suddenly as it had begun, it died away and all was quiet again. Even then we were not quite happy in our minds and uneasily waited for the dawn.

A few minutes before six a.m., zero hour, a buzz ran along the line.

"Here they come."

In the dim light, the vast bulk of the tanks could be faintly seen moving towards the line.

Almost as though a warning-bell had been rung by the approaching tanks, so precise was the synchronisation, a thousand guns at that moment flamed into activity. With an ear-splitting roar the barrage came down and the infantry, rising to their feet, followed their protecting tanks.

The German barrage replied, but it was paltry in comparison with ours and many of the German guns were put out of action after firing a few rounds. Rockets and S.O.S. signals flared from every point of the enemy line, calling for help where no help was to be found.

Quickly the first line of wire was reached, trampled and crushed down by the tanks. Through these lanes the infantry poured and leapt down on to the panic-stricken defenders, who put up their hands and surrendered, almost without firing a shot.

On again, meeting with little opposition, the tanks moved forward towards the second and third lines, followed by laughing, cheering soldiers. This was a proper sort of battle, they thought; lots of fun and little danger.

TANK ADVANCING THROUGH WIRE ENTANGLEMENTS

Only at a few points was serious resistance encountered, though in one case a heavy loss of tanks occurred, partly through evil fortune, partly through the heroism of one single German officer, and partly through a somewhat "ca' canny" attitude on the part of the accompanying infantry.

The tanks, followed at too great an interval by the infantry, topped a slope outside the village of Flesquières. On the far side of the crest stood the relics of a German field battery. One gun and one officer alone remained. With splendid devotion and self-sacrifice, this officer fired his gun at point-blank range as the top of each tank appeared above the crest-line and knocked out no less than sixteen of them before he himself was killed beside his gun.

The result of this check was far-reaching. The triumphant advance was badly delayed and much valuable time lost. It was not only vexatious in the highest degree, but doubly so in that the incident should never have taken place.

General Harper, commanding the 51st Division, the troops concerned in the Flesquières attack, had, as I pointed out above, never had any faith in the scheme of operations. He had laid down a system of co-operation with tanks which was, essentially, based on disbelief. If all went well with the tanks, "my little fellers," as he affectionately called his division, could take advantage of the situation; if things, however, fared badly, then his men would not be implicated in any disaster; and would suffer no heavy losses.

The result of this method of "co-operation" was that the tanks outdistanced the laggard infantry and were massacred by the action of a single man whom one well-directed bullet would have settled. If the whole-hearted faith of the 62nd Division had been displayed by the commander of the 51st Division, the check at Flesquières would never have taken place and no "regrettable incident" would have marred our progress.

Nobody could help admiring the great courage of the German artillery officer, but to us it appeared somewhat tactless, to put it mildly, for the British commander-in-chief specifically to mention him in dispatches. We all regarded this commendation as a direct incentive to others "to go and do likewise," a consummation sincerely to be deprecated at any rate by the Tank Corps. I feel sure that hundreds of German officers gladly would have laid down their lives if, by their self-sacrifice and devotion, they could merit the distinction of being mentioned in enemy dispatches.

Chivalry to the fallen is much to be admired, after it can do no harm, but any inducement to raise the courage of your foes is poor policy.

As a German naval officer is reported to have said at the beginning of the war, when saved from drowning at the imminent risk of his rescuers:

You English will always be fools and we Germans will never be gentlemen.

7

On other parts of the line, the battle had gone forward with equal success, though there, too, unfortunate incidents had occurred A bridge across a canal gave way and further progress in that direction was held up. On the whole, however, things had gone as favourably as we had dared to hope and one of the most remarkable victories in the annals of the British Army had been won.

But, it will be asked, what of the cavalry? Surely masses of galloping squadrons had passed through the "gap" and were riding *ventre à terre* through village and hamlet, cutting down the fleeing enemy amid loud cheers from the down-trodden and enslaved peasantry.

Not a bit of it.

The cavalry, after blocking all the roads for miles, sat down behind a hill, remained there all day and then returned homewards, again blocking up the roads which were desperately needed to bring up every sort of supplies for tanks and infantry.

What a chance that day was missed! Never before and never again was such an opportunity offered.

On each section of the front, gaps in the wire, a quarter of a mile or more wide, had been made; the "going" was splendid, and from midday onwards, except in a few isolated spots, organised resistance had ceased to exist.

Bourlon Wood, Bourlon Village, even Cambrai could have been captured. The only reason why the 62nd Division failed to capture Bourlon Village was solely due to exhaustion.

Tanks, their crews perched outside on the roof, pushed on a long distance in front of our high-water mark without meeting any opposition, but the infantry, eager and victorious though they were, were physically incapable of going any farther.

Why, then, did not the cavalry avail itself of this golden opportunity?

It is a difficult question to answer, though one fact which is known, has an important bearing on the subject namely, that the cavalry leaders were strictly prohibited, from taking action without the permission of superior authority.

This, in itself, largely explains their astounding inactivity, but it does not explain why such orders were issued.

The first Cavalry Division, under Major-General Mullens, was allotted to the front on which I was working, and he and every officer and man of the division were eagerly looking forward to coming to grips with the enemy once more.

And yet the only cavalry-man whom I saw that day was the cavalry liaison officer attached to the First Brigade of the Tank Corps, who sent back message after message reporting the successful progress of the battle. At the end of the day he was almost in tears of disappointment and mortification. The one great chance in the war for mounted men came and went on the 20th November 1917, never to recur.

By the next day, enemy reinforcements had been rushed down to the threatened points and resistance stiffened throughout the defensive line. The first onrush had spent itself, the all-important element of surprise had disappeared and there were no fresh troops to carry on the assault, without giving the enemy time to breathe.

The original intention had been that the attackers should burst on the enemy, inflict the maximum of damage with a minimum of loss to themselves, and retire to their previous starting-point; in other words, it was to be a gigantic raid.

In one day, an advance of seven miles had been accomplished, eight thousand prisoners had been made and more than a hundred guns captured. The total losses suffered by the British amounted to four thousand, less than one-half of the enemy losses, excluding the dead.

If the original intention had been rigidly carried out in its entirety, all would have been well, but G.H.Q., dumbfounded by this totally unexpected success, lost its sense of proportion and altered the whole conception of the scheme. It was unthinkable to them to give up territory thus cheaply gained. It had taken three solid months of blood and slaughter to achieve an equal advance on the Ypres front. No. The new positions must be retained and consolidated, although it was obvious to the most inexperienced eye that a very dangerous salient in the German line had been created. However, that was not the affair of the Tank Corps, and orders were issued to clean up and execute the necessary repairs before retiring to our new quarters for rest and winter training.

Congratulatory messages were showered upon us in almost embarrassing quantities, and, if the pressing recommendations of the infantry commanders had been complied with, every officer of the Tank Corps would have received a D.S.O. and every N.C.O. and man a D.C.M.

It was, indeed, a difficult task to choose from the mass of recommendations for awards that confronted me. The only thing I could do was to put aside, however regretfully, all those which told only of duty splendidly done. That duty I regarded as what was expected from the officers and men of the Tank Corps and I confined my recommendations to those who had, in some manner, exceeded the high standard of behaviour demanded. Even then my list was relatively large, but I am proud to say that not one single recommendation ever put forward by me failed to bring its reward.

8

A few days later, the 30th November, the Germans launched a vigorous attack at each end of the salient created, with a view to cutting off the entire slice. On the left, where my brigade was situated, the line held: firm and inflicted heavy losses on the enemy; on the, right, however, a rapid advance was made and several villages were captured. So sudden and unexpected was the assault that one divisional commander is reported to have made his escape in his pyjamas!

The Second Brigade of the Tank Corps added fresh laurels to those already gained, by its splendid work in assisting to stem the enemy's onrush. Most of their, machines were in various stages of *déshabille,* but, within an incredibly short space of time, from twenty to thirty tanks moved forward to meet the enemy and took part in the heavy fighting.

For a couple of days or more the attack continued though we, on the left, our line holding in its entirety, took no active part.

By a miraculous piece of luck, I happened to visit the Third Army Headquarters on the morning of the 4th of December. After discussing my business with Major-General (now Sir Louis) Vaughan, I got up to take my leave.

"This withdrawal is rather disappointing," he said, as he wished me goodbye. "But you'll get all your tanks out all right, I hope."

"What do you mean?" I asked. "I haven't heard anything about a withdrawal."

"What?" he exclaimed. "Orders were sent to Elles this morning, telling him that the line was being withdrawn to the original position tonight, and that all tanks must be clear by eleven o'clock."

"Elles went into G.H.Q. early this morning. I saw Fuller, but he knew nothing about it. How was the envelope addressed?"

"To Elles, personally, by name. That probably accounts for it. You'd better rush back to Tank Headquarters, and see that orders are issued immediately."

Hastily I dashed off to Albert, where I told Fuller what had happened, and we found the orders lying unopened on Elles' table. In a few minutes urgent messages were dispatched to all tank units warning them of the coming move. Many valuable hours had already been lost, and it looked as though a large number of tanks, which had been dismantled for the purpose of repairs, would have to be abandoned.

Feverish activity prevailed throughout the afternoon and evening, until the last possible moment. Many of the tanks were put into condition to enable them to move, but many also, alas! had to be left, although attempts were made to render them useless to the enemy by blowing them up.

It was a tragic finale to a memorable battle, but we of the tanks had the satisfaction of knowing that we had accomplished all we had set out to do and more.

The tanks had completely justified the confidence placed in them, and had made for themselves a secure position in the British Army.

A new era in warfare had dawned, but only a few deep thinkers were aware of it.

CHAPTER 16

Awaiting the Enemy's Onslaught

1

The winter of 1917-18 was a period of waiting and suspense. The Russian Front had ceased to exist and an enormous number of British troops were being employed in innumerable "side-shows," in which the politicians still maintained their childlike faith. Until the American Army arrived, the Germans would possess a considerable superiority in numbers.

It was obvious to everybody that the enemy would put in a heavy blow at one or more points of the line. It was his last chance before the Allies once more out numbered him.

In addition to this, the more stringent rigour of our blockade, now that the Americans, having entered the war, had discovered that a blockade was fully justified and, for the time being, had forgotten about "the freedom of the seas," was making itself very thoroughly felt in Germany. Letters and diaries taken from prisoners revealed how serious was the state of their internal affairs, the only remedy for which was victory.

The situation for the Allies, generally, was an anxious one, but for the British, in particular, it was doubly so.

In response to urgent pressure by the French, our Home Government had, in face of strenuous opposition from Sir Douglas Haig, agreed to take over another forty miles of front, though the number of troops at his disposal had not been sensibly increased.

Here again, as in the case of the Third Battle of Ypres, policy overrode strategy, and the result might have been far more disastrous, even to the extent of losing the war, if the enemy had appreciated more fully the lessons of the Retreat from Mons and had realised that it is

Sir Douglas Haig with General Joffre and Marshal Foch

exhaustion both of men and supplies, rather than the resistance of the defenders, which brings an offensive to a standstill when the opposing force is in full retreat. A hundred tanks and a thousand lorries, loaded with machine gunners and their necessary equipment, would have delivered Amiens and Abbeville into their hands, dividing the French from the British, with results that might, and probably would, have been fatal.

This was the third, and last, chance of the Germans to win the war.

2

The Tank Corps, training and refitting, was scattered over a large area that rendered supervision difficult. The battalions of the First Brigade were dotted about between Amiens and Albert, my headquarters being established in the Château of Henencourt.

The winter of 1917-18 was one of intense cold, and though the house, built and floored entirely with white stone, must have been a charming spot in summer, in December and January it was the chilliest and draughtiest building I have ever known.

For a week or more after Christmas we were completely snowed in, but my staff and myself managed to keep ourselves warm and amused by skating on the small artificial pond in the grounds.

We were also enlivened later by a visit, for a fortnight or more, of three of the principal members of the French Tank Corps Staff.

It is popularly supposed that the English are the poorest linguists in the world, but, personally, I am of the opinion that the French are far worse. I am not speaking of the travelled, idle class, but of the vast middleclass, which constitutes the bulk of a nation.

Wherever I went, whether it was to a French Army Headquarters, a Machine Gun School, or a Tank Training Centre, I found that no one, with very rare exceptions, was able to speak a word of English.

Fortunately two of the staff of the First Brigade could speak French fluently and two others could "carry on" in the language, for none of the three French officers knew any English at all.

They were all charming men and bursting with enthusiasm to learn. They wished to see everything and to visit every battlefield on which the tanks had ever fought. It was a busy fortnight for us, as we had not only to satisfy their insatiable craving for knowledge, but we had, also, to attend to our ordinary work.

In the early days of the visit, before we had shed some of our superlative politeness and were able to discuss matters more frankly, they insisted, much to our embarrassment, in shaking hands on every possible and impossible occasion. The average number of "shake-hands" daily averaged seven times. As there were five of us and three of them, each occasion called for fifteen "shake-hands," a total of a hundred and five *per diem*.

This was altogether too much and, after a few days, when we were on more intimate terms, I asked the senior officer, a colonel, why they did it.

"Because it is the English custom," was the astonishing reply.

I asked, also, how it was that none of them spoke English, but, apparently, they had not been taught English at school and, since, had had no opportunity to learn.

The Intelligence Officer, an exceedingly capable, quickwitted boy, confided in me that he had made up his mind to learn English and was already trying to pick up what he could of the language.

One morning he came into the breakfast-room. His face was beaming and his eyes were bright with excitement. He came to my chair and held out his hand.

"Good noight!" he said triumphantly.

3

One other French visitor I entertained, but only for a night.

Late one afternoon, there arrived at the *château* an exceedingly dirty and dishevelled *poilu,* who said he wished to speak to me.

The man was shown into my office, and, to my astonishment, addressed me in perfect English. I was, also, surprised when he asked me if I might spend the night in the house, with which he seemed strangely familiar. However, I took him to be a steward of sorts and consented to his request. He thanked me cordially and hoped that we were comfortable and so forth.

The man was obviously well educated and had good manners, so I asked him to dine in our mess. He accepted gratefully and disappeared.

At dinner-time he reappeared, looking much cleaner and more respectable. In each hand he clasped a bottle of Burgundy.

"A little celebration," he explained.

When dinner was over, he rose from his chair, and, murmuring his excuses, left the room.

In a few moments he returned, bearing a cobwebby bottle of old brandy.

"There are but few left in the cellar," he said, "but this is an occasion."

"Won't anybody object to your handing out the wine like this?" I demanded.

"Only my wife," he replied, with a smile. "But she is quite safe. She is in the South of France."

"Who are you, then?" I asked.

"I am the Marquis de R——, the owner of this *château* and very much at your service," he answered, with a little bow.

4

In February 1918 the symptoms of a tremendous enemy offensive became more and more evident. The main question resolved itself into a problem of where he would strike. There were many points strategically convenient and it was, at first, impossible to decide which of these he would select.

Every man, every gun, would be needed to stem his onslaught, and although, up till now, tanks had been regarded as a purely offensive weapon, some use might be made of them in defence.

Our training, therefore, was abruptly terminated and brigades were moved forward to the armies to which they had already been allotted.

The First Brigade was placed at the disposal of the First Army at Ranchicourt, in the Lens area, and plans were drawn up for co-operation with the infantry.

The army commander, General Sir H. Horne (now Lord Horne, G.C.B., K.C.M.G.) had had no experience of tanks in battle, but like everyone else, he had been greatly impressed by the successful Cambrai Battle. Both he and his chief of staff, Major-General Anderson (now Lieutenant-General Sir Hastings Anderson, K.C.B.) were most helpful and it was a matter of regret to me that no occasion arose when tank action was possible, although for many weary weeks the crews, much against my earnest representations, fought with the infantry in the line as Lewis gun detachments.

There was little we could do but wait.

My headquarters were established in Nissen huts, in a wood not far from Ranchicourt, with the battalions spread out along a wide front. Various classes and courses of training were held, but there was little for senior commanders to do when once the dispositions for battle had been decided and put into effect.

The task of giving lectures on tanks had devolved on myself and, owing to the universal interest created by the Cambrai Battle, I was frequently called upon to lecture to all sorts of Schools of Instruction.

Strictly speaking, I should have performed this duty only within the First Army area, but, by an accident, the giving of lectures outside also fell to my lot.

In the winter of 1916-17, while I was still in command of "C" Battalion, I happened one afternoon to be at Tank Corps Headquarters, where I found Elles greatly perturbed in his mind by the fact that he was "billed" to lecture on tanks to the Staff College Course at Hesdin. He insisted upon my accompanying him to the school.

Arrived there, we had a cup of tea with the *commandant*, Colonel Hare, in his private room.

At five o'clock, Hare got up from his chair and announced that everybody was in the lecture-hall, ready to begin.

"By the way, Hare," said Elles, "Baker-Carr is going to give the lecture instead of me."

"But I've never given a lecture on tanks in my life," I began. "I haven't got a note—"

My expostulations were cut short by Elles, who thrust into my hand a sheet of note-paper with half a dozen hieroglyphics written on it.

"Here are my notes," he said. "Use them."

Further protest was impossible, as Hare was already leading the way into the lecture-hall, where the seventy or eighty students were assembled.

Before I knew what was happening, Hare had begun to address the audience.

"Gentlemen, the lecture this evening on tanks was to have been given by General Elles. It will be given instead by Colonel Baker-Carr."

He motioned me towards the lecture-table and seated himself on one side of the platform, with the ideal chairman's expression on his face of "Now we're in for a real treat!"

Inwardly cursing Elles, I took my place at the table and spread the sheet of note-paper in front of me.

"What the deuce am I going to talk about?" I thought to myself, as I tried to decipher Elles' so-called "notes."

I could make out, by the aid of some guess-work, that the first heading was "Machines not miracles."

Here at any rate was a cue, and off I started.

The lecture-platform possesses one privilege, at least, in common with the pulpit (though the pulpit enjoys it even more than the lecture-platform), namely, that the audience is usually polite enough to listen in silence and credits the speaker with some inside knowledge of his subject.

I gained confidence after a moment or two when I remembered that, little though I myself knew of my subject, my hearers knew infinitely less.

As I progressed, I called to mind an article, recently appearing in the *Daily Mail,* which purported to be the diary of a tank officer, giving the most outrageous and grotesque account of a week's continuous fighting, during the Battle of the Somme, in a tank.

This "diary" I quoted at some length and begged my audience not to believe one word of it.

"The article," I said in conclusion, "is stated to have been written by 'a young Australian.'"

Immediately there was a roar of merriment and of shouts of 'Good old 'Orace!"

I was somewhat startled by this outburst, as I did not at that time know that a young Australian officer was going through the Staff Course who, while universally popular, afforded enormous amusement to his fellow-students by his boastful manner, and was affectionately known as "'Orace."

The main thing, as far as I was concerned, was that I had my hearers laughing. If you can do that in the first five minutes of a lecture, the rest is easy.

As we drove back in the car to Bermicourt, Elles turned to me.

"Thank goodness!" he said with a sigh of relief. "That settles it. You'll give all lectures on tanks in future, Baker."

One lecture I remember in particular, given to all the corps, division, and brigade commanders and staffs of the First Army.

It was, in many ways, a difficult audience to address, as, of necessity, the lecturer must lay down the law somewhat, and my hearers were, almost without exception, considerably my seniors.

After the lecture, which apparently was a complete success, an informal talk took place. A great deal of discussion ensued and many theories were advanced. General Braithwaite, my best friend of the

Cambrai Battle, who was now commanding an army corps, was one of those present and expressed in most generous terms his opinion of the value of tanks. He even went so far as to attribute his own advancement to the great help he had received from them.

This tribute, though far from being the actual case, was especially welcome, as many commanders, after a battle, were prone to arrogate all the credit to the units under their own command.

5

Still we awaited the impending blow. Everything now pointed to an attack on the new line, taken over recently from the French by our Fifth Army, under the command of General Sir Hubert Gough.

It was an obvious point to assault.

The defence line, which the French had organised, was lacking in almost every particular. The trenches were poor, the machine gun arrangements faulty, and the barbed-wire entanglements conspicuous by their absence.

The troops at General Gough's disposal were totally inadequate for the length of front to be held. A protest had been entered by him and more men had been urgently demanded, but none were forthcoming and the pessimistic prognostications of the were regarded with disbelief.

The correctness of his judgment was proved on the 21st March 1918.

Once again, "*Unser Gott*" was on the side of the Germans. The weather, which up till now had been bright and clear, became foggy and rendered observation by our artillery almost impossible.

Under the protection of a dense mist and a terrific barrage of gas-shells and high explosive, the German attack moved rapidly forward. Thanks to the low visibility and the thinly held line, the enemy was able to make gaps in our defences with amazing speed. Profiting by our mistakes, he had staked everything on the element of surprise and was fully justified in the result.

Along the whole front of the Fifth Army, bodies of troops, specially trained and magnificently led, made holes in our defensive line. There was no semblance of the old method of continuous waves of attackers, and each group moved forward to its objective independently. Fresh masses of troops were constantly being pushed on and, as soon as one body was spent, another was ready to take its place.

So rapid was the advance that confusion reigned and organised resistance broke down. Communications were destroyed and orders were unable to be transmitted. The headquarters of corps, divisions, and brigades were moved in haste to the rear and touch with units was completely lost.

For nearly a fortnight chaos reigned. Huge gaps in our line existed and nobody knew, from day to day, precisely what was the real position.

The action of the tanks of the Fourth Brigade, attached to the Fifth Army, during this *débâcle* was, of necessity, extremely limited, but everything was done that could be done to cover the retirement of the infantry. Most of the tanks, however, had soon to be abandoned, after hasty demolition by the crews, owing to a bridge across the Somme being destroyed by our own troops. The personnel, salving only their Lewis guns and ammunition, was organised into sections and lent valuable aid in rear-guard actions.

The enemy offensive extended also to other portions of the line on the front of the Third and First Armies. Although progress there was not so rapid as in the first instance, it was rapid enough to cause much confusion and alarm.

At that time, the British Army, stretched out almost to breaking-point along too wide a front, possessed little in the way of reserves. Even if a moderate number of reserves had been available, it would have been difficult to know where to throw them in, when so many holes, which needed damming, existed. The French, it is true, had a number of divisions in reserve, but they, too, were expecting a heavy attack and were disinclined to denude themselves for our benefit.

The system of *imperium in imperio* was soon to be found wanting, but it was only after the decision to appoint Marshal Foch as *Generalissimo* of the Allied Forces, that steps were taken to form a general pool of reserves, to be used, irrespective of nationality, wherever they might be required.

All the brigades of the Tank Corps, except the First Brigade, were mixed up in the retirement.

Spread out along a vast front, they proved only of purely local value. Two or three tanks, especially when the infantry are retreating, can accomplish little, except to slow up the enemy's rate of progress. Time after time this was done, but it usually ended by the crews being compelled, by the exhaustion of their petrol, to abandon their machines, after destroying them to the best of their ability.

The small, light tank, the Whippet, as it was named, took part in

Whippet tank on the Western Front

one or two successful actions and inflicted heavy loss on the enemy. It was, at this time, an unknown quantity and its encouraging *début* was a great source of gratification to everybody and big things were hoped of it when the position was reversed and the Germans, instead of the British, were in retreat.

The First Brigade, strung out along the front of the First Army, was fortunate in that the enemy was unable to make rapid headway on this section. No tanks took part in the fighting and none were lost, but I was called upon to form Lewis gun detachments from the personnel and distribute them along the line to assist the infantry.

At the time, I strongly opposed this decision and, willing and anxious though I was to lend any aid I could, it appeared to me to be a sinful waste of valuable, highly trained men to send tank crews into the line to be killed without adequate return.

The total number of tank personnel in the brigade, available for this work, did not exceed seven hundred and fifty, including officers, N.C.O.s, and men. Although the actual fire-power of these Lewis gun detachments was out of all proportion to their small number, yet their value outside a tank was infinitesimal in comparison with that inside a tank.

These detachments, dotted about on a front of several miles, could have but little real worth. It is true that we had "our backs against the wall," but the relatively small help that these diminutive parties could give was out of all proportion to the inestimable assistance which they would be able to afford as tank crews, when tanks once more could be employed to advantage.

The members of a tank crew were the most highly and most widely trained men in the British Army.

Every man was a skilled machine-gunner most of them were trained six-pounder gunners; most were fully competent drivers; most, if not all, were able to read a map and steer by compass; every single man was, to a greater or lesser degree, a mechanic.

It took many, many months to train a man to be a competent member of a crew, even from the theoretical standpoint. Actual experience in battle was further needed before he could be regarded as a real, reliable tank man.

Each tank crew was a definite, permanent entity and was encouraged to regard itself as such. Tremendous rivalry existed between crews, with the happiest results to efficiency. If, through casualties in action, sickness, promotion, or any other cause, a tank crew lost one or more of its members, some little time elapsed before that crew regained its previous standard of efficiency and the mutual confidence which was essential for its welfare.

Almost every day, new casualties among my Lewis gun detachments were reported and, almost every day, I begged the Army Commander to let them go, but, Pharaoh-like, he constantly put me off, promising me that, before long, they should be relieved.

The front of the First Army, less seriously attacked than in the south, managed, for the most part, to hold, although in many places it was forced to bend back.

Several times I put forward plans for offensive action by tanks with infantry co-operation, but, for various reasons (chiefly lack of available troops), these schemes never came to fruition.

One plan, in particular, I urged upon the First Army and, for a long time, it seemed as though it might be put into effect.

The enemy had created a big bulge in our line in the neighbourhood of Merville, forming, for them, a dangerous salient. Very briefly, my scheme was to send fifteen or twenty Whippet tanks, followed by a number of heavy tanks, up the road that ran at the back of the salient and connected the flanks of the bulge. The infantry, with a large body of tanks, was then to attack the front of the salient and drive back the enemy on to the line of the Whippets and their accompanying heavy machines. The attack was to be carried out, on the St. Julien principle, without artillery preparation and relying mainly on surprise and audacity.

The army commander was favourably inclined towards the project and all the preliminary plans were drawn out.

But, alas! counsels of "playing safe" once more prevailed and the scheme was reluctantly abandoned.

6

Meanwhile, the German offensive continued, though, of necessity, at a much reduced rate of progress, but one began to wonder if anything could ever stop it.

Then came the historic Conference at Doullens and Sir Douglas Haig, with splendid and unselfish patriotism, agreed to Marshal Foch being placed in supreme command of all troops on the Western Front.

Now, for the first time in the war, an undivided programme of offensive and defensive action was capable of being put into effect.

The situation, up till now, had been that of a game of chess, in which the player of black was pitted against two players of white, each independent of the other and mutually distrustful. Black had called "check" and white's king was in imminent danger. Almost at any moment "check-mate" might be called and the game irrevocably lost.

At such a moment only one course was possible, but it needed a self-sacrificing courage to take the necessary step. Happily for England, Sir Douglas Haig was a big enough man to realise that by means of this solution, and of this solution only, the saving of the game might yet be accomplished. He handed over to his partner the entire control of white's future moves.

Sanction for the formation of a General Reserve was given and, after some slightly acrimonious discussion, the ratio of the relative number of divisions to be supplied from the French and British Armies respectively was decided.

The Supreme Council at Versailles, also, came into being, with Henry Wilson, by special request of Marshal Foch, as Chief British Representative.

The appointment of Henry Wilson was inevitable. Of all the British generals he was the only one in whom our Allies had any real faith.

From the very beginning, he had been regarded by the French as our one really competent soldier, and Poincare, with childlike candour, speaks, in the last published volume of his monumental work, of the efforts made by his compatriots in 1914 to put Henry Wilson in command of the British Expeditionary Force in place of Sir John French.

At Versailles Wilson was destined to remain until he was summoned to England to take up the post of Chief of the Imperial General Staff. His tenure of the appointment on the Supreme Council was coincident with the lowest ebb of the Allied fortunes.

The outlook was discouraging in the extreme.

British G.H.Q., despite their brave outward show of confidence, was in reality a prey to the gravest apprehensions. The French, as a nation, were weary to death of the war and trembling on the brink of catastrophic internal troubles. The position in Italy was critical in the extreme.

If any man in the world realised the anxiety and; perplexity of the situation to the full, that man was Henry Wilson. But never for one instant did he allow his calm, serene demeanour to be disturbed, and

Marshal Foch

he planned and schemed and toiled with the same imperturbability that he had already shown during the Retreat from Mons.

A truly great man.

7

By mid-April the position seemed almost desperate. The promised reinforcements, despite all statements made to the contrary, had not arrived. On almost every part of the line considerable penetration had been effected and still the tide of invasion flowed.

Throughout all this seeming evidence of disaster, Foch steadfastly pursued his theory of war. Many years previously, when chief of the French equivalent of our Staff College, he had laid down that, in a deadlock, it is the side which in the end possesses an efficient reserve which wins.

This theory was now to be put to the supreme test of war.

While British G.H.Q. was bewailing the loss of so many towns and villages captured, so many thousands of acres of fresh territory passing into enemy's hands, Foch was carefully keeping count of the numbers of German divisions engaged, used up, and withdrawn. To him the loss of a few thousand yards of devastated country was as nothing in comparison with the fact that half a dozen fresh enemy divisions had been employed and worn out.

Behind our line, a vast army of reserves lived and had their being in motor buses and lorries.

This mobile reserve moved up and down the front to any spot where danger threatened. As soon as the crisis was past, this "travel-ling-circus" was dispatched to some other threatened point in case of need, but usually the onslaught, having spent itself in the capture of another mile or so of barren and useless territory, came to a standstill without the intervention of the reserve force.

British G.H.Q. was far too liable to attribute importance to ter-ritorial losses and gains and, in spite of all our boasts concerning the "killing of Germans," great stress was always laid on the actual ad-vancement of our line.

On a front of a thousand yards, we have advanced our line to a depth of two hundred yards.

How often did one read such a statement in the official *communi-que!* But what on earth was the value of this gain?

Unless some tactical advantage, such as the acquisition of high

239

ground, was secured by this advance, it merely meant that more trenches had to be dug, more wire put up, longer communications were entailed and, possibly, a nasty little salient created.

Conversely, the loss of ground weighed heavily on their mind, though such ground might be absolutely and utterly valueless. The old Somme battlefield, for instance, a shell-pitted, desolate wilderness from Bapaume to Albert, could be of no real value to either side. By all means let us inflict on the enemy a maximum of casualties in his efforts to capture it, but do not let us lament the loss of the actual terrain, which could not benefit him one iota.

At the end of April, a decision was taken by G.H.Q. which, if put into effect, would have had far-reaching and calamitous results.

Every man in France belonging to the British Army, who could bear arms, had been hurried into the trench line and still the cry was for more.

Was there no source of supply which had not yet been fully drained?

Yes. There was one, the Tank Corps. It was, it is true, only a drop in the ocean, a mere four or five thousand fighting men, but, in these desperate days, even that small number was something.

The immediate and pressing needs of the moment seemed to have blinded British G.H.Q. to the requirements of the future when, if the war was to be won, offensive action would once more be the order of the day.

In the minds of some of the highly placed individuals at G.H.Q. there still lingered doubts about the ultimate importance of the tank. It was still regarded in certain quarters as a "stunt" weapon and one which, having once been disclosed, had lost most, if not all of its efficacy.

The Battle of Cambrai had been a perfect God-send, of success after the wallowing for months in the bloody morasses of the Salient and a generous tribute had been paid to the achievement of the tanks.

On the other hand, the consensus of opinion at G.H.Q. was that the tank had shot its bolt. "A splendid show," as Elles was told, after the battle of the 20th November, by the Chief of the General Staff, Sir L. Kiggell, seated in a Mahatma-like atmosphere of isolation and contemplation in his office at Montreuil, "but one that can never be repeated."

However, cogent and pressing though the situation was, the event

Mark V Tank

proved that the decision of G.H.Q. to reduce the number of tank battalions by one-half was a grave mistake and only to be explained by a counsel of despair.

Elles, naturally, was terribly disturbed on receiving the news. Both he and Fuller, with admirable foresight and imagination, were already looking forward to the time when the Tank Corps, armed with the immensely superior new model, the Mark V, would, in conjunction with the infantry, fall upon the battle-spent enemy divisions and hurl them back as quickly as they had come.

This proposed reduction threatened not only a considerable diminution in the numbers of trained personnel which would, in his opinion, be urgently needed for our counter-offensive, but the production of new machines, now at length coming forward in satisfactory quantity, would be completely dislocated and would take many months to get into working order once more.

"Give me three days' leave to go to Paris," I said, when Elles informed me of the decision.

"What for?" he asked.

"Never you mind," I replied.

"All right," he said at length. "But I should like to know what you're up to."

"Better you shouldn't. I'll go tomorrow."

The next day I started, arriving in Paris in the afternoon. I at once rang up an old and trusted friend, one of the British officers attached to the Supreme Council at Versailles, and asked myself to lunch with him. He gladly assented and told me that a French Cabinet Minister was also coming and would call for me at the Ritz Hotel to bring me down in his car.

On the morrow the Cabinet Minister duly arrived. Whether he thought that I belonged to the inner councils of the British, I do not know, but during the drive to Versailles he gave me all sorts of information that would have come as a horrible shock to the general public.

In the first place, the French nation, he told me, was so war-weary that it was prepared to accept almost any terms which the enemy might offer. The army, according to him, was in an appalling condition and on the very verge of mutiny. Whole units had left their trenches, taken possession of railway trains and proceeded to Paris. There the troops, ordered to round them up, had defied authority and joined the deserters. Senegalese black troops had eventually been called upon to take action and had responded nobly. The "strike" of waiters and *midinettes,* which was made much of in the papers, was merely a clever piece of camouflage to conceal the true situation.

At the time I was inclined to think that the picture he painted was unduly alarmist and pessimistic, but, in view of what has since transpired, it seems to be a very moderate and accurate statement of facts.

After lunch I retired to my friend's private room and; laid before him the proposed plan of reduction of the Tank Corps. W——, as we will call him, was deeply perturbed. Even at this early date, a scheme for an Allied counter-offensive was being prepared and in this schemes tanks were to play an important part.

After some discussion, W—— left the room and, in a few minutes, returned in company with a French officer, who stood extremely high in Marshal Foch's; confidence. To him was related the decision of the British High Command.

He listened attentively to what we had to say and, after asking a few questions, took his leave, assuring me that the matter would be laid before the *generalissimo* at the earliest possible moment. I, too, departed, thoroughly satisfied with the result of my interview.

No more was ever heard of a reduction of the Tank Corps and, shortly afterwards, a polite "instruction" was received by G.H.Q. from Marshal Foch, requesting that further formations of tank units should be brought into being as soon as possible and every effort made to accelerate delivery of new machines.

8

By the beginning of May 1918, the high-water mark of the German offensive had been reached. Through sheer lack of impetus from the rear, the force had spent itself and the two armies, both of them exhausted and battle-worn, lay gasping and glaring at each other.

Now was the time when a fresh effort, backed by tanks that could move faster than a foot-sore, weary infantryman, would in all probability have given victory to the Germans.

In a half-hearted manner, the enemy had attempted to follow our lead, and a few tanks had been constructed, more as a sop to public opinion than as the result of the considered policy of the High Command. These tanks were much inferior to ours and possessed defects which, at the cost of much toil and tribulation, experience had taught us to eliminate. It may be stated here that the few appearances of the

GERMAN TANK "SCHNUCK"

German tanks in battle were woefully unsuccessful and soon ceased altogether.

The fact that the Germans had built tanks and, also, had put into fighting trim some of those captured from us in the precipitate retirement after the Cambrai Battle and during the March offensive, was well known throughout the British Army and many were the conjectures as to the results which they would achieve. The personnel of the Tank Corps was keenly looking forward to a tank-*versus*-tank combat, but our own infantry, having seen the machines in action against the Germans, was not so anxious to encounter them on the opposing side.

One day I was sent for in haste by First Army Headquarters. Aeroplane reports had been received that an enemy tank had been seen moving along the road from Albert in the direction of Doullens. If one tank was reported, in all probability a dozen more might be expected to follow.

Great excitement prevailed, not to say consternation.

I was instructed forthwith to take what steps I could to deal with the situation.

Giving orders for the nearest tanks of my command to be prepared to start at a moment's notice, I dashed off in my car, accompanied by one of my staff, to prospect. As we approached the spot indicated, we got down from the car and proceeded on foot.

It was not long before we heard the sound of steel tracks on the hard, metalled road. Breathlessly we waited, till the "tank" came into view.

The "tank" was a plough-tractor, part of the equipment of the Agricultural Department, and saved from, falling into the enemy's hands by dint of considerable courage and audacity on the part of the driver and his mate.

CHAPTER 17

The End

1

Throughout May and June the situation was still fraught with considerable anxiety, though the crisis was now definitely past. The German offensive had been based mainly on the ability to make a swift and complete breakthrough and, when the first impetus was spent, was brought to a complete standstill. The large reserves under Foch's hand still remained almost intact, and, as soon as the moment was ripe, our counter-stroke would be launched.

As far as the Tank Corps was concerned, the interval between the climax of the German attack and the first British counter-offensive was one of great activity. Many casualties among the personnel had been suffered, mostly while acting as Lewis gun detachments, and not only had the losses to be replaced, but new formations were to be brought into being. A large number of machines had been destroyed or abandoned, but supplies of the new pattern were arriving from England in satisfactory quantities.

Already attacks on a limited scale were being made by us on various parts of the enemy line, mostly with a view to testing its strength.

One particularly successful attack early in July, in which tanks co-operated, was carried out by the Australians in the neighbourhood of Villers Bretonneux, a few miles in front of Amiens. One month later this same part of the line was to be the scene of the first "full-dress" battles which were to culminate in the final defeat of the enemy.

There still persisted some doubt about tanks in the mind of the Australians, who had not forgotten the disastrous little action at Bullecourt a year previously. The success, however, with which they met on the 4th of July and the splendid work of the new Mark V machines, dissipated evil memories for good and all and the Australians thereafter were numbered among the most enthusiastic supporters of the tanks.

The First Brigade had been withdrawn from the First Army area and billeted in the neighbourhood of Tank Corps Headquarters, for refitting purposes, preparatory to taking part in the coming offensive. It was somewhat of a disappointment to us to find that the supply of Mark V machines did not permit of all the brigades being re-equipped with them, and as the First Brigade was the only one which still possessed its full complement of tanks, it was naturally decided that it should be the last to be re-armed. As it proved, one of the battalions of the First Brigade was still equipped with the Mark IV when hostilities ceased.

2

After refitting was completed, the brigade was moved up into the Third Army area and I found myself under the command of General Sir Julian Byng.

From now onwards until the end, I was to receive my orders from General Byng and his chief staff officer, Major-General Vaughan.

During those four months of almost incessant fighting, with short, hectic intervals for "rest" and refitting, I received from General Byng and General Vaughan the most generous appreciation of our efforts and the most sympathetic consideration. Not only did General Byng already possess great confidence in tanks, due to his previous experience as the director of the Cambrai Battle, but he was kind enough to place full trust in my judgment and, on every single occasion, accepted my opinion on tank matters as final.

Sometimes, during the ensuing months, I was to find myself in opposition to corps commanders as to the best method of employment of tanks. Usually I was able to gain my point without appeal to higher authority, but, in one instance, I was forced to make such an appeal to General Byng, who, without a moment's hesitation, gave orders that he approved of my dispositions and that they were to be carried out.

Yet once again, I found myself working in association with "Uncle" Harper, now commanding an army corps. "Uncle," after his experience with tanks, first at the Arras Battle, then in the Third Battle of Ypres, and finally in the Cambrai Battle, felt that he knew more about tanks than any living man, and at his Corps Conferences, had no hesitation in saying so.

General Sir Julian Byng

"I know far more about tanks than anybody else, Baker," he usually began, "and this is what you are to do."

He then proceeded to outline a scheme which was utterly impossible to carry out. Such trivialities as time and space were completely ignored and the tanks were ordered to dash about a battlefield, like a terrier in a cornfield chasing rabbits. Only on one occasion did he prove obdurate to my arguments and I was forced to appeal to higher authority.

The Canadian Corps, after the Battle of Amiens, was placed under the orders of General Byng and, like the other great Colonial Corps, the Anzacs, it became a most enthusiastic supporter of the tanks. The commander, Lieutenant-General Sir Arthur Currie (familiarly known as "Guts and Gaiters") was a huge man with a vast expanse of pallid, clean-shaven countenance. In private life, in Canada, he was a real-estate agent, but he was possessed of considerable military abilities, not the least of which was an imaginative mind, completely free from hampering tradition and prejudice.

With him, too, I was destined to have a serious difference of opinion, but, with the aid of General Byng's good sense and tact, the difficulty was smoothed over satisfactorily and our relations of mutual confidence were re-established.

3

On the 8th of August the first big British offensive took place. Four hundred tanks of the Third, Fourth, and Fifth Tank Brigades co-operated with the infantry, the majority of which, in the initial stages, consisted of the Anzacs and the Canadians.

The battle was fought on the lines of the Cambrai Battle without artillery preparation, and the utmost secrecy was enforced in all the preliminaries.

From the very commencement, everything went well. Even the weather, for almost the first time since the Retreat from Mons, was favourable to us. A dense ground-mist enveloped the countryside and, as had happened during the first day of the enemy offensive in March, the defenders were taken completely by surprise and overwhelmed.

Another innovation was tried for the first time during this battle, but proved, for unexpected reasons, to be only moderately successful.

Some infantry-carrying tanks had been manufactured similar in every respect to the Mark V, except that they had been lengthened by several feet in order to allow ten or fifteen machine-gunners, with

GENERAL CURRIE

their equipment, to be carried inside. The idea was that the tank, after reaching its objective, should decant its passengers, who would then proceed to occupy the captured position.

In theory this was an excellent plan, but, in practice, it failed to come up to expectations.

The atmosphere inside a tank, when going into action, and when every aperture is closed, in a very short time becomes impregnated with the exhaust gases from the engine and the fumes of cordite. By habit, the tank crews had become more or less inured to the condition of things and were capable of enduring it for ten or twelve hours or even longer.

The infantry, however, for the first time subjected to the test, were almost at once overcome by the noxious gases. Within a short time, those who had not already collapsed completely were in the throes of violent sickness. When, at last, the destined point had been reached, the unhappy passengers were disembarked, not caring very much what happened to them, but with their opinion of the joys of being in the Tank Corps considerably changed.

The Battle of Amiens, as it came to be called, was a complete and overwhelming success. For four days the battle continued, though resistance stiffened as the element of surprise disappeared and enemy reserves were flung in.

Over twenty thousand prisoners and four hundred guns were captured, the biggest haul of the war, and by this victory the morale of the British Army was much increased, while that of the enemy was correspondingly lowered.

At long last, the tank had come into its own.

Every report from the army commander downwards paid eloquent tributes to its services. From now onwards, no question ever again arose concerning its merits; indeed, the only question was how many of them each commander could manage to obtain for co-operation with his infantry.

If our own troops now appreciated their true value, the Germans, also, did and had no hesitation in attributing the defeat, which they had suffered, solely to the use of the tanks. Their dispatches, orders, and memoranda were filled with references to tanks. Stringent orders were issued on the subject and Ludendorff, in his; *Memoirs,* refers to the "tank panic," which seized the German troops when attacked by these machines.

Before the enemy could recover from this devastating blow, another heavy attack was launched, this time by the Third Army towards Bapaume on the 21st August, the First and Second Brigades of the Tank Corps co-operating.

Once more the weather was in our favour. A heavy mist enveloped the front and, though it made the steering of tanks difficult, it enabled us again to fall upon the enemy and take him completely by surprise.

The artillery preparation, which until the Battle of Cambrai had been regarded as indispensable, was now completely discarded. The enemy, entirely in the dark as to the spot chosen for our next attack, was unable to mass his reserves behind the threatened point. The initiative lay in the hands of the British, and we could strike when and where we wished, without giving our opponents the least inkling of our intentions.

Although the German High Command was anxiously endeavouring to discover an antidote to the tank, it was too late. Anti-tank rifles with armour-piercing ammunition were issued to the troops, but, partly owing to their clumsiness and weight partly owing to the disinclination of the soldier to fire a weapon which possessed a terrific "kick," little real use was made of them. Light anti-tank field guns were placed in advanced positions in the line, but, though causing considerable damage, were not effectual in stopping a tank attack. "Booby-traps," also, were laid, but, as the Germans apparently were still under the misapprehension that tanks were chiefly confined to roads, were almost ludicrous in their inefficacy.

4

Late in 1917, several staff officers of the American Tank Corps had been attached to the British Tank Corps for the purpose of acquiring as much information as possible, and early in 1918, my "opposite number" in the A.E.F., Colonel Conrad Babcock, commanding the First American Tank Brigade, had been a welcome guest at my headquarters for a fortnight.

In August 1918, the first heavy Tank Battalion of the American Expeditionary Force arrived in France, and for a month or more formed part of my brigade. I was much honoured to be the first British officer to, have, under his direct command, an American unit.

This battalion was eventually moved south to take part in the attacks made by the American Army, and never went into action under my orders, but I was much impressed by their remarkable keenness and their ability. Every single man was a trained mechanic and, from a

CIVILIAN BOY WITH AN ANTI-TANK GUN

technical point of view, their training left nothing to be desired.

On the other hand, their idea of discipline was somewhat different from ours.

The relations between officers and men of the British Army are of the very best, and are admirably suited to our national characteristics. The relations between the officers and men of the American Army appear to us to be distinctly lax, but it is not for us to judge them by our own particular standard. It was, however, always somewhat of a shock to me to hear a private soldier address his company commander as "Say, Cap!"

The commander of this battalion was almost embarrassing in his protestations of inexperience in military matters and his desire to learn. He told me that he knew that, from our point of view, the discipline of his unit was terribly bad and begged me to pay it the honour of treating it in exactly the same way as one of my own. I assured him that I would do everything in my power to assist.

The first thing was to hold a little ceremonial parade and give the men a short address.

On the day appointed, accompanied by my staff captain, I drove in my car to the quarters they were occupying in the old German line. The battalion commander and his adjutant were waiting for me by the roadside.

I got down from the car and the little procession moved slowly and statelily to the parade-ground, where the battalion was drawn up in three sides of a hollow square.

As I drew near, the second-in-command called the parade to attention.

Every man in the ranks took a final whiff of his "fag," threw it on the ground in front of him and expectorated generously. He then adjusted his cap and stood more or less to attention.

It was difficult to repress a smile as I gravely took the salute; it was so very different from the ceremonial parade to which one had been used.

I walked slowly down the ranks, stopping now and again to ask questions concerning the training, profession, or experience of some of the men.

The first thing that struck me was the astounding lack of uniformity of their "turn-out." One man had his cap over his left ear, one over his right, another on the back of his head; one man wore *puttees*, another canvas gaiters; some wore their haversacks over the right shoulder, some over the left. Hardly ten men out of the four hundred on the parade were dressed identically.

After I had inspected the ranks, I made a short speech, telling them how proud I was to have them under my command and that I was going to pay them the compliment of treating them exactly in the same way as one of my own battalions. I wound up by saying that I knew they would worthily uphold the tradition of the great American nation.

For one awful moment I thought that they were going to cheer, but there was only a loud buzz of conversation along the ranks.

The parade dismissed, I visited their quarters and had little informal conversations with some of the men, who invariably addressed me as "Gen," a diminutive, I presume, for "General."

There was no doubt but that they knew their work very thoroughly, but, at times, I did wish that they would be a little less careless in their habits.

On several occasions I was taken to task by General Harper, whose Corps Headquarters were only half a mile away, for various iniquities committed by what he called my "barbarians."

Some of these iniquities were merely breaches of etiquette, whereas others were of a more serious nature.

In the old German lines, which the Americans inhabited, were many relics of the previous occupants, including a good deal of warlike equipment, which aroused much interest among the new tenants.

It was extremely disturbing to hear two or three machine guns suddenly being fired off, until one realised that it was only the Americans "trying-out" another German gun they had found in the trenches. This was dangerous enough in all conscience, though fortunately no casualties occurred; but, on one occasion, a tragedy nearly did take place.

While searching about among the *débris,* two of my Americans found some German rifle grenades. These they proceeded to fire off at random. After firing a few rounds, they looked about for a target and, observing someone about a couple of hundred yards away, let off two grenades in his direction. Luckily, the human target was not damaged, but it was a near thing.

Once more I was in trouble on account of my "barbarians," for the "target" turned out to be one of the senior officers of General Harper's Corps Staff.

Colonel Mitchell, who succeeded Colonel Babcock in command of the First Brigade American Tank Corps, was for several weeks attached to my Headquarters.

One morning, after making the most transparently false excuses, he told me that he was going away for a few days. I was well aware that the American Army was about to attack the St. Mihiel salient, but I did not think it tactful to let him find out that the secret he guarded so carefully was already known to me.

When he returned, I was much interested to hear how the battle had gone.

"Hell!" he said, almost indignantly. "That wasn't a *reel* battle. When we attacked, we found that every son of a gun of a German had his 'grip' already packed and had got his surrendering pants on."

I was sorry when my Americans were ordered south to join their own army. At times they were a source of anxiety, but they were a splendid lot of men and I should have much liked to command them in battle.

They suffered somewhat heavily on the first occasion when they went into battle, partly through inexperience, partly through their over-impetuous desire "to knock the block off those gol-darned Dutchmen."

Generally speaking, the American troops in France were only too ready and anxious to learn from the British and never did I encounter the least symptom of that detestable boastfulness, the prerogative of the "man-who-stayed-at-home," who, after the war was safely over, wore in his coat a button bearing the legend "After England Failed," a pleasing and tactful variation of "American Expeditionary Force."

5

There was no doubt but that, at last and in actual fact, the German morale was breaking down. The enemy infantry was now composed of a very different calibre from that previously. The prisoners often consisted of elderly men and young boys, and, time after time, large numbers surrendered without firing a shot.

It was the German machine gunners who did the fighting. They were a veritable *corps d'élite* and put up the most heroic defence. Again and again detachments were called upon by the tanks to put up their hands; but they refused to do so, and the tanks had, literally, to crush gun and gunners into the ground beneath their tracks to stop them firing.

The officers were no less brave and stubborn. On one occasion two or three of my tanks found themselves in a "nest" of machine guns in a small, isolated valley. They called upon the crews to surrender. Several did so, but the officer in command drew his revolver and endeavoured to force them to continue fighting. His efforts proving unavailing, he put his revolver to his head and shot himself. Useless perhaps, but demonstrating a fine spirit.

Almost every day attacks were launched on different portions of the front of the Third and Fourth Armies. In all of these attacks tanks took part in greater or lesser numbers.

The story of these battles was one of continuous success, the resistance encountered and the number of prisoners and guns captured providing the only variants. In many cases the enemy machine guns put up a splendid fight, but our advance on a thirty-mile front remorselessly pushed its way forward to a depth of nearly twenty miles.

But the tanks, which had been almost without respite in action and had, including their approach-marches to the starting-off places and their withdrawal after battle, travelled well over a hundred miles, were in urgent need of rest and refitting. Consent, at last, was given for them to be brought into Army Reserve, much against the wishes of the infantry commanders.

For a fortnight tank units toiled unceasingly to get their machines into righting trim in order once more to take their share in the fighting.

Before us still lay the much-vaunted Hindenburg Line, "the last ditch" of the enemy. If this could be captured, then, indeed, would the enemy be in a bad way. Nothing had been prepared behind this line and, in the event of a breakthrough, no time would be given him to dig a new system of defence.

The Third Army was confronted with an obstacle to their advance on which the enemy confidently relied as "an insuperable barrier to tanks," the dry bed of the Canal du Nord.

Once more the First Brigade found itself in familiar country, though regarding it from a totally new angle. In front of us again we could see Bourlon Wood and Bourlon Village, the high-water mark of the Cambrai Battle, but now, instead of having the canal as a protection on our flank, we found ourselves faced with the necessity of crossing it.

It was, indeed, a difficult problem that lay before us. The enemy held the near bank in full strength and innumerable machine guns

Tanks in the Canal de Nord, near Mœuvres, 27th September, 1918

had been mounted in its face. The Canadian Corps, to which the task of capturing and crossing the canal had been assigned, would, without doubt, have succeeded in forcing a passage without the aid of the tanks, but only at terrible loss. I was determined that tanks should take part, if it were in any way possible, though everybody, except a few optimists like myself, had ruled the crossing of the canal as definitely out of the question.

The first thing to do was to collect every scrap of information concerning the canal itself.

By means of daring personal reconnaissances, carried out by Williams-Ellis, Macavity (the head of the Intelligence Department of the Canadian Corps), and Oswald Birley of the First Army Staff, much valuable data was obtained. Low-flying aeroplanes, at great risk, took dozens of photographs and the original drawings of the designers were carefully studied.

In spite of all this, however, we were still in ignorance of the one fact which really mattered, *viz.* Could or could not the tanks cross the canal?

Having thoroughly digested every fragment of information that could be gathered, I decided that such a crossing was possible. Having made up my mind, I proceeded to act. Orders were drawn up, in conjunction with the Staff of the Canadian Corps, for an infantry and tank attack.

For the first and only time in two years, my plans were taken exception to by Tank Corps Headquarters.

Elles happened to be in England on a special mission for a day or two and no one had been appointed to take his place during his short absence. If he had been in France I do not think he would have seen fit to intervene.

However that may be, Colonel Karslake, who had recently been appointed in place of Fuller (transferred to the War Office as Tank Representative there), came out to my headquarters with the avowed intention of stopping me from wasting tanks on an impossible task. He pointed out to me how disastrous from every point of view a failure would be and how certainly such a failure must take place in view of the obstacle before us. I told him that my reconnaissance officer and the battalion commander concerned, Lieutenant-Colonel Fernie of "G" Battalion, were as confident of success as I was and that we were going to carry out our plans as arranged.

Being unable to issue orders to me, he contented himself with ominous predictions of disaster and took his departure in the deepest gloom.

A possible alternative method of crossing the canal was put forward by some genius, who suggested that half a dozen "time-expired" tanks should be specially fitted up and strengthened and should form a bridge across the bed of the canal. Over this improvised bridge the fighting tanks were to crawl and emerge in safety on the other side.

This plan, improbable of success though it appeared, I decided to attempt, but the bridge-tanks proved entirely too "time-expired" and failed even to get within several miles of their proposed last resting-place.

6

The attack took place at dawn and the tanks moved forward in front of the infantry. Each machine had been allotted a spot, where it was thought that breaches had been made in the banks, through or over which it could pass.

It was an anxious moment for the commander and staff of the First Brigade, who had all but pledged themselves to the ability of the tanks to cross the obstacle.

But we had not long to wait in suspense.

First one, then another, then two or three at a time, negotiated "the insuperable obstacle" and appeared going strong on the far side. Only one machine failed to emerge; it had stumbled upon a "booby-trap" placed by the enemy in a breach of their own making, and had exploded a small land-mine beneath its tracks. No member of the crew was injured and the machine itself only slightly damaged.,

Bourlon Wood and Bourlon Village fell into our hands after some resistance. It was a happy coincidence that "G" Battalion of the First Brigade, which had attacked it at the time of the Cambrai Battle, should be the battalion which now took part in its final capture.

From the wooded heights we could look down over our former battlefield and reconstruct the action, which marked a turning-point in the history of war. We could make out Havrincourt Wood and *château*, Flesquières of evil memory, and all the various landmarks. How great, we thought to ourselves, was the transformation the tanks had undergone since that 20th day of November when their very existence was at stake!

7

It was during the last month of the war that my difficulty with the commander of the Canadian Corps took place.

At my request the First Brigade of the Tank Corps had been withdrawn into Army Reserve in order to refit. Both crews and machines were worn out with ceaseless fighting and marching. It was absolutely essential that a few days' respite should be granted. I pointed out to General Byng that, while the infantry were relieved after a few days of leading the attack, it was always the same Tank Battalion that went into action with them.

The Army Commander readily agreed and notification was sent out to corps that no tanks would be available until further orders. The same afternoon I received a peremptory summons to proceed to Canadian Corps Headquarters immediately.

On arriving there I was ushered into the presence of General Currie, who lost no time in making manifest his extreme displeasure at the withdrawal of the tanks and was, to tell the truth, extremely rude to me.

I must admit that the circumstances were of a nature to disturb the equanimity of the most urbane and courteous commander.

It appeared that one of the divisions of the Canadian Corps had been ordered to make an attack in three days' time and that the G.O.C. had stoutly refused to do so unless assisted by tanks. Why, he argued, should he lose three thousand men when, with the help of tanks, he would only lose three hundred?

"It is by the army commander's orders, sir," I replied, "that the tanks have been withdrawn."

General Currie seized the telephone and demanded to be put through to General Byng without a moment's delay.

In a couple of minutes he was "through" and talking with the army commander. After he had discussed the situation down the telephone, he turned to me once more.

"General Byng wishes to see you at once."

I departed and made all speed to Army Headquarters, at that time established in a railway train.

"Look here, Baker-Carr," began General Byng, with his charming, sympathetic manner, "this is rather serious. I don't want to tell G.H.Q. that one of my divisions refuses to fight. I won't *order* you to put in tanks, but, as a personal favour to me, can't you do something?"

"I'll manage somehow, sir," I replied, "though to be quite frank, I don't know how it's going to be done."

"I'm very grateful to you. Let me know what you can do."

Australian troops in action, Hindenburg Line, 18th September, 1918

I drove off to where my battalions were "resting" and called for volunteers. Every man responded and, out of two battalions, I was able to collect twelve "scratch" tanks, manned by twelve "scratch" crews. The tanks were in a miserable state of efficiency and the crews, through overwork were equally unfitted for the task. However, there it was and it was the best I could do.

I next called upon the commander of the division concerned and told him that twelve tanks would be at his disposal, though I would take no responsibility whatever that a single one got even as far as our own front line.

"That's splendid," he said gratefully. "I'll let the corps commander know."

Of the twelve "crocks," eight managed to get into action and did good work. The division captured all objectives and suffered even less than the estimate of their commander, who issued a special order of thanks to us.

Thus was fulfilled General de Lisle's prophecy, made after the Arras Battle, eighteen months previously, namely, that the time would come when infantry would become so dependent on tanks that they would refuse to fight without them.

8

By the middle of October, we were nearing the little town of Le Cateau, the first abode of G.H.Q. in August 1914.

The Hindenburg Line, after fierce resistance, lay behind us, and open warfare, after four long, weary years, was once more the order of the day.

The enemy were still putting up a good fight, almost entirely by the aid of machine guns of which apparently he possessed an incalculable number.

The First Brigade of the Tank Corps was on its last legs.

Day after day, fresh casualties to machines were reported and those that could still move were in a bad way, but it was evident that the end of the war was in sight, and that it was only a question of weeks, perhaps even days, before the enemy collapsed.

The last action fought by the First Brigade was a small one in itself, but demonstrated to the full the tank's principal and most valuable quality, its ability to save life.

In front of us lay a valley, down which ran the River Selle between low, marshy banks. The stream itself was only a few feet wide, but the swampy land on either side rendered it impassable for tanks. Furthermore, on the other side, two or three hundred yards distant, ran a railway embankment, teeming with enemy machine guns. It was a position of extraordinary strength and one which, without the help of tanks, could only be captured at terrific loss.

The corps commander, General Harper, called upon me to put in a tank attack against the embankment.

"Certainly, sir," I said. "But I must have a causeway built across the Selle. Without it, it is impossible."

"But you can't build a causeway. The Germans are only a couple of hundred yards away," he objected.

"No causeway, no tanks, sir. Not one would get across."

The chief engineer of the corps was called in and consulted. No decision could be arrived at, but I still adhered to my opinion.

The army commander was asked for his views, and the Chief Engineer of the Army arrived on the scene.

It was eventually agreed that a causeway could be built, but that the builders would suffer appalling loss while engaged on the work.

"Which is it to be, Baker?" demanded General Harper, "If we build the causeway, will you guarantee that it is worth the loss of the builders?"

"I can't guarantee anything, sir. All I can say is that, if a causeway is built, my tanks will be able to cross and will clean up the railway embankment."

"The decision rests with you. If you say that the causeway must be built, it shall be done. Yes or no?"

Strictly speaking, the responsibility should not have been mine. The corps commander, after hearing my views, should have decided which was the right policy.

In my own mind, however, I was absolutely convinced that the only thing to do was to build the causeway, even though it might cost many lives to make. The number of lives lost in an attack by infantry without tanks would be at least ten times as great.

"Very good, sir," I replied, after some consideration. "In my opinion the causeway should be built."

After dark, on the night preceding the attack, building operations commenced. Sand-bags were filled under cover, carried to the stream and laid in position.

Soon the enemy detected activity and machine gun fire was poured on to the gallant company of Royal Engineers. Man after man fell, but still the work went on. All the officers were killed or wounded and of the two hundred men who had started but few remained.

But the work was not yet completed. Another company of R.E. was summoned and the causeway finished, but not before the fresh workers, also, had paid a heavy toll.

At dawn the tanks moved across the causeway and, breasting the hill, climbed the railway embankment. They turned right and left and worked along it, killing and destroying the defenders. Masses of machine guns were found, in one place seventy guns in the space of less than half a mile.

The infantry, following the tanks at a short interval, suffered almost no loss whatever, and the gallant sappers, splendidly upholding the tradition of their corps, had saved hundreds upon hundreds of the lives of their comrades.

9

My last headquarters were situated in the pleasant little town of Caudry.

The town was untouched when I entered it, soon after the tanks had passed through. I proceeded to the *mairie,* where I was embraced on both cheeks by *Monsieur le Maire.* The inhabitants, after four years of enslavement, were almost delirious with joy and I was escorted by a happy, cheering crowd to the best house in the town, owned by a big lace-manufacturer, who received me with open arms. The house was mine and everything in it.

From a hidden store, which had remained undetected throughout the entire occupation, he produced a bottle of excellent wine and we toasted one another with great enthusiasm.

He told me of all the tribulations he had suffered, and how all his machinery had been stolen. His chief grievance, however, was on the subject of eggs.

"Imagine to yourself, *Monsieur le Général,*" he exclaimed indignantly. "For every fowl that I possessed each day must I bring one *egg* to the German *kommandantur.*"

"But it is impossible for a hen to lay an egg every day," I protested. "What happened if the number fell short?"

"Then, *Monsieur le Général*" he replied, "I was fined one *franc* for each egg deficient.'"

I am afraid my amusement must have been visible in my face, for my host hastened to assure me that it was no laughing matter. Some of his hens were very old and had cost him hundreds upon hundreds of *francs*.

For several days I stayed in this house, a most welcome guest, until one night a 5.9 German howitzer shell arrived and wrecked the back of the building, nearly killing my staff captain, Tapper, who was buried beneath the *débris*. We retired to the cellar for the remainder of the night, in deference to the tearful entreaties of our host.

It was the last shell I heard in the war and I sincerely trust that it will be the last I shall ever hear in my life.

Only two tanks were now left fit for action and, a few days later, my brigade was withdrawn in Army Reserve.

For over a year I had had no leave, and a few days before the Armistice, I arrived in London.

On the 11th November I stood in Piccadilly and watched the yelling, cheering mob go by.

Peace had come at last, and I was filled with a deep feeling of thankfulness and pride, that I had been privileged to play my part, small and unimportant though it was, in the achievement of the Great Victory.